P9-CJC-188

TO: Mommy
LOVE: Toto ♡

This book contains
all the places the
two of us are
going to go before
we die! ☺

love you, and
merry Christmas
XOXO
Tot

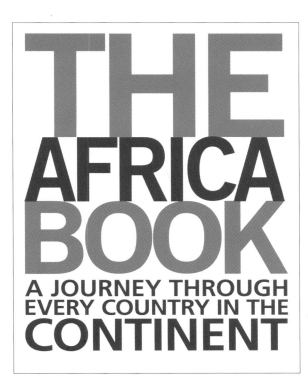

THE AFRICA BOOK

A JOURNEY THROUGH EVERY COUNTRY IN THE CONTINENT

CONTENTS

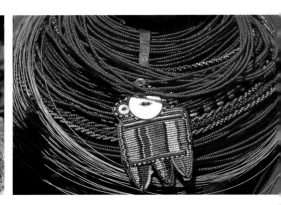

FOREWORD

AFRICA IS A DESTINATION FULL OF DREAMS FOR THE TRAVELLER: VAST AND DIVERSE LANDSCAPES, COLOURFUL AND MYSTERIOUS CULTURES, ICONIC WILDLIFE AND A CHARACTER DEFINED BY EXTREMES OF BEAUTY, CELEBRATION AND HARDSHIP.

Africa for me is still largely unexplored. So far the only country on the continent that I have visited is Egypt, an iconic place that houses one of the world's oldest civilisations, situated at the source of the great African Nile and nestling at the axis of Africa, Europe and the Middle East. Still, somehow this country doesn't represent the 'Africa' of the popular imagination. This quirk reminds us that Africa – a continent of 54 individual nations – is so much more than those eternal images of majestic wildlife on a vast savannah. It is a characteristic of the continent that it somehow exists in duality, divided between the 'imagined' – a series of images and impressions that we hold in our mind's eye – and the 'real' – diverse peoples and cultures that have extended their roots and influences the world over.

Many of us will admit to entertaining a host of dreams about Africa: an undulating canvas of stunning mountains, rainforests, canyons, deserts and deltas, lakes and waterfalls; a collection of diverse social groups each with their own languages and cultures; a place to experience and commune with the most iconic and rare creatures on the planet. And for the traveller, there's a unique opportunity to see and experience a mix of these things.

I've been dreaming of visiting Africa for many years, and am currently in the final stages of planning my 'big trip' this year. My dining room table is littered with travel brochures and this trip is my singular topic of conversation at the moment, unfortunately for my friends and family. My journey begins in Uganda, where I'll join a trek to meet the mountain gorillas in the wonderfully-named 'Impenetrable Forest' in Bwindi National Park. From there, I'll travel through Kenya, if I feel brave enough taking the so-called 'lunatic express' from Nairobi to Mombasa. I'll definitely check out the flamingos on Lake Nakaru, and visit the Masai Mara National Reserve, and then it's onto Tanzania where I'll go on an organised safari through the Serengeti and Norongoro Crater.

At the risk of sounding like one of those brochures I mentioned, the options for travel in Africa are limitless and planning a trip is both exciting and painful, because choosing one thing inevitably involves excluding another. I hope that this book will provide you with a great starting point for discovering Africa – in it we have brought together a selection of stunning images which bring each country to life and evocative text that explores the characteristics of each country, as well as contributions from our travellers who have sent us their stories and pictures of travel in Africa, sharing with us what their experiences have meant to them.

Keeping the traveller in mind, we've divided this book into five regions with the countries of each ordered by a logical travel route. For the traveller, the experience of each of these countries is unique, with its own sights, sounds, people, trademarks and surprises.

There are unifying themes to Africa, and we've explored some of these in the essays at the end of this book – you can join our authors on an in-depth tour of the culture and spiritual traditions of Africa, take a whirlwind ride through high-adrenaline adventures; reflect on the soul and significance of music in African cultures and, of course, marvel at the sheer diversity and majesty of wildlife on the continent.

In Swahili, the word for journey is *safari*. Many journeys have gone into the creation of this book, and we hope that it will inspire you to plan your own *safari* to this remarkable place where dreams and reality meet.

ROZ HOPKINS,
PUBLISHER, TRADE & REFERENCE,
LONELY PLANET PUBLICATIONS

INTRODUCING AFRICA

Africa was dubbed the 'Dark Continent' by Henry Stanley (of 'Dr Livingstone, I presume?' fame) in the late 19th century. Stanley chose this epithet not because Africa was perceived as malevolent, but rather because it was a place into which few outsiders had ever ventured – and a place nobody fully comprehended. Today, despite looming large in the global consciousness as its challenges are widely discussed in the world's media, Africa continues to be misunderstood.

AFRICA, THE IMAGE

To those with a penchant for adventure, romance or wildlife documentaries, Africa holds a lifetime's worth of dreams: tracking legendary animals across acacia-dotted plains, encountering remote cultures that time seems to have forgotten or exploring the monumental remains of past empires. To those who keep their heads out of the clouds and focussed on the apocalyptic hype created in the news, Africa is a place of incessant nightmare: famine, poverty, crime, corruption, disease and war. To *all* who visit – experienced Africa travellers included – each step into the 'Dark Continent' brings further enlightenment on the true nature of this fascinating place.

AFRICA, THE REALITY

Considering Africa's vast size (the Sahara alone could swallow most of the United States) and its diversity of wildlife, landscapes and cultures (how does 1800 spoken languages sound?), the only African reality is that there are countless realities. Cape Town's gleaming shopping arcades welcome the affluent while poverty and constant struggle continue unabated in suburbs nearby. Harvest cycles and family life in rural villages carry on at the same tempo as that of their ancestors. Remote tribes, like those on Lake Turkana's shores, exist in harsh environments yet exhibit pride and happiness that would make those in materially rich societies blush. Yes, poverty is widespread, but sadness and wanting are not.

The dire realities of famine and war still plague parts of Africa, but they are anything but commonplace. Cease-fires and peace deals in recent decades have brought peace to former trouble spots – Mozambique is a stellar example, with others such as Rwanda, Burundi and (more tentatively) Angola slowly following suit. Meanwhile, Africa's famines through the years have achieved such notoriety that many countries remain scarred by the images of starvation and drought long after famine has ended. The biggest victim of this phenomenon is Ethiopia. Despite being one of the most traditionally fertile and well-watered nations (it supplies over 80 per cent of the Nile's water), travellers, with images from Live Aid still on their mind, continue to phone the world-class Ethiopian Airlines to enquire whether there will be food available during their flight.

Africa's landscapes, such as the mind-numbing Namib dunes and the resplendent Rift Valley, are no less spellbinding than its cultures. The sublime stature and equatorial glaciers of Mt Kenya have even led the Kikuyu people to

deify the extinct volcano. Although a multitude of Africa's landscapes are artworks in their own right, many consider them simply backdrops to another of Africa's masterpieces: its fabled wildlife.

THE PAST

The history of Africa's people is a long and storied one. After all, Africa is considered to be the birthplace of humanity, where 'ape men' branched off – or rather let go of the branch – and walked on two legs down a separate evolutionary path. Since those very early beginnings, numerous empires and civilisations have risen and fallen across the continent. While the influence of the ancient Egyptians is widely known, the prowess of other civilisations – such as Ethiopia's Aksumite kingdom, which spread Christianity into Arabia and gained tremendous wealth by trading with Egypt, Syria and India – is little known. As well as shaping many of Africa's present-day cultures, the empires of old left behind many physical traces of their grandeur: the pyramids of Egypt, the stelae and rock-hewn churches of Ethiopia, and the ruins of Great Zimbabwe, to name only a few.

Africa's modern history has been more turbulent – the 16th to 19th centuries were not kind to the continent, with the slave trade and colonialism rearing their ugly heads. And while the 20th century brought independence to most African nations, the ensuing grim economic realities – often due to old colonial policies and foreign loans with strings attached – meant that many countries were more financially shackled to the West than they were during colonial times. Worse, the power vacuum created by the end of colonialism led to numerous civil wars, some of which still continue today. But the greatest blight of the 20th and early 21st century is the HIV/AIDS epidemic, which affects Africa more than any other place on the planet: 5500 Africans die from the disease every 24 hours.

THE FUTURE

Although Africans could easily despair in the face of the HIV/AIDS catastrophe, many are looking to the future with optimism. The G8's debt relief to date is already showing dividends in many nations, including Tanzania, which has used its savings to fund education and eliminate school fees – three million children have returned to school. Now, if only the West would remove the trading shackles from Africa, Africans would have a truly fair chance to pull themselves out of their current morass. Some Africans cringe at the idea of economic growth, globalisation and the Westernisation of their traditional cultures, but others question why they should be held back from the same financial prosperity experienced by many Western nations. But in some areas, such as northern Kenya, pioneering remote communities are showing that it's possible to blend both worlds. They are thriving thanks to novel ecotourism projects designed to preserve both their vibrant culture and their surrounding wildlife, which would otherwise be under threat. So it just may be that sustainable ecotourism is the key to retaining the essence of local cultures in an Africa that is becoming more and more globally aware.

TIMELINE

14,000–9500 BC »
The Sahara region is covered with verdant vegetation and plays host to early agricultural societies.

2755–2255 BC »
The pharaohs of Egypt oversee the construction of the Pyramids of Giza; huge advances are made in navigation, astronomy and medicine.

2500 BC »
The rains decrease in North Africa and the Sahara starts to form.

1323 BC »
King Tutankhamun and his treasures are laid to rest in the Valley of the Kings.

1100–146 BC »
Phoenicians rise to create the capital of Carthage; they dominate the Mediterranean from the 6th century BC until conquered by the Romans in 146 BC.

AD 300–325 »
The Aksumite kingdom of Ethiopia accepts Christianity.

639 »
Islam starts its inexorable sweep across North Africa.

700–1000 »
The Ghana empire flourishes in West Africa.

1000–1200 »
The Shona dynasty rises in southern Africa and creates the trading city of Great Zimbabwe; when resources are exhausted in the 15th century the city is abandoned.

1250 »
The vast Mali empire rises to power and rules from present-day Senegal to Niger until its eventual collapse 300 years later.

1348–51 »
The Black Death kills 25 per cent of North Africa's population.

1490–1543 »
Ethiopia's Christian highland people endure and eventually defeat the Muslim raiders.

1510 »
Spain's King Ferdinand authorises the systematic transportation of African slaves to Spanish colonies in South America.

1593 »
The Portuguese build Fort Jesus in Mombasa (Kenya); the garrison is massacred in 1631.

1834 »
Slavery is abolished in the British Empire; the French do the same 13 years later.

1835–40 »
Afrikaners abandon their Cape colony and commence the Great Trek North.

1848 »
Johannes Rebmann becomes the first European to see Mt Kilimanjaro.

1867 »
The first diamonds are found in South Africa.

1869 »
The Suez Canal is completed.

1871 »
Henry Stanley meets David Livingstone in Tanzania (or Burundi) and utters the immortal line, 'Dr Livingstone, I presume'.

1884–85 »
Africa is divided up between European nations at the Berlin Conference.

1896 »
Gold discovered on the Witwatersrand, South Africa

1896 »
Ethiopia routs the Italian armies at Adwa and avoids being colonised.

1910 »
Union of South Africa created, with no voting rights for blacks.

1951-80 »
Fifty African nations are granted independence from European powers. Seventeen countries were granted independence in 1960 alone.

1990 »
Nelson Mandela is released after 27 years of imprisonment and apartheid effectively ends.

1994 »
The Rwandan genocide occurs while Western governments sit on their hands.

2003 »
Niger officially bans slavery.

2006 »
Andrew Hawkins, a descendant of England's first slave trader, kneels in chains before 25,000 Africans in The Gambia to apologise for the slave trade, and is officially forgiven.

2010 »
South Africa will become the first African nation to host the FIFA World Cup.

AFRICA AT A GLANCE

△ THE ZAMBIAN SIDE OF VICTORIA FALLS

△ IN AMONG IT ON A FOUR-WHEEL DRIVE SAFARI, SOUTH AFRICA

△ REAPING THE DEPTHS OF LAKE TANGANYIKA, TANZANIA

POPULATION 910.8 MILLION
With a population growing faster than anywhere else on earth, Africa's 910.8 million account for 14 per cent of the world's people.

AREA 30.1 MILLION SQ KM
Africa's beauty stretches over 30 million square kilometres, which is just over 20 per cent of the earth's land area.

COUNTRIES 54
LANGUAGES 27 OFFICIAL, 1800 SPOKEN

BEST NATURAL FEATURE
Dotted with volcanoes, lakes and exquisite escarpments and stretching across a total of 12 African nations, the Rift Valley is the world's most stunning scar.

HIGHEST MOUNTAIN
The snow-capped stratovolcano Mt Kilimanjaro (5982 metres) rises magnificently from Tanzania's plains.

BEST WATERFALL
Victoria Falls – at almost two kilometres wide and 100 metres tall, this mind-blowing waterfall is justifiably ranked as one of the world's seven natural wonders.

BEST OUTDOOR ACTIVITY
A no-brainer – Africa is blessed with the most entertaining wildlife on the planet and spectacular backdrops, so you can't beat a safari.

LARGEST LAKE
At 68,000 square kilometres, Lake Victoria has the second-largest surface area of any lake in the world; three countries – Kenya, Tanzania and Uganda – meet at its sultry shores.

DEEPEST INLAND BODY OF WATER
Lake Tanganyika's 1470 metres, courtesy of Rift Valley tectonics, make it one of the planet's deepest lakes; it's also fringed with beaches, forests and wildlife.

MOST BEAUTIFUL TREK
The 41-kilometre five-day Otter Trail, along the sublime shores of Tsitsikamma Coastal National Park in South Africa, is pure bliss.

MOST EXTREME ENVIRONMENT
In the Danakil Depression, a primordial region of salt flats, volcanic vents and sulphur fields in Ethiopia, temperatures often soar past 50°C. It's the home of the world's only permanent lava lake.

OLDEST MAN-MADE FEATURE
Olduvai Gorge's stone circle easily beats the step pyramid of King Zoser in Egypt and all of Africa's ancient rock art for age – it's believed to be the base of a 1.8 million-year-old hut.

BEST OFF-THE-BEATEN-TRACK DESTINATION
Arquipélago dos Bijagós is a little-visited Unesco International Biosphere Reserve in Guinea-Bissau with unique wildlife.

MOST STUNNING CITY
Lapping at the base of Table Mountain's striking sheer bluffs is the sophisticated and cosmopolitan South African city of Cape Town and its bounty of beautiful beaches.

BEST CUP OF COFFEE
Ethiopia is the birthplace of the bean and coffee isn't just consumed there, it's celebrated – a coffee ceremony is a thing to enjoy.

STRANGEST ANIMAL
The aye-aye: with the face of a ferret, the teeth of a rodent, the ears of a bat, massive middle fingers and the hair of Albert Einstein, this lemur is an odd sight indeed.

BEST HANG-OUT
Zanzibar – dine on seafood at the seafront in historic Stone Town, laze on powdery white beaches and swim in crystal-clear waters.

BEST ADVENTURE ACTIVITY
Hands down, it has to be trekking – Ethiopia, Tanzania, Kenya, Uganda and South Africa are just a few of the prime locations.

SOUTH AFRICA'S OTTER TRAIL, AFLAME WITH COLOUR »

AFRICA'S HEART BEATS TO THE RHYTHM OF DRUMS »

ALL EARS: A BABY AYE-AYE »

GREAT JOURNEYS

IN EARLY 1796, GERMAN Frederick Hornemann approached the African Association of London with the idea of a grand North African adventure. His pitch was successful and he arrived in Cairo in September 1797 to study Arabic, but was confined by the Egyptians to the Citadel of Cairo when the French invaded in 1798.

Freed by the French, and now fluent in both Turkish and Arabic, Hornemann received the support of Napoleon and finally set out on his long-awaited expedition on 5 September 1798. He managed to join a caravan returning from Mecca to the Fezzan (a region in central Libya) by concealing his Christian religion and assuming the character of a young Muslim *mamluk* (a slave soldier of Turkish origin).

The caravan travelled through the eastern Egyptian oasis of Siwa and the Libyan oasis of Aujila (between present-day Ajdabiya and Jalu). From there, it crossed rocky black sections of desert and finally reached Murzuk on 17 November 1798. Hornemann lived in Murzuk for seven months before travelling to Tripoli to send his journals back to Europe. He then returned to Murzuk and set off in the hope of locating the region of the Hausa people, in present-day Nigeria.

Although he was never heard of directly again, there are reliable reports that he made contact with the Hausa and settled in Caina (now Katsina, Nigeria). It's believed he died in 1819 while visiting Nigeria's Nupe tribes. Today, Hornemann is regarded as the first modern European explorer to cross the northeastern Sahara.

Although logistics and bureaucracy make it impossible to trace Hornemann's route step by step, it is possible to visit some of his stamping grounds. In Egypt, you'll still find the citadel dominating the skyline at the southern end of Islamic Cairo, the mangled mud-brick walls of Shali, the 13th-century fortified town within the oasis town of Siwa, and some serious dunes, deep-blue lakes and mountains looming on Siwa's horizon.

Border-crossing bureaucratic festivities are only possible on the coast, meaning you'll have to bypass the Great Sand Sea along the Libyan border, though you'll get a glimpse of similar sands southwest of Murzuk. While Italian influence has changed the face of Tripoli since Hornemann's time, its infectious Arabic spirit and decidedly North African disposition have likely changed little.

Separating Libya and Katsina in Nigeria are two of Niger's most time-tested natural features: the desolate Djado Plateau and the stunning Ténéré Desert. The Nigerien town of Zinder, just north of the Nigerian border and northeast of Katsina, has some of the best Hausa architecture in Africa.

This journey is undoubtedly one of the toughest on the continent – it will require a couple of months, some serious logistical planning, at least two sturdy four-wheel drives (going alone isn't permitted in certain areas) and deep pockets.

⌃ ROSE-RED ZINDER AND ITS WEALTH OF HAUSA ARCHITECTURE, NIGER

FRANCE'S GRIP ON WEST AFRICA was as vast as it was strong, and the French left a linguistic legacy and much more. However, it's the vibrancy and diversity of the traditional West African cultures that make this region one of Africa's most fascinating.

Where better to start in West Africa than at its westernmost point, Pointe des Almadies, just outside Dakar? Besides offering entrancing nightlife and some of West Africa's best live music, Dakar's cosmopolitan centre (love it or loathe it) gives you a taste of the African urban future. A trip to nearby Île de Gorée provides a look back at the region's painful slave-trade past. Before leaving Senegal for Guinea, you can pop in to visit The Gambia, a petite former British colony that straddles the Gambia River. Also be sure to visit the lush Niokolo-Koba National Park, in Senegal's southeast corner.

Hike over the verdant hills of Fouta Djalon, recline on the beaches of Îles de Los, let loose to Conakry's renowned music and track wildlife in Guinea's south before slipping east into Mali. There, visit Djenné's celebrated mud mosque and shop for salt slabs at Mopti's river port before delving into Dogon Country. Before entering Niger, you can detour up to the legendary city of Timbuktu (Tombouctou) or take the long route via Burkina Faso.

Burkina Faso's highlights include Gorom-Gorom's famed market, Bobo-Dioulasso's old quarter and the Sindou Peaks. And we'd be remiss if we didn't mention that a visit to Africa's most evocatively named capital, Ouagadougou, is worthwhile. This route also allows you to take in two of West Africa's more intriguing countries, Togo and Benin. Togo is the home of the unique Tamberma architecture, a plate-licking cuisine and a lively capital, Lomé. As for Benin, the fact that it's the birthplace both of voodoo (it's still a hotbed of voodoo worship) and the Atlantic slave trade should be enough to tweak your interest.

Once in Niger, enjoy a few sunsets on the surface of the Niger River before heading north to the mystical Saharan city of Agadez. From there, you can explore the astounding Aïr Mountains and the Ténéré Desert, two of the Sahara's most beautiful assets. After that, slide south to Zinder and wander among the Birni quarter's historic Hausa architecture. Cameroon is next – reach it via Nigeria or, if you have more patience than you know what to do with, make your way via the remote northern rim of Lake Chad. Cameroon's highlights include Waza National Park, the remote peoples around Bamenda and the Atlantic coast's beaches.

To complete this 9000-kilometre-plus foray, you'll need about six months.

⌃ GETTING A GROOVE ON, ÎLE DE GORÉE, SENEGAL

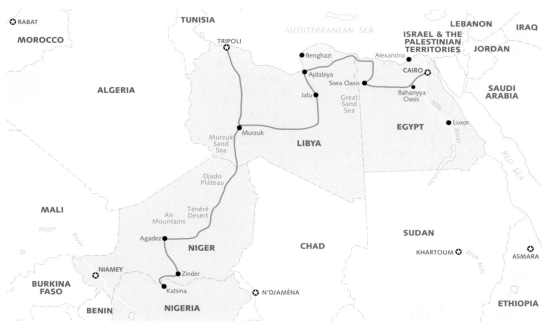

THE SAHARA
HISTORICAL JOURNEY

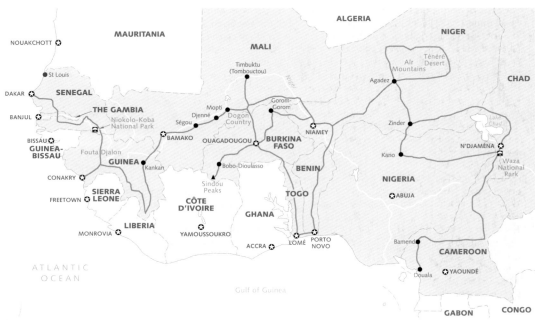

WEST AFRICA
A FRENCH FORAY

NORTH AFRICA
A MEDITERRANEAN MEANDER

EAST AFRICA
A SWAHILI SAFARI

SOME OF NORTH AFRICA'S finest sands are a world away from the dramatic dunes of the Sahara – they line the Mediterranean's shores. Throw in vestiges of Egyptian, Greek, Roman and Carthaginian history and you have one special North African journey.

Start in the shadow of the Sphinx in Cairo and get your fill of the unearthly pyramids, before hitting the coast at Alexandria. Although it was founded by Alexander the Great and was once home to the Pharos lighthouse (one of the seven wonders of the world), the city today is characterised more by its time under French rule, with colonial buildings and elegant coffee houses. Sample some of the beaches between Alexandria and Sallum before jumping into Libya with both feet.

Travelling in Libya can be infuriating as well as intriguing, due to laws requiring you to travel in the company of an official tour agency. Once you get over that fact, however, it's usually smooth sailing. As you move west towards Shahat, you'll flirt with the prettiest sections of Libya's coast – Ras al-Hilal is not to be missed. Near Shahat are the Graeco-Roman ruins of Cyrene, where you can rub shoulders with Zeus and step over mosaics that would be under glass if they were in Europe. Wander Leptis Magna, the best-preserved Roman

city in Africa, before breathing in the Arabic and North African air of Tripoli.

Next, enter Tunisia and leave the Libyan limitations on independent travel behind. Take some sun on Jerba's beaches before visiting El-Jem's honey-coloured Roman amphitheatre and contemplating the fate of those who didn't leave the stadium alive. Continue north to Tunis, where you can sink into its mazelike medina and sip espresso or mint tea calmly, in the knowledge that getting lost is fun and never permanent. Northeast of Tunis are the remarkable remnants of the Punic and Roman city of Carthage. East of Carthage, on Cap Bon, are some of Tunisia's finest white-sand beaches. Before you leave Tunisia for Algeria, explore the well-preserved Roman city of Bulla Regia, which is famous for its underground villas.

Sandwiched between the Mediterranean and the Tell Atlas mountains, Algeria's beautiful and little-visited coast offers more Roman ruins as well as the kicking capital city of Algiers. From here, you can either catch a ferry to France or delve deep into the Sahara. Unless you take to the air, Morocco is out of the question (the border remains closed).

For your Mediterranean meander, you'll need about three months and a whole lot of sunscreen.

EL-JEM'S HONEY-COLOURED ROMAN AMPHITHEATRE, TUNISIA ≪

ALTHOUGH SAFARIS ARE A highlight of East Africa, there's plenty more on offer. With the plethora of air connections in Nairobi, it's a convenient place to start your journey.

Perhaps the best way to introduce yourself to East Africa's famed wildlife is on foot at Hell's Gate National Park. Another way to stretch your legs is to tackle Mt Kenya's valleys, craggy cliffs and steep summits. Although it's 696 metres shorter than Kilimanjaro, Mt Kenya provides some of the most rewarding and scenic trekking in East Africa. With a sturdy four-wheel drive it's then possible to make a loop north from Mt Kenya to take in Samburu National Reserve and the gloriously desolate Lake Turkana.

From Kenya, move west into Uganda and do some white-water rafting on the Nile near Jinja. With water oozing from every pore, continue west to Kampala, where the overwhelming crowds at the bus park will squeeze you dry. Ten minutes of Kampala's frenetic nightlife and you'll be soaked again, this time with sweat. If Mt Kenya didn't give you your fix of glaciers and summits, western Uganda's Mountains of the Moon (Rwenzori Mountains) certainly will.

Your next high will be a Rwandan one, standing metres away from rare mountain gorillas on the slopes of the Virunga volcanoes at the Parc National des Volcans. Then come down to earth with a soul-bruising visit to Rwanda's poignant genocide memorials.

If you don't have a penchant for travelling through countries with fragile peace agreements,

your next move will be straight to Tanzania. More intrepid travellers may, however, want to take the opportunity to discover Burundi, recently emerged from its long civil war. The country offers an exciting capital city, Bujumbura, and rather gorgeous tropical beaches on Lake Tanganyika's shores.

Moving on from Bujumbura, make your way into Tanzania, and then down along the shore of Lake Tanganyika. This route will give you access to the little-visited region of western Tanzania and the Mahale Mountains, which are home to a population of chimpanzees.

Moving east across Tanzania, it would be foolish for any visitor to miss out on seeing the celebrated Serengeti Plains, the setting for the awe-inspiring annual mass migration of wildebeest. It would be equally unwise to skip the Ngorongoro Crater or Mt Kilimanjaro, Africa's mightiest mountain. After a short stop in Dar es Salaam, take to the Indian Ocean for a trip to Zanzibar. Whether you lounge on the island's white beaches, linger in its turquoise waters or get lost in the shadows of Stone Town, Zanzibar is glorious.

Next, it's back to Kenya and the historical port of Mombasa, where you can meander through the old town's maze of narrow streets and enjoy the laid-back Swahili atmosphere.

Finish your journey by boarding the Mombasa–Nairobi train and riding in colonial style back to where you began three or four months earlier.

ELEPHANTS IN KENYA ARE DWARFED BY MAWENZI, A PEAK OF MT KILIMANJARO ≪

NO, WE HAVEN'T MIXED up our bangers with our crepes and mistakenly squeezed in the portly English city of Plymouth instead of posh Paris – this is no Paris–Dakar Rally! For starters, this rally has nothing to do with speed – something people who live along the route are thankful for.

Through the years, the Paris–Dakar Rally has been criticised for killing locals and their livestock, as well as providing little for communities along the route besides clouds of dust. The Vatican newspaper, *L'Osservatore Romano*, went as far as to say that the race was a 'vulgar display of power and wealth in places where men continue to die from hunger and thirst.'

Unlike the Paris–Dakar's souped-up money machines, this rally's cars (known as 'bangers') must not cost more than £100 to procure and £15 to make Sahara-worthy, according to the entry rules. What's the goal? Simply to get your vehicle to the finish line, and to raise money for charities in The Gambia. The rally typically takes a team between three and four weeks to finish, depending on the banger's talent for handling the abuse thrown at it.

As with its costly cousin, the Plymouth–Dakar's first few days are spent reaching Africa from Europe. The journey begins with teams taking a ferry from Plymouth to St Malo in France. From there, it's two days and almost 2000 kilometres worth of driving to reach Gibraltar, where they catch their breath and get their first glimpse of Africa.

After a short ferry crossing to Morocco, teams slide 280 kilometres along the Atlantic coast to the capital, Rabat. The next rest point, Marrakesh, is 333 kilometres south. When they've finished shopping for cheap auto parts, competitors have the joy of wandering the city's medieval bazaars and stuffing themselves at the nightly food stalls on the Djemaa el-Fna, one of Morocco's most atmospheric city squares.

The next leg takes teams 280 kilometres further south to Agadir and its much-loved beach. With some sand in their shorts, teams make the mighty 700-kilometre jaunt south to Laâyoune. The following day's 467 kilometres sees the bangers hugging the tops of bleached coastal cliffs and teams gazing out over the blue Atlantic, before entering Mauritania and repairing their road-weary cars in Nouadhibou.

With the tarmac behind them and the dunes stretching out before them, the next three days and 700 kilometres are always memorable. The Sahara's sublime sand structures are as entrancing as the driving is difficult – sand ladders anyone? The last 93 kilometres to Nouakchott, Mauritania's dusty capital, is along the beach, so it must be done at low tide.

The next port of call, 306 kilometres south, is Senegal and the charming colonial town of St-Louis, where the Senegal River meets the sea. Rested and repaired, teams make the final jaunt (612 kilometres) to Banjul in The Gambia, where their vehicles are auctioned to raise money for various charities. Where does Dakar fit into all this? Besides in the catchy name, nowhere! You can wave as you drive past it if you like; just another quirk in what must be Africa's quirkiest rally.

⤊ DRIVING A £100 CAR THROUGH THE SEARING SAHARA – AFRICA'S ODDEST RALLY

THIS IS THE GRANDADDY of all African itineraries, stretching more than 12,000 kilometres from Table Mountain in Cape Town to the Pyramids of Giza in Cairo, and taking around a year to complete. One of the toughest hurdles is simply starting, leaving the cape's coast, wineries and nightlife behind. Before your foot hits the pedal, you'll also have to make the difficult decision of which route to take north into Malawi.

Venture due north into Namibia and you'll be able to gaze over the Fish River Canyon, stare up at the Namib Desert's massive dunes at Sossusvlei, throw yourself from a plane in Swakopmund and glimpse rhinos in the dark at Etosha National Park. Botswana's transcendent Okavango Delta and Chobe National Park are next, then get soaked rafting the Zambezi at Victoria Falls in Zambia. Before you move on to Malawi, visit the South Luangwa, Kafue and Lower Zambezi National Parks.

The other route to Malawi from Cape Town is east, along South Africa's gorgeous Garden Coast and to Transkei and the Wild Coast. The Drakensberg Range and Lesotho make a perfect side trip. Dip into Swaziland for some rhino-spotting and perhaps a royal wedding or two, then head to Mozambique's capital, Maputo; though you could briefly detour back into South Africa to visit the celebrated Kruger National Park. Get your fill of the Indian Ocean at Mozambique's Bazaruto Archipelago, and go on to Malawi via Gorongosa National Park.

Mt Mulanje, Liwonde National Park and Lake Malawi's northern shores are Malawi musts; in Tanzania, Zanzibar Island, Mt Kilimanjaro and the Serengeti take centre stage. After moving north into Kenya (and surviving Nairobbery with your wallet intact), visit some of the splendid Rift Valley parks and trek past equatorial glaciers on Mt Kenya. En route to Ethiopia, sneak a peek at Samburu National Reserve – the adventurous can travel via the Jade Sea (Lake Turkana).

A long climb from the African plains puts you in the cool Ethiopian highlands. Explore Lalibela's rock-hewn churches, one of the continent's greatest marvels, and visit the 17th-century castles of Africa's Camelot at Gondar. Then trek the sublime Simien Mountains before descending west into Sudan. Witness the meeting of the Niles in Khartoum and head north to the mystical Meroitic pyramids at Meroe. By the time you reach Wadi Halfa on the Egyptian border, you'll be entirely convinced Sudan has Africa's most hospitable people.

In Egypt, sail along one of the Nile's prettiest stretches at Aswan, then head north to Luxor and indulge in history at the Valley of the Kings and the temples of Karnak. Next, follow the Nile Valley further north to Cairo and the finish line. When faced with the Sphinx and the transcendent pyramids, you'll be in awe both of what's before you and of the continent you've just put behind you – the perfect way to finish your epic African journey.

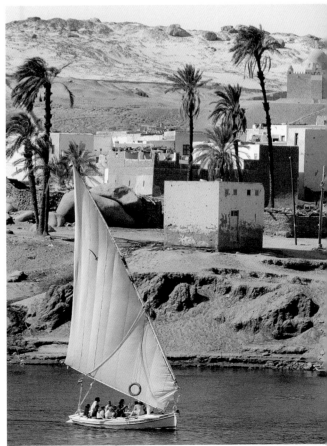
⤊ FELUCCA FANTASY – SAILING ONE OF THE NILE'S ICONIC STRETCHES AT ASWAN, EGYPT

PLYMOUTH–DAKAR RALLY
ADVENTUROUS JOURNEY

CAPE TO CAIRO
CLASSIC JOURNEY

NORTH AFRICA

PUSHED HARD UP AGAINST THE MEDITERRANEAN SEA BY THE SAHARA, NORTH AFRICA IS WHERE AFRICA MEETS THE MIDDLE EAST AND GAZES LONGINGLY ACROSS THE WATERS TOWARDS EUROPE.

This is a region where the landscape dominates. All across North Africa, the parched climate and terrain drive people into the sometimes idyllic, sometimes dying oases of Libya, Egypt and Algeria. Or they congregate in the fertile Nile Valley of Egypt. Or they crowd into Cairo, one of the greatest cities on earth and known as 'the Mother of the World'.

It has always been this way, ever since the ancient Egyptians built their splendid monuments along the Nile Valley. Further west, in modern-day Tunisia, the Carthaginians dominated the Mediterranean region before yielding to the Greek and Roman empires. These empires, in their turn, established magnificent cities all along the North African coast, from Volubilis in Morocco to El-Jem in Tunisia and on through Sabratha, Leptis Magna and Cyrene in Libya.

The great European civilisations of antiquity were unable, however, to penetrate the formidable Sahara and as a result they left the rest of the African continent largely untouched; the armies of

Islam proved themselves more adept in their conquest of land, hearts and minds. When Islam first arrived in North Africa in the 7th century, it swept all before it, racing across Africa's northern rim and implanting the Arab population which now dominates the human landscape of the region. As they carried Islam across the desert sands, they began an enduring transformation of Africa.

The Berbers, North Africa's original inhabitants, were largely supplanted by the Arabs. Most of those that remain live in the Atlas Mountains in Morocco and Algeria and in the Jebel Nafusa of eastern Libya. They are a fiercely traditional and independent people, and provide travellers with some of the most memorable instances of the hospitality for which the region is famed.

The legacy of the past may be everywhere evident in North Africa, but these are also lands of incomparable, vibrant cities whose names – Marrakesh, Fès, Casablanca, Algiers, Tripoli and Alexandria – resonate with African magic. Cities

such as these have become essential North African stopovers for the independent traveller, even as European package tourists arrive in their hundreds of thousands along the Mediterranean coasts of Tunisia and Morocco or the Red Sea resorts of Egypt's Sinai Peninsula. The southern parts of Algeria, Libya and Tunisia are home to the best that the Sahara has to offer, with remote seas of sand and eerily beautiful desert massifs which conceal millennia-old rock art.

The region is, of course, not without its problems, not least of which are the deaths by drowning of thousands of Africans trying to reach Europe in leaky boats. But with a new openness sweeping through Morocco, Algeria's civil war largely consigned to the past and Libya finally emerging from the isolation of long years of international sanctions, visiting North Africa is easier than it has been in decades.

TEXT: ANTHONY HAM

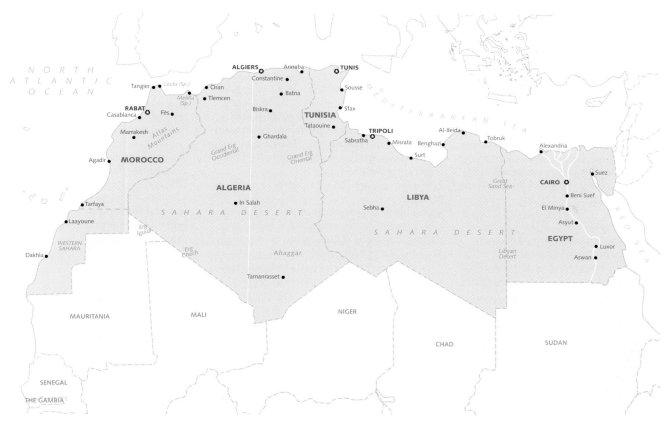

NORTH ATLANTIC OCEAN

MOROCCO
Tangier
Ceuta (Sp.)
Melilla (Sp.)
Oran
Tlemcen
RABAT ✿
Fès
Casablanca
Marrakesh
Atlas Mountains
Agadir
Tarfaya
Laayoune
WESTERN SAHARA
Dakhla
Erg Iguidi

ALGERIA
Grand Erg Occidental
Biskra
Batna
Constantine
ALGIERS ✿
Annaba
Ghardaïa
Grand Erg Oriental
SAHARA DESERT
In Salah
Erg Chech
Ahaggar
Tamanrasset

TUNISIA
TUNIS ✿
Sousse
Sfax
Tataouine

LIBYA
TRIPOLI ✿
Sabratha
Misrata
Benghazi
Surt
Al-Beida
Tobruk
Sebha
SAHARA DESERT
Libyan Desert

MEDITERRANEAN SEA

EGYPT
Alexandria
CAIRO ✿
Suez
Beni Suef
El Minya
Asyut
Luxor
Aswan
Great Sand Sea
RED SEA

MAURITANIA
MALI
NIGER
CHAD
SUDAN
SENEGAL
THE GAMBIA

TEXT SIONA JENKINS

EGYPT

EGYPT HAS FASCINATED VISITORS FOR THOUSANDS OF YEARS, AND ITS MIXTURE OF INCREDIBLE ANCIENT MONUMENTS, FRIENDLY PEOPLE AND NATURAL BEAUTY CONTINUE TO MAKE IT ONE OF THE WORLD'S MOST COMPELLING DESTINATIONS

CAPITAL CITY CAIRO   POPULATION 78.9 MILLION   AREA 1 MILLION SQ KM   OFFICIAL LANGUAGE ARABIC

LANDSCAPE

Egypt is a land of geographical extremes: the Nile is virtually the country's only source of water and it irrigates less than three per cent of its million square kilometres. Almost all Egyptians live in or on the edge of this lush strip of green. The remaining 97 per cent of the country is arid, sparsely populated desert. Rainfall is minimal throughout the country, and temperatures are high in the summer and moderate in the winter.

HISTORY IN A NUTSHELL

Human civilisation first took off when the Nile's bounty gave Egyptians enough leisure time to develop a sophisticated and wealthy society, and for nearly 3000 years Egypt was the world's superpower. In an attempt to guarantee themselves a continuation of their earthly pleasures in the hereafter, the Egyptians developed complicated religious rituals, already ancient and diluted by outside influences by the time the Romans arrived. It was Christianity that first supplanted Egypt's pagan beliefs, but Islam arrived soon after that. Egypt's past glory was gradually buried or forgotten and the country was occupied, first by the Ottomans and then by the Europeans. In 1952 Gamal Abdel Nasser became Egypt's president and ended foreign rule. In the half-century since then, misrule by military dictators more concerned with security than governance has left Egypt grappling with issues of overpopulation, economic stagnation and a repressive political system that has provoked violent religious opposition.

PEOPLE

Egypt is remarkably homogeneous. Ninety-eight per cent of the population is ethnically 'Egyptian'. One per cent is a mixture of Berber (most of whom live in Siwa), Nubian (in the southern Nile Valley), Bedouin (in Sinai and along the northwest coast) and Beja (a sub-Saharan group concentrated close to the Sudanese border). The rest are a European melange, mostly of Armenians, Greeks, Italians and French. Ninety per cent of all Egyptians are Sunni Muslim and about 10 per cent are Christian (of which roughly 90 per cent are Coptic).

MARKETPLACE

Although it's a middle-ranking economy (annual GDP per capita is estimated to be US$3900), Egypt is Africa's largest aid recipient. Thanks largely to its geopolitical importance it receives US$1.7 billion a year from America alone (albeit most comes in the form of military assistance). Tourism is also a significant earner, despite sporadic attacks in tourist centres. Government outgoings total US$27 billion per year, equating to nearly three per cent of the UK's annual expenditure. Yet 20 per cent of Egyptians are officially estimated to live below the poverty line (unofficial estimates are far higher) and, despite attempts to reform the creaking centralised economy, they seem likely to remain there for the foreseeable future.

TRADEMARKS

o Pyramids
o The Nile
o Mummies
o Temples
o Tombs
o Mt Sinai
o The desert
o Baksheesh
o King Tut
o Belly-dancing

A BOY RENTS INNER TUBES AS FLOTATION DEVICES ON ALEXANDRIA'S CORNICHE »

⌃ A FORMAL FIGURE BLENDS WITH THE HIEROGLYPHICS AT THE FUNERARY TEMPLE OF RAMSES III ON LUXOR'S WEST BANK

MARK WEBSTER // LONELY PLANET IMAGES

⌃ A SCHOOL OF ANTHIAS BROWSING OVER BRAIN CORAL IN THE RED SEA'S RAS MOHAMMED NATIONAL PARK

⌃ BERBER CHILDREN IN CONTRASTING MOODS, SIWA

CAFÉ CONTENTMENT: A MAN SMOKES A SHEESHA IN ESNA ≫

SPLASHES OF COLOUR ON A LUXOR STREET ≫

FROM THE TRAVELLER

Being in Egypt means a visit to the pyramids is a must. I wanted to capture how they look from a distance, surrounded by the desert, but after walking about five kilometres away, a thunderstorm arrived. With nowhere to run, I waited in the heavy rain for about 10 minutes. When the rain was over, miraculously the sunlight soon returned and I saw a rainbow across the pyramids.

RR UKIRSARI MANGGALANI SOEPIJONO-BRODJOKALOSO // INDONESIA

RANDOM FACTS

o The ancient Egyptians didn't invent the wheel until 1000 years after they built the pyramids.

o In 17th-century Europe, Egyptian mummies were believed to have healing powers and were ground up and eaten or made into poultices.

o Fifty-four per cent of Egyptians watch more than five hours of TV each day.

NATURAL BEAUTY

One of the greatest pleasures in Eygpt is sitting beneath a palm tree or on the deck of a boat and watching the Nile's inexorable flow northward through lush farmland. Beyond this icon, however, are some varied and stunning desert landscapes, from the dunes of the Western Desert's Great Sand Sea to the barren crags of Sinai's mountains. In the Red Sea lie some of the world's most famous coral reefs, frequented by an equally impressive variety of marine life.

ON PAPER

o *The Alexandria Quartet* by Lawrence Durrell

o *The English Patient* by Michael Ondaatje

o *Death on the Nile* by Agatha Christie

o *The Levant Trilogy* by Olivia Manning

o *The Blue Nile* and *The White Nile* by Alan Moorehead

o *An Egyptian Journal* by William Golding

URBAN SCENE

Cairo is Egypt's beating heart, a chaotic agglomeration of 16 million people on the banks of the Nile. So central is it to the consciousness of Egyptians that its name in Arabic, Masr, is the same as the word for Egypt. Dusty, polluted, crowded and noisy, it's a mad mixture of flyovers, high-rises and monuments; the seat of government, engine of the economy and centre of culture, and one of the world's great cities.

MYTHS & LEGENDS

For centuries the Pyramids of Giza were thought to have been built by slaves – a belief that persists despite plenty of archaeological evidence to the contrary. The myth began when Egyptian priests told the tale to the Greek historian Herodotus, who arrived in Egypt in the 5th century BC. The priests must have smiled when the gullible Greek recorded their yarn that the pharaoh Khufu (Cheops) forced thousands of slaves to build the Great Pyramid and prostituted his daughter to raise money for its construction.

TOP FESTIVAL

At the full moon each October, hundreds gather in remote Siwa Oasis for the Siyaha Festival, a three-day celebration of community. Most of the oasis decamps to Jebel Dakrour, a small mountain on the edge of the desert. Visits are exchanged, outstanding disputes resolved and, after noon prayer each day, huge communal feasts of rice, meat and bread are consumed. Later, under the light of the moon, the men gather in huge circles for *zikr*, long, mystical sessions of chanting and dancing in praise of God.

IMPORT

↗ *Aida* (the opera commissioned for the opening of the Suez Canal in 1869)

↗ Archaeologists

↗ Camels (from the Persians)

↗ Peugeot taxis

↗ Wheat (Egypt is one of the world's biggest importers)

EXPORT

↖ Political Islam

↖ Beer (the pharaohs did it first)

↖ Pharaonic Revival architecture

↖ *Sheesha* (water pipe)

↖ Belly-dancing (no matter what other Arab countries claim)

↖ Arabic-language soap operas

↖ Long staple cotton

ECOTOURISM

Cairo may be choking on smog, but there are 21 protected areas away from the capital. Ecolodges are rapidly emerging in oases and deserts, with projects in Siwa Oasis and the St Katherine Protectorate (Sinai) leading the way in preserving the environment and ensuring indigenous minorities benefit from tourism.

FUTURE DIRECTIONS

Without profound political change, Egypt is likely to continue on its present course: getting by but failing to reach its potential, with a small minority using violence to try to change the status quo. Egyptians may become increasingly religious unless enlightened change offers them hope of a brighter future, and most will keep their heads down and survive with humour, as they have done for millennia.

ESSENTIAL EXPERIENCES

o **Savouring your first view of the pyramids and wishing they were not on the edge of a polluted megalopolis**

o **Dragging your hand through the water as you float along the Nile in a felucca**

o **Joining the faithful to watch the sunrise on top of Mt Sinai**

o **Getting ripped off by a Cairo taxi driver**

o **Swimming among the rich corals off Sinai's Ras Mohammed National Park**

o **Losing yourself amid the papyrus columns of Karnak Temple's hypostyle hall**

o **Being awestruck by the ancient treasures in the Egyptian Museum**

o **Braving the spiral staircase of Cairo's Bab Zuweila for a panoramic view of the city's medieval core**

o **Sweating profusely while exploring the incomparable, but perennially hot, tombs in the Valley of the Kings**

o **Sloughing off the sand in a desert hot spring in Siwa**

≫ EYES FOLLOW YOU ON THE STREETS OF CAIRO

MAP REF // O3

BEST TIME TO VISIT **OCTOBER TO MAY**

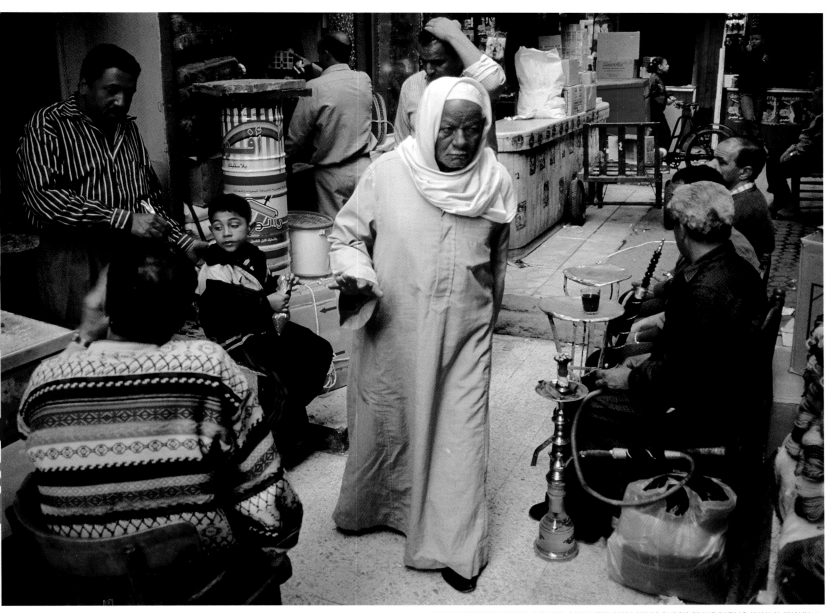

NAVIGATING THE NARROW AND WELL-POPULATED PASSAGES OF CAIRO'S GRAND BAZAAR, KHAN AL-KHALILI ⤢

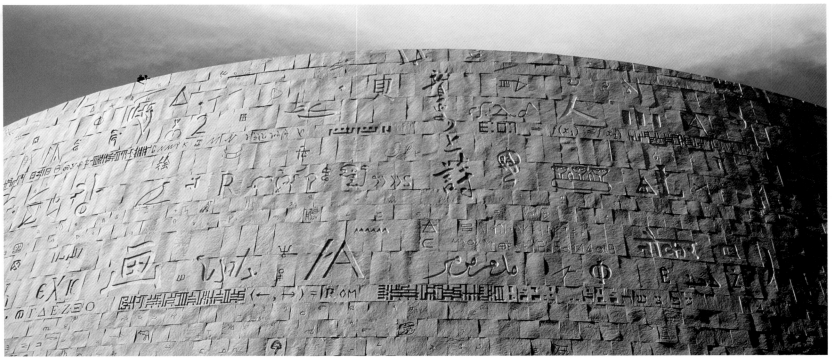

SYMBOLS FROM AROUND THE WORLD DECORATE THE NEW ALEXANDRIA LIBRARY ⤢

TEXT ANTHONY HAM

LIBYA

LIBYA IS A DESTINATION WITH CACHET – COASTAL RUINS AND INCOMPARABLE DESERT TERRAIN MAKE IT THE ADVENTURE DESTINATION OF CHOICE FOR THE DISCERNING TRAVELLER.

CAPITAL CITY TRIPOLI   POPULATION 5.9 MILLION   AREA 1.8 MILLION SQ KM   OFFICIAL LANGUAGE ARABIC

≫ RICH TONES FOR A BARREN LANDSCAPE: MEN IN DESERT HEADGEAR, SAHARA DESERT

LANDSCAPE

Libya, Africa's fourth-largest country, is dominated by the Sahara – plateaus of rock scoured by sandy winds and sand seas larger than many a small European country. The country also does a good line in mountains, with no fewer than three mountain ranges: the Jebel Acacus in the remote southwest, the Jebel Nafusa in the northwest and the northeastern Jebel Akhdar (Green Mountains), which drop steeply into the Mediterranean.

HISTORY IN A NUTSHELL

Until about 4000 years ago, the Libyan Sahara was a temperate paradise of vast inland lakes and forests. Northern Libya later became a playground and battleground for the great empires of antiquity – Punic, Roman, Greek and Byzantine – while the home-grown and highly civilised Garamantes made the desert bloom in the south. In 643, however, Islam swept all before it, and a succession of Islamic dynasties, including the Ottoman Empire, ruled Libya until the Italians arrived in the 20th century. During World War II Libya again became a battleground for other countries' wars, before the British brought Italian colonial rule to a close. The country achieved independence in 1951, but Libyans had to wait until 1969 for young Colonel Muammar Gaddafi to arrive on the scene. Gaddafi – his regime at once eccentric and authoritarian – has worn many guises since, from international pariah to responsible world citizen.

PEOPLE

Libya is one of Africa's most homogeneous nations: 97 per cent of its people are of Arab or Berber origin. Other small groups include the Tuareg, the indigenous people of the Sahara, and the Toubou. More than 95 per cent of the population are Sunni Muslims and up to 90 per cent of Libyans live in urban centres. And while Gaddafi is in his sixties, almost half the country's population is under 15.

MARKETPLACE

Oil, oil and more oil. Libya is one of Africa's largest oil producers, and oil has propelled the country from grinding 1950s poverty to its current status as Africa's richest country. As a result, Libyans enjoy a highly respectable per capita GDP of US$11,400 (compared to US$900 in neighbouring Niger). But pity the day that Libya runs out of oil: although there are reserves of natural gas for export, 75 per cent of its food is imported. Oil is what keeps the nation afloat, and amounts to a staggering 95 per cent of exports.

TRADEMARKS

- Colonel Gaddafi
- World heritage–listed ancient cities
- Idyllic palm-fringed lakes amid sand dunes
- Ancient rock art
- Friendly souqs

NATURAL BEAUTY

The Libyan Sahara is the desert you thought existed only in the imagination. In the country's south, the Ubari and Murzuk Sand Seas are daily sculpted by the wind into splendid shapes. In the former are the Ubari Lakes, surrounded by soaring sand dunes and swaying palm trees – a miracle of water in the desert's heart. In the southwest, the Jebel Acacus consists of towering stone monoliths rising from the sands; the east boasts the black aftermath of the long-extinct volcanoes of Waw al-Namus and Haruj al-Aswad.

RANDOM FACTS

- Deserts cover 95 per cent of the country.
- Twenty per cent is covered by sand dunes.
- A quarter of the population died as a direct result of Italy's colonial rule.
- The 10 years of international sanctions have cost Libya $US30 billion.

EXIT STAGE LEFT: THE LEPTIS MAGNA AMPHITHEATRE »

KNOBBLY BASALT FORMATIONS POPULATE THE JEBEL ACACUS »

URBAN SCENE

Tripoli has long been known as the 'White Bride of the Mediterranean' – it's one of North Africa's prettiest cities. The Ottoman-era medina is a secret world of souqs and labyrinthine lanes which conceal the grand mansions of colonial times behind high white walls. There's a 1st-century AD Roman triumphal arch, and lording it over all is Tripoli's Red Castle, a sturdy fortress which houses one of the best museums in Africa. But it's in the evening that Tripoli is most seductive, when the breeze sweeps in off the sea and you have all the city's fine restaurants to choose from.

LIBYA'S GREAT MAN-MADE RIVER

Libya has plenty of oil but a critical shortage of water. Colonel Gaddafi's solution? Use the revenues of the former to pipe water from the vast underground reservoirs beneath the Sahara to Libya's thirsty coastal cities – and then call it the 'Eighth Wonder of the World'. One of the most ambitious infrastructure projects anywhere in the world, Libya's Great Man-Made River will outlive its creator – though not by much. The water, some of which has been beneath the desert for 38,000 years, is expected to disappear in around 50 years, just as Libya's oil reserves run dry.

SURPRISES

○ Tobruk, one of World War II's most famous battlefields, is in Libya
○ Libya is one of Africa's safest countries
○ Colonel Gaddafi as the West's New Best Friend

TUAREG ORIGINS

The nomadic Tuareg people of the Sahara were originally Berbers from the Libyan oasis of Awjila, but the arrival of Arab armies in the 7th century and the 11th-century invasion by 200,000 Arab families drove many Berbers deeper into the desert where, over the centuries, they became known as Tuareg. All Tuareg, whether in Libya, Algeria or Niger, claim descent from a single woman of noble birth named Lemtuna, the same ancestress claimed by the Berbers of Ghadames.

FUTURE DIRECTIONS

Libya is a country on the upswing and its stunning re-emergence from decades of international isolation has transformed Libyans into Africa's most optimistic people. Libyans have a spring in their step and eagerly embrace all that's new, impatient for their government to loosen the economic and political shackles. It won't happen overnight, but it will happen.

☆ A CAREFUL WALK THROUGH TRIPOLI

FROM THE TRAVELLER

In this photo, a local stands in the light at the end of a long corridor with a sand floor, wooden roof and white walls. I was in a traditional house in Ghat – in the south of Libya – and just as I was going outside I saw this man (my guide) waiting for me just beyond the door in the hard sun of the desert like a mirage... and I knew I couldn't miss this striking picture!

ROMAIN DELORME // FRANCE

ESSENTIAL EXPERIENCES

○ **Wandering through Leptis Magna, the best-preserved Roman city in Africa**

○ **Getting lost in the labyrinth in the wonderful Saharan oasis of Ghadames**

○ **Rubbing shoulders with Zeus in the Graeco-Roman ruins of Cyrene**

○ **Discovering 12,000-year-old rock art deep in the desert massif of the Jebel Acacus**

○ **Meandering through the medina in Tripoli with its whitewashed architecture and refreshingly nonexistent sales pitch**

○ **Falling off the end of the earth at the remote black-sand volcano of Waw al-Namus**

MAP REF // M3

BEST TIME TO VISIT **NOVEMBER TO MARCH**

☆ A LARGER-THAN-LIFE COLONEL GADDAFI IN GREEN SQUARE, TRIPOLI

THE INTERIOR OF QASR AL-HAJ'S MASSIVE FORTIFIED GRANARY 》

PASSING THE TIME AT GURGI MOSQUE IN TRIPOLI 》

THE MUSHROOM ROCK, ONE OF THE WORKS OF EROSION IN THE JEBEL ACACUS 》

TUNISIA

TRANQUIL TUNISIA – HEMMED BETWEEN UNRULY NEIGHBOURS – IS A BIG COUNTRY PACKED INTO A SMALL ONE, WITH DESERTS, FORESTS, MOUNTAINS, BEACHES AND SETTINGS WEIRD ENOUGH TO BE USED AS *STAR WARS* LOCATIONS.

CAPITAL CITY **TUNIS**   POPULATION **10.2 MILLION**   AREA **163,610 SQ KM**   OFFICIAL LANGUAGES **ARABIC, FRENCH**

⌃ MEN ENJOY A GAME OF DESERT HOCKEY AT THE SAHARA FESTIVAL, DOUZ

LANDSCAPE

Tunisia has 1400 kilometres of Mediterranean coastline. The Tunisian Dorsale (the continuation of Morocco and Algeria's dramatic Atlas Mountains) is the main mountain range, which tapers off to form the Cap Bon Peninsula. North of this spine lie bountiful plains and the Medjerda River valley, beyond which are the Kroumirie mountains. South of the Dorsale, a barren plain meets endless salt flats, which give way to the rolling dunes of the Grand Erg Oriental. Tunisia has hot, dry summers and mild winters, but the further south you go, the hotter and drier it gets. Though it's an astonishingly diverse country, ever since the Romans started clearing woodland the environment has suffered, with forests shrinking from 30 per cent of the country then to two per cent today.

HISTORY IN A NUTSHELL

Carthage, the Phoenician imperial capital, dominated the Mediterranean from the 6th century BC until it was destroyed by arch-rival Rome 146 BC. Vandals and Byzantines invaded next, then Islam arrived in the 7th century with the Arabs, followed by centuries of Islamic Arabian dynasties. In the 16th century Tunisia became part of the Ottoman empire. The French had control from the 19th century until Habib Bourguiba led the country to independence in 1956. Socialist, secular, autocratic Bourguiba ruled for 32 years, until current president Ben Ali headed a 1987 coup. He's continued along socialist, secular, autocratic lines, winning subsequent elections with a Soviet-style 95 per cent or so of the vote.

PEOPLE

After 14 centuries of intermarriage, the indigenous Berbers and more recently arrived Arabs are thoroughly entwined. Arab-Berber Muslims form 98 per cent of the population, the other two per cent being Jews and Christians. You're most likely to see Berber culture in the south.

MARKETPLACE

Tunisia has one of Africa's strongest economies. However, in 2002, growth slowed due to drought and tourism slackening in response to 9/11. Better rains from 2003 to 2005 improved matters, and tourism has bounced back since the official end of the Iraq war. GDP per capita is now US$8300 (it's US$29,900 in France, by comparison), and government spending is US$8.3 billion a year compared to the French US$1.144 trillion.

TRADEMARKS

- Jasmine
- The desert
- More women's rights than any other Arab nation
- The Hand of Fatima (a symbol made into charms or used to mark doorways to ward off the evil eye)
- White-sand beaches
- *Star Wars* settings
- Beach gigolos

NATURAL BEAUTY

South is the Sahara of your dreams, undulating southwest into Algeria: silent, shifting gold. North of the famous desert lie the great salt lakes, weirdly flat surfaces that refract mirages and blister in the heat, with drifts of salt that sparkle like snow. Around the coast, limpid Mediterranean waters lap at pearly sands – there are some particularly impressive beaches in the north of Tunisia, around Cap Bon and also on the desert island of Jerba. The Tunisian Dorsale peaks rear up from the plains surrounding them like ghostly islands. Jugurtha's Table is the eeriest, a flat-topped mountain used as an ancient fortress, with steps hacked up one side. Further north, the Kroumerie range is on an alpine scale, blanketed in tall cork-oak forest.

THE NEED FOR SPEED: A BERBER HORSEMAN PERFORMS AT THE SAHARA FESTIVAL, DOUZ »

RANDOM FACTS

○ It gets so hot and so cold that both the Romans and the Berbers resorted to living underground.
○ In the Middle Ages, Monastir was said to be the first step on the road to paradise.
○ Tunisia has stood in for any number of other places on film: Cairo, Jerusalem, Tatooine. *Star Wars: A New Hope* (1977), *Star Wars: The Phantom Menace* (1999), *Star Wars: Attack of the Clones (2002), The English Patient* (1996), *Raiders of the Lost Ark* (1981), *Life of Brian* (1979) and *Jesus of Nazareth* (1977) were all filmed here.
○ From Tunis on the north coast to Tataouine deep in the desert is only a 10-hour journey.
○ The French were so attached to the port of Bizerte that they stayed for six years after independence.

URBAN SCENE

The capital Tunis is a cross-cultural marriage between wide, tree-shaded, French-style boulevards and the North African medina's tangle of souqs and lanes. This curious cultural sandwich isn't just architectural: young women in Western fashions swish past elderly men in *chechia* (red felt hats) and women in headscarves and slippers.

In central Tunisia, Kairouan, Islam's fourth holiest city, was once the Arabian capital of North Africa. Here all roads lead to the beautiful Great Mosque, surrounded by a whitewashed maze of streets, where flashes of blue and green brighten the doors and windows and elderly women hurry along in dusty black.

IMPORT

↗ Islam
↗ Western values and architectural fashions
↗ Roman mosaics
↗ World War II armies
↗ Film crews
↗ French bread and croissants
↗ Disgraced former Italian prime minister Bettino Craxi (avoiding corruption charges)
↗ Tourists
↗ Yasser Arafat and the PLO (from 1982 to 1994)

EXPORT

↖ Cheap labour
↖ Dates
↖ Almonds
↖ Carpets
↖ Numidian marble
↖ Hannibal and his elephants

⌃ SHEEP FOR SALE AT THE WEEKLY ANIMAL MARKET IN DOUZ

CUISINE

In Tunisia, fiery food is equated with hot passions. The nation's favourite spice is harissa, a hot chilli paste that real men eat with everything. The national dish, of course, is couscous, steamed with a vegetable, meat or fish sauce. It's traditionally eaten communally, with the whole family delving into a large bowl. A Tunisian peculiarity is the addictive *briq*, a fried pastry envelope usually filled with a satisfying slurp of runny egg. Eating it without getting splattered is a specialist skill.

SURPRISES

○ Ancient cultures, remote mountains, desert and unspoilt beaches add up to so much more than a package-holiday heaven.
○ Tunis' Bardo Museum has the world's greatest collection of Roman mosaics.
○ Tunisia banned the *hejab* (headscarf) in schools and public administration in 1981, over 20 years before France did.

ESSENTIAL EXPERIENCES

○ **Threading through the labyrinthine Tunis medina and sipping mint tea laced with pine nuts**
○ **Wandering around Roman underground houses – as if their residents just popped out – at Bulla Regia**
○ **Watching mirages flit across the Chott el-Jerid salt lake**
○ **Imagining the crowd erupting at El-Jem's stadium, the most spectacular Roman monument in Africa**
○ **Camel trekking across the Grand Erg Oriental's golden blankness**
○ **Exploring Berber underground houses and hilltop granaries that look like they were built by aliens**
○ **Observing Roman minutiae in the Bardo Museum's incredible mosaic collection**
○ **Getting scrubbed by an enthusiastic elderly masseur in a *hammam* (bathhouse)**
○ **Watching the sun set over Dougga, a hilltop Roman town amid ancient wheat fields**
○ **Using your imagination to reconstruct Carthage's legendary civilisation**

MAP REF // K1

BEST TIME TO VISIT MID-MARCH TO MAY FOR THE NORTH, NOVEMBER FOR THE SOUTH

⌃ AN EYE-CATCHING WHITE MOSQUE NEAR CHENINI

WOMEN ADMIRE EXPENSIVE BRIDAL GOWNS IN THE WINDOW OF A TUNIS SHOP »

AN ELEGANTLY DETAILED DOOR IN THE MEDINA, TUNIS »

THE GHORFA (GRANARY) AT KSAR OULED SOLTANE WILL SEEM ODDLY FAMILIAR TO *STAR WARS* FANS »

TEXT VESNA MARIC

ALGERIA

VAST DESERT, OASIS TOWNS, TRIBAL CULTURES AND A ROCKY MEDITERRANEAN COAST MAKE ALGERIA ONE OF THE MOST VERSATILE PLACES TO VISIT, BUT A DIFFICULT HISTORY MEANS THAT ONLY TRULY INTREPID TRAVELLERS MAKE IT IN.

CAPITAL CITY ALGIERS   POPULATION 32.9 MILLION   AREA 2.4 MILLION SQ KM   OFFICIAL LANGUAGES ARABIC, FRENCH, BERBER

⌃ YOU NEVER KNOW WHO YOU'LL MEET IN THE NARROW STREETS OF GHARDAÏA

LANDSCAPE

Algeria is Africa's second-largest country, after Sudan. About 85 per cent of the country is taken up by the Sahara, while the mountainous Tell region in the north makes up the balance. The Tell is made up of two main mountain ranges: the Tell Atlas, which runs right along the north coast into Tunisia, and the Saharan Atlas, about 100 kilometres to the south. The area between the two ranges is known as the High Plateau. Summer in the north is hot and humid, and the winters are mild and wet. Summer in the Sahara is ferociously hot. Daytime temperatures seldom fall below 25°C in winter, but nights can be very cold, particularly in the Hoggar. Rainfall ranges from over 1000 millimetres per year in the northern mountains to zero in the Sahara.

HISTORY IN A NUTSHELL

Algeria's original inhabitants were Berbers; the Arabs conquered North Africa in the 7th century. After the 12th century, coastal Algeria, together with Tunisia, was one of the main outposts for pirates operating in the Mediterranean. The pirates were only truly beaten with the arrival of the French, centuries later. In the 16th century the Ottomans waltzed into the country and established themselves as rulers. The French took over in 1830, much to the displeasure of the Algerians. Their struggle for independence began in 1954, headed by the National Liberation Front, which came to power once independence was achieved in 1962. Following civil protest in the 1980s, the Algerian politics of the 1990s were dominated by the struggle between the military and Islamist militants. In 1992 a general election won by an Islamist party was annulled, starting a civil war in which more than 100,000 people were killed. Upon being elected in 1999, Abdelaziz Bouteflika pronounced an amnesty, leading many rebels to lay down their arms. Though Algeria is now a peaceful country, Bouteflika's government, elected again in 2004, continues to struggle with issues of high unemployment and corruption, the minority Berber community's demands for autonomy, and extremist militant activity.

PEOPLE

An estimated 99 per cent of Algeria's population are Sunni Muslims; the majority are Arab-Berber and live in the north of the country. Berber traditions remain best preserved in the Kabylie region southeast of Algiers, where people speak the local Berber dialect as their first language, French as their second and Arabic as their third. After sustained protests and rioting, Berber was finally recognised as an official language in 2002. The Tuareg people of the Sahara are also Berbers, but they speak their own tribal language, Tamashek.

MARKETPLACE

Algeria is potentially a wealthy country – it possesses the seventh-largest reserves of natural gas in the world and is the world's second-largest gas exporter. It also ranks 14th in oil reserves. But this economic potential has failed to translate itself into a higher living standard for the majority of the population, and despite the government's continued efforts to diversify the economy through attracting foreign and domestic investment outside the energy sector, the country's high unemployment rates and low living standards remain.

TRADEMARKS

- Tuareg desert nomads
- Sahara sand dunes
- Algiers' old quarter
- Hoggar Mountains
- Raï music

A WOMAN BEDECKED IN SILVER FOR THE TAFSIT SPRING FESTIVAL »

- The Tuareg are known as 'blue men' because they colour their faces with indigo for celebrations.
- On a visit to the hot spring of Hammam Meskoutine, on the Mediterranean coast, it's traditional to cook an egg in the 98°C water and eat it.
- In the Ibadite town of Beni Isguen, women are allowed to show only their left eye in public.

NATURAL BEAUTY

Algeria has two contrasting sides to it: the Mediterranean coast and the parched Sahara. Both are beautiful, but it's the Sahara that epitomises all the exotic and mysterious ideas of the desert, and what fascinates most visitors to the country. It covers a great range of landscapes, from the classic S-dunes of the great *ergs* (sand seas) to the rock-strewn peaks of the Hoggar Mountains in the far south. The vast empty space is interrupted by volcanic hills and mountains and oasis towns.

URBAN SCENE

Algiers, the country's capital, is a kicking urban centre, with sprawling French mansions stretching from the Ottoman medina. There's a real mix of the traditional and the modern, with old men fishing at the port, fez-wearing salesmen making their pitches at the medina, and youngsters in designer outfits strolling down the wide boulevards.

IMPORT

- French architecture
- Ex-soldier turned missionary Charles de Foucauld
- Designer outfits
- European food
- Marseille ferries

EXPORT

- Natural gas
- Petroleum
- *Raï* music king Cheb Mami
- Sublime Saharan stories
- Football player Zinedine Zidane

A BOY BOUNDS AHEAD, IN SALAH

CUISINE

Meals are a big deal in Algeria, and family larders are full of wonderful things like couscous, seafood and lamb, prepared with vegetables, herbs and spices that your tastebuds will crave forever once you've tried them. Family meals are usually elaborate and enjoyed over a few hours, and big festivities like Eid or weddings are an occasion for a three-day feast. Algerian dishes include the amazing lavender couscous, orange and onion salads, spicy octopus soup, lamb bombarded with olives, and chicken sautéed with diced pumpkin – not to mention exquisite pastries such as the semolina-flour *ghribia*.

ECOTOURISM

Algeria's vast, undeveloped and untouched landscape is still relatively little visited, and there are many people who would like to see things stay that way. However, as Algeria's political situation becomes more stable, exploring the country is becoming relatively easier. Concerted efforts are being made, for the most part by individuals and private agencies, to preserve the Saharan landscape and emphasise ecofriendly tourism.

ESSENTIAL EXPERIENCES

- **Cruising on a walking expedition with the Tuareg through the desert, eating by the campfire, seeing incredible desertscapes and sleeping under the stars**
- **Climbing up onto Assekrem, the highest peak of the Hoggar mountain range, playing dominoes with the Tuareg and watching the sunrise**
- **Seeing 8000-year-old rock art in Djanet and Taghit**
- **Trying to work out who's who in the sea of veiled 'blue men' in the Tuareg capital, Tamanrasset, deep in the Sahara**
- **Admiring the beautiful terracotta architecture and getting to know the wonderful people of the oasis town of Timimoun**
- **Taking in the Ibadite town of Beni Isguen, where 1000-year-old Islamic traditions survive, men and women live completely separate lives, and no non-Muslim visitor can go in alone or stay the night**

MAP REF // 13

BEST TIME TO VISIT **MARCH TO JUNE**

CURVES AND LINES IN THE ABDELKADER DISTRICT OF ALGIERS

THE MARTYRS' MONUMENT SWEEPS SKYWARD IN ALGIERS »

A CUP OF THE UBIQUITOUS MINT TEA »

THE GRAND ERG OCCIDENTAL, A MASSIVE YET GRACEFUL TIDE OF SAND, SEEMS ABOUT TO OVERWHELM KERZAZ »

TEXT ANTHONY HAM

MOROCCO

MOROCCO IS THE CROSSROADS OF EAST AND WEST, A BRIDGE BETWEEN AFRICA AND EUROPE THAT POSSESSES THE BEST OF ALL POSSIBLE WORLDS.

CAPITAL CITY RABAT **POPULATION** 33.5 MILLION (INCLUDING THE ANNEXED REGION OF WESTERN SAHARA) **AREA** 712,550 SQ KM **OFFICIAL LANGUAGE** ARABIC

LANDSCAPE

Morocco's fusion of rock, sand and sea gives it some of North Africa's most diverse topography. In the north, the limestone-and-sandstone Rif Atlas Mountains shoot up from the Mediterranean coast to a decidedly steep 2200 metres. Further inland, forming the backbone of Morocco, tiered mountains rise first to the 3340-metre summit of the Middle Atlas Mountains, before yielding to the greater might of the High Atlas and the dizzying heights of Jebel Toubkal (4167 metres), the highest peak in North Africa. And then it all drops away, down, down, down into the vast Sahara.

HISTORY IN A NUTSHELL

The Berbers, Morocco's original inhabitants, thought that they had seen off all comers – Phoenicians, Romans, Vandals and Byzantines – until the Arab armies of Islam arrived in the 7th century and never got around to leaving. Later, home-grown Berber dynasties such as the Almoravids and Almohads put Morocco firmly on the Islamic map. Morocco's strategic importance drew the attention and armies of France and Spain, who each ruled parts of Morocco. After they withdrew and Morocco regained independence in the 1950s, it claimed sovereignty over the Western Sahara, much to the indigenous Sahrawis' chagrin. Since it achieved independence, Morocco has had a remarkably stable history: on a continent where revolving-door governments are standard, it has had just two leaders (King Hassan II and his more liberal-minded son, Mohammed VI) in the last 45 years.

RANDOM FACTS

- In 1975 King Hassan II led 300,000 unarmed Moroccans in the 'Green March' to claim the Western Sahara.
- One third of all Moroccans are under 15.
- The last Barbary lion in captivity died in the 1960s.
- Morocco's birth rate has fallen from 6.9 births per fertile woman in 1970 to just 2.8 in 2006.
- The adult literacy rate is 50.7 per cent.

PEOPLE

Morocco could lay claim to the title of Africa's most homogeneous country: 99.1 per cent of the population are Arabs or Berbers. A mere 98.7 per cent are Muslim. The population of Morocco is also overwhelmingly young – the average age is only 23.9 years, compared to 39.9 in Spain – and many of the country's brightest young stars, frustrated by a lack of opportunities in their home country, seek their fortunes abroad.

MARKETPLACE

Despite a crippling debt of US$15.6 billion (72.3 per cent of GDP) hanging over it, there are high hopes for the future of Morocco's economy. In a move of which most African countries can only dream, all trade barriers between Morocco and Europe will be removed by 2012, and a similar trade agreement has also been signed with the US. Morocco's GDP per capita is US$4200, which is not much compared to that of former colonial rulers Spain (US$25,500) and France (US$29,900).

TRADEMARKS

- Mint tea and couscous
- Carpets and carpet-sellers
- Bogart and Bergman in *Casablanca*
- Kasbahs
- Last stop before Europe
- Magical medinas
- Marrakesh

≫ MUSICIANS PLAYING UP A STORM, ESSAOUIRA

≫ CONTRASTING LANDSCAPES LEAD DOWN TO THE KASBAH OF AÏT ARBI IN THE DADÈS GORGE

≫ A MAN AND HIS DONKEY MAKE STEADY PROGRESS IN FÈS EL-BALI (OLD FÈS)

JOHN ELK III / LONELY PLANET IMAGES

CHILLING OUT AT THE ENSEMBLE ARTISANAL, HIVERNAGE, MARRAKESH »

FROM THE TRAVELLER

Wandering through the Fès medina one morning, I was suddenly shoved to one side, a sympathetic hand steadying me on the kerb. A caravan of laden donkeys hurtled out of the murky depths of the marketplace. They were bringing carpets from remote mountain villages to sell to the shops. I snatched a photo, and they were gone. The crowd closed behind them as quickly as it had parted.

BENEN HAYDEN // IRELAND

THE WATER'S FINE: A RITUAL BATHING POOL IN AN ANCIENT MEDERSA (ISLAMIC SCHOOL), FÈS »

WILD THINGS

Most Moroccan animal species are endangered, from the shy addax antelope that defies the desert's dictates and can survive its whole life without water, to the equally reticent leopards which are thought to cling to remote mountain redoubts. However, there are some success stories among the active preservation programmes, including pulling the Dorcas gazelle, Barbary sheep and bald ibis back from the brink of extinction. Sadly, the iconic and abundantly maned Barbary lion was last seen (and shot) in the Atlas Mountains in 1922.

IMPORT

↗ 4.2 million tourists every year
↗ Henri Matisse, William Burroughs and Paul Bowles
↗ The Western Sahara
↗ The Rolling Stones, Robert Plant and Jimmy Page to play with the Master Musicians of Joujouka
↗ Moroccans returning home from Europe, keen to recreate the country in their image

EXPORT

↖ Thousands of illegal immigrants to Europe every year
↖ Fatima Mernissi, one of the world's most respected feminists
↖ *Gnawa* music
↖ Marijuana from the Rif Valley
↖ Moroccan Jews
↖ Couscous

URBAN SCENE

Marrakesh marches to a different beat. It's a vibrant, beautiful city of exquisite mosques, peaceful gardens and stately palaces, and the energy of the city's souqs – each of which is a city in itself – never seems to subside. This is a medieval bazaar *par excellence,* with every conceivable handicraft – Moroccan lamps, carpets and traditional clothes – on display and on sale. By night the Djemaa el-Fna is transformed into one of the most intoxicating places in the world, as storytellers, musicians, street performers and wonderful outdoor restaurants illuminate the night.

TOP FESTIVAL

Whirling dervishes and sacred orchestras take the stage in June every year for the Fès Festival of World Sacred Music. Not only does the festival draw world-class performers, but it has also found a perfect home in a medieval city replete with venues that include acoustically rich palaces and gracious old homes. Staged for the first time in the aftermath of the first Gulf War, the festival has one very simple aim: to make peace through music by bringing together the musicians of the world regardless of cultural or religious background.

CUISINE

Eating in Morocco is taken very seriously, so much so that hours each day are set aside for the purpose. From the Middle East, Moroccans developed a taste for meze, that Arab equivalent of tapas or antipasto. From North Africa's deserts, Moroccans adopted *mechoui*, an entire lamb or calf stuffed with all sorts of delicious goodies and slow-roasted to perfection. But Moroccans have also exported their own dishes around the world, most notably tagines (stews cooked in a clay pot), which all North African countries have adopted as their own. Other Moroccan staples incorporate any kind of meat, dates and chickpeas and no Moroccan dinner table would be complete without couscous.

IN FILM

Morocco has long been a star of the silver screen, which has lodged the country in the Western imagination as at once exotic and familiar. *The Tragedy of Othello* (1952), starring Orson Welles, was filmed in Essaouira, while Alfred Hitchcock found the perfect backdrop in Marrakesh for *The Man Who Knew Too Much* (1956). Since then, *Lawrence of Arabia* (1962), *Alexander* (2004), *Gladiator* (2000), *The Sheltering Sky* (1990), *Jesus of Nazareth* (1977), *The Last Temptation of Christ* (1988), *Asterix & Obelix: Mission Cleopatra* (2002) and *Hideous Kinky* (1998) were all filmed, at least in part, in Morocco.

SURPRISES

○ Morocco and Spain nearly went to war in 2002 over an uninhabited island.
○ Not one second of *Casablanca* (1942) was filmed in Morocco.
○ Moroccan women were granted the right to vote in 1963.

FUTURE DIRECTIONS

All eyes are on Mohammed VI, Morocco's youthful king. Alienation among the country's youth is the single most pressing issue facing the king and his country – if young Moroccans are responsible for more terrorist attacks in the future, such as those perpetrated in Casablanca in 2003 and Madrid in 2004, the world can expect the king's tentative liberal reforms (which include more democracy and women's rights) to stall.

ESSENTIAL EXPERIENCES

○ **Winding your way down through the magical medina of Fès to the leather-dyeing pits awash with bright colours**
○ **Getting swept up in the vibrant night market in Marrakesh's Djemaa el-Fna**
○ **Catching a breeze on a groovy Essaouira rooftop by an expansive sweep of beach**
○ **Scrubbing all your troubles away in an authentic Moroccan *hammam* (bathhouse)**
○ **Trekking deep into the spectacular Berber heartland of the High Atlas Mountains to discover fairytale kasbahs**
○ **Soaking up the solitude of a desert sunset amid the sand dunes of Merzouga**

⌃ A KEYHOLE VIEW IN THE MAUSOLEUM OF MOULAY ISMAIL, MEKNÈS

⌃ HANDLE IN MOUASSINE MOSQUE, MARRAKESH

⌃ HIS AND HERS: SLIPPERS OUTSIDE THE MAUSOLEUM OF MOULAY ISMAIL, MEKNÈS

MAP REF // G2

BEST TIME TO VISIT **OCTOBER TO APRIL**

A STREET IN CHEFCHAOUEN «

A HOTEL IN ERFOUD BARELY HOLDS BACK THE DESERT «

WEST AFRICA

IF THERE'S ONE PLACE WHERE THE PEOPLE PUSH THE USUAL AFRICAN ATTRACTIONS INTO A BLURRY BACKGROUND, IT'S WEST AFRICA. MUSIC SETS LIFE'S RHYTHM HERE – WEST AFRICANS BREATHE IN THE SULTRY AIR AND EXHALE THEIR SOUL'S SONG. CREATIVITY IS KING AND EXPRESSION IS EVERYWHERE.

Amid the dust of the frenetic markets are striking masks, basketwork, jewellery and leatherwork, all examples of the region's rich artistic heritage. Nearby are artisans honing their skills, perfecting age-old patterns or adapting traditional materials to make something truly unique and their own. Rising from areas of rough and featureless terrain are houses that look more like pottery. Although nature's artwork is brilliant in its own right – the fiery soils' rich reds, the wavering trees' glowing greens and the orange waters of the Niger River at sunset – it's the creations of West Africa's people that shine brightest.

Most West African borders were drawn up hastily by greedy French, British, German and Portuguese colonialists, so they hardly reflect the distribution of West Africa's diverse peoples. Yes, West Africans are now incredibly nationalistic – you only need to watch the African Cup of Nations to see that – but cultural identities go further back than the borders, back to West Africa's great empires: the Mali and Songhaï empires that stretched across the Sahel from present-day Niger to the Atlantic; the Kanem-Bornu empire of Nigeria, Niger, Cameroon and Chad; Burkina Faso's Mossi kingdom; and Ghana's Ashanti empire, to name a few.

In fact, of West Africa's 18 most populous, well-known and colourful peoples, nine are spread over international boundaries. The Fulani people stretch from Senegal to Cameroon; the Tuareg blanket sections of Mali, Niger, Burkina Faso and North Africa; the Malinke call Mali, Guinea, Côte d'Ivoire, Senegal and the Gambia home; the Senoufo live in Côte d'Ivoire, Burkina Faso and Mali; the Lobi inhabit Burkina Faso, Côte d'Ivoire and Ghana; the Ewe people are found in Togo and Ghana; the Songhaï straddle Niger and Mali; the Hausa people reside in Nigeria and Niger; and the Yoruba live in Nigeria and Benin. Although each group has its own strong cultural identity, most cohabitate in peace – a phenomenon that is less common in other regions of the continent.

Religion also plays an enormous role in West Africa. About half the population is Muslim, with Islam dominating much of the desert and Sahel regions. Christianity is limited to the southern coastal countries. Hundreds of traditional religions (most of which are animist) remain strong in sections of West Africa, and voodoo, which was born in Benin, also lives on.

Sitting beneath the religions, the artwork, the song, the hundreds of ethnicities, the countless languages and the openness and smiles of the people, is a massive landscape that has one foot baking in the Sahara's sands and the other cooling its toes in the Atlantic. Caught between the Sahara and the coast's beaches and forests is a southern belt of savannah, with rolling plains freckled with trees, and a northern belt of Sahel or semidesert. Flowing through it all, bringing life to the land and soothing refreshment to all those singing voices, is the mighty 4030-kilometre-long Niger River.

TEXT: MATT PHILLIPS

N O R T H
A T L A N T I C
O C E A N

MOROCCO

Erg
Iguidi

ALGERIA

LIBYA

Erg
Chech

Zouérat

Taoudenni

Nouâdhibou

Ouarâne

MAURITANIA

MALI

NIGER

CHAD

NOUAKCHOTT ✪

Azaouâd

Massif
de l'Aïr

Ténéré

CAPE
VERDE

Rosso

Senegal

Aoukâr

Timbuktu
(Tomboctou)

Agadez ●

Gao

PRAIA ✪

SENEGAL

Kayes

THE SAHEL

DAKAR ✪ ● Thiès

Segou

Mopti

NIAMEY ✪

Zinder

Lake
Chad

SUDAN

BANJUL ✪ THE
GAMBIA

BURKINA FASO

Sokoto

Maiduguri ●

BISSAU ✪

BAMAKO ✪

OUAGADOUGOU ✪

GUINEA-BISSAU

Labé ●

Sikasso ●

Bobo Dioulasso ●

BENIN

Kano ●

GUINEA

Kankan ●

TOGO

Tamale ●

Kaduna ●

Maroua ●

CONAKRY ✪

NIGERIA

FREETOWN ✪

Bo ●

Nzérékoré ●

CÔTE
D'IVOIRE

GHANA

Parakou ●

ABUJA ✪

Benue

Garoua ●

SIERRA LEONE

Harbel ●

YAMOUSSOUKRO ✪

Kumasi ●

PORTO
NOVO

Ibadan ●

Enugu ●

CENTRAL
AFRICAN
REPUBLIC

MONROVIA ✪

LIBERIA

Abidjan ●

ACCRA ✪

LOMÉ ✪

Lagos ●

Adamawa
Highlands

CAMEROON

Port Harcourt ●

Douala ●

Gulf of Guinea

YAOUNDE ✪

EQUATORIAL GUINEA

DEMOCRATIC
REPUBLIC OF
CONGO
(ZAÏRE)

SÃO TOMÉ & PRINCIPE

GABON

CONGO

TEXT JEAN-BERNARD CARILLET

MAURITANIA

A MAGNETIC PLAYGROUND FOR WANNABE EXPLORERS, MAURITANIA HAS VAST DUNE FIELDS, GIDDYING CANYONS, EYE-POPPING PLATEAUS, A WILD STRETCH OF COAST AND ENOUGH OASES TO CALM THE MOST STRESSED MINDS.

CAPITAL CITY NOUAKCHOTT   POPULATION 3.2 MILLION   AREA 1 MILLION SQ KM   OFFICIAL LANGUAGES HASSANIYA (ARABIC), FRENCH

⌃ MINERAL-DERIVED REDS, YELLOWS AND WHITES ARE TRADITIONALLY USED TO DECORATE HOUSES

LANDSCAPE
In Mauritania, wild coast meets Saharan dunes. Desert, rocky plateaus and sand dunes are Mauritania's signature landscapes, but the country also boasts 700 kilometres of shoreline, including the Banc d'Arguin National Park, one of the world's greatest bird-viewing venues and a World Heritage natural site.

HISTORY IN A NUTSHELL
From the 3rd century AD the Berbers established trading routes all over the Western Sahara, including Mauritania. In the 11th century the Marrakesh-based Islamic Almoravids pushed south and, with the assistance of Mauritanian Berber leaders, managed to destroy the Empire of Ghana, which covered much of present-day Mauritania. The descendants of the Almoravids were finally subjugated by Arabs in 1674. In 1904 the French made Mauritania a colonial territory. Independence was fairly easily achieved in 1960, but the first 40 years of the country's autonomy were not particularly rosy (read: repressive regimes, coups, guerrilla wars and ethnic tensions). The year 2005 marked a turning point for Mauritania, when it gained a government led by Ely Ould Mohamed Vall. He won popular support during a transition period leading up to presidential elections in 2007 that were considered to be a step towards the establishment of a proper democracy. The elections' victor was Sidi Ould Cheik Abdallahi, a former cabinet minister.

PEOPLE
Of Mauritania's estimated 3.2 million inhabitants, about 60 per cent are Moors of Arab and Berber descent. The other major ethnic group consists of black Africans, who are ethnically split into two groups. The Haratin, or black Moors, are the descendants of people enslaved by the Moors. They have assimilated the Moorish culture and speak Hassaniya, an Arabic dialect. The other group are the Soudaniens, black Mauritanians who live in the south of the country along the Senegal River. They are mostly Fulani people (also known as Peul) or the closely related Tukulor, and speak Pulaar (Fula). There are also Soninke and Wolof minorities.

MARKETPLACE
Mauritania is poor, but not as poor as some – its GDP per capita is US$2200 (whereas Niger's, for example, is US$900). Mauritania's main resource has traditionally been iron ore, which currently accounts for nearly 40 per cent of total exports, but the discovery of oil reserves in 2001 could bring a new impetus to the country's economy; commercial oil production in offshore fields off Nouakchott began in 2006. The nation's coastal waters are among the richest fishing areas in the world, but overexploitation by foreigners is a major concern.

TRADEMARKS
- Camel trips in the desert
- Ancient Saharan towns
- Endless servings of tea in a Moorish tent
- The world's longest train: 2.5 kilometres long
- The sand dunes in the Adrar
- The Banc d'Arguin National Park

URBAN SCENE
Nouakchott, the capital, is a discombobulating city that reflects the geographical duality of the country. Though it's only five kilometres inland from the Atlantic, it's more a city of the interior than of the coast – yet it boasts the most active fish market in West Africa. Every day between 4pm and 6pm hundreds of colourful fishing boats return and innumerable teams of men drag heavy fishing nets onto the beach. Nouakchott has modern amenities, a couple of hip restaurants serving French cuisine, the

FORTRESS OF LEARNING: THE GUARDIAN OF THE LIBRARY »

odd bar and comfortable hotels – bliss after the austerity of the desert.

TOP FESTIVAL

The whole country goes gaga during the much-awaited *Guetna* (date-harvesting) season from June to August. The heat is stifling, with temperatures reaching 45°C, but it's a very festive time, and many Mauritanians from the cities return to their tribes and take part in the harvest. There's a mellow atmosphere and a great deal of socialising, drinking of tea and *zrig* (unsweetened curdled goat's or camel's milk), playing games and dancing. There are also virtually no tourists – it's the perfect time to sample Mauritanian hospitality at its best.

RANDOM FACTS

○ You can travel for free in the open-topped wagons of the iron-ore train – if you can survive the dust.
○ Nouakchott's fish market is the most colourful in West Africa.
○ Although slavery was declared illegal in 1980, it still exists in pockets of Mauritania, according to human rights groups.
○ The coastal waters of Mauritania have one of the world's highest densities of fish.

NATURAL BEAUTY

In the north of the country, the Adrar is the jewel in Mauritania's crown. For desert lovers, this area is a must, with mighty sand dunes that look as if they've been sculpted by an artist, ancient Saharan towns, mellow oases and grandiose basaltic plateaus. To the south, the Tagânt region is even more spectacular. Compared with the Adrar, it's much less touristy and virtually untouched.

WILD THINGS

Between Nouâdhibou and Nouakchott, the Banc d'Arguin National Park is a paradise for twitchers. It's one of the best bird-watching venues in the world – an important stopover and breeding ground for multitudes of birds migrating between Europe and Southern Africa. Most birds nest on sand islands in the shallow ocean.

FUTURE DIRECTIONS

Oil, oil and oil! The oil boom that began in 2006 with the exploitation of offshore fields off Nouakchott should foster growth and have a positive impact on the country. More investments and more expats mean more jobs and a growing need for infrastructure and a greater choice of activities, both in the capital and in the desert. But it's also synonymous with inflation.

☆ GONE FISHING IN THE BANC D'ARGUIN NATIONAL PARK

☆ ANOTHER BRICK IN THE WESTERN WALL OF OUADÂNE

☆ CLEAN ARCHITECTURAL LINES IN CHINGUETTI

ESSENTIAL EXPERIENCES

○ **Getting up at the crack of dawn to catch a glorious sunrise from the labyrinthine lanes of the old city of Chinguetti**

○ **Experiencing the magic of the Sahara, via either a four-wheel-drive tour or a camel trip: sleeping beneath the star-studded skies at the saffron dunefields in the Adrar region, then cooling down in Terjît, a palm-filled oasis**

○ **Looking through your binoculars at vast flocks of birds from a traditional pirogue at Banc d'Arguin National Park**

○ **Admiring the elaborate decorative paintings that adorn the traditional houses in Oualâta, one of Mauritania's best-kept secrets**

○ **Hopping on the iron-ore train, the world's longest train, for an epic journey through the Sahara**

MAP REF // F4

BEST TIME TO VISIT **OCTOBER TO MARCH**

A BOY AND HIS DONKEY GET A SPLASHDOWN ON THEIR WAY TO THE LOCAL MARKETS »

A DASH OF GREEN IN THE DESERT TOWN OF OUALÂTA

THE SHIPS OF THE DESERT CROSS A RED SEA, NEAR NOUAKCHOTT »

SENEGAL

BETWEEN SOLITARY PLAINS IN THE NORTH AND LUSH TROPICAL LANDS IN THE SOUTH, SENEGAL'S HECTIC CAPITAL DAKAR IS A FINE SLICE OF URBAN AFRICA, PERCHED ON A BEACH-LINED PENINSULA.

CAPITAL CITY DAKAR   POPULATION 12 MILLION   AREA 196,190 SQ KM   OFFICIAL LANGUAGE FRENCH

LANDSCAPE

Senegal is a patchwork of classic African landscapes. Northern Senegal lies just south of the Sahara, and the desert's hot, dusty breath leaves its mark. In the south is the Casamance, a lush zone of tropical forests and swelling rivers. West are the beaches of the Atlantic coast; eastwards, towards the Malian border, are flat, dry plains dotted with mighty baobabs. The only kind of topography missing is mountains – the country's highest peak, in the southeastern corner of the Bassari lands, 'looms' a whole 580 metres.

HISTORY IN A NUTSHELL

Over the centuries Senegalese lands have been home to some of West Africa's major empires, like the Tekrur, Jolof and Mali. In the 15th century, lured by stories about West Africa's vast gold reserves, the Portuguese established a trading post for goods and slaves at Île de Gorée, but soon lost control of it to the French. The first French settlement in West Africa, St-Louis in northern Senegal, later became the capital of Afrique Occidentale Française (French West Africa). In 1960 president (and poet) Léopold Sédar Senghor led Senegal to independence; governments have since changed twice in peaceful and democratic elections.

PEOPLE

The Wolof are the largest ethnic group in Senegal, comprising around 43 per cent of the population, and unifying much of the nation through their language and culture. Parts of the northern area along the Senegal River are home to substantial groups of Tukulor (12 per cent) as well as smaller Soninke populations. The Serer (14 per cent) are another important ethnic group, inhabiting large parts of the Siné-Saloum Delta. The Casamance is dominated in the west by the Diola (nine per cent), and in the east by the Malinke (nine per cent) and Fulani (10 per cent). Kedougou is the only area with substantial Bassari and Bedik populations. More than 90 per cent of Senegal's population is Muslim.

MARKETPLACE

When you see the gleaming four-wheel drives on the streets of Dakar, you might be tempted to think that Senegal is doing reasonably well economically, but a short stroll through the heaving urban suburb of Pikine or a tour around the country's rural communities will quickly dispel that idea. With a GDP per capita of around US$1800, Senegal is still one of the poorest nations in the world. The most important branches of its economy are the groundnut industry and fishing, which are closely followed by the growing area of tourism.

TRADEMARKS

o Youssou N'Dour
o *Car Rapides* (Dakar's colourful minibuses)
o Île de Gorée
o Colourfully painted wooden pirogues
o Football
o Hospitality

NATURAL BEAUTY

Senegal's mighty Oiseaux du Djoudj National Park – a 16,000-hectare expanse of wetlands, marshes and mud flats, cut through by numerous channels and lakes – is the third-largest bird sanctuary in the world and one of the best places on the planet to see migrant birds escaping the European winter. A few kilometres further south, conveniently close to the windswept Grande Côte, are the rolling desert dunes of Lompoul. The Siné-Saloum Delta is another one of Senegal's impressive natural zones: the Saloum River meets the Atlantic Ocean in a maze of mangrove swamps, tiny estuaries, islets and lagoons.

⌃ GOT THAT SWING: A BOY SWINGS FROM THE HULL OF A BEACHED FISHING BOAT IN ST-LOUIS

NIC BOTHMA/EPA /EPA // CORBIS

⌃ A FISHERMAN CATCHES A WAVE IN HIS PIROGUE

⌃ WRESTLER IBOU CISSE GRAPPLES WITH AN OPPONENT IN DAKAR

RACING THROUGH A CLOUD OF LOCUSTS, DAKAR »

LIGHT TRAFFIC ON THE STREETS OF ST-LOUIS »

LABOUR OF LOVE: A CRAFTSMAN RESTORES THE MOSQUE AT TOUBA »

IN ART & CULTURE
○ The entire catalogue of prolific film director Ousmane Sembene.
○ The Afro-eccentric fashion displays of Oumou Sy
○ *So Long a Letter*, Mariama Ba's beautiful novel about women in polygamous marriages.
○ *Immigrés*, an early, rumbling Youssou N'Dour hit that shifted Senegal into the consciousness of African-music lovers worldwide.
○ The reverse glass paintings *(sous-verre)* of Babacar Lô.
○ The urban paintings of Senegal's spiritual leaders Cheikh Amadou Bamba and Cheikh Ibra Fall, which adorn walls, cars, shop fronts and T-shirts across the country.

TOP FESTIVAL
In Senegal, and particularly in Dakar, one music festival chases the next. But Dakar's queen of festivals doesn't tease the ears so much as the eyes; the famous Dak'Art Biennale is one of Africa's main celebrations of contemporary art, and it drowns the town in colour. Hundreds of galleries and public spaces around the city announce imaginative fringe programmes, featuring artists from across Africa. It's the only time of year that Dakar counts more artists than street hustlers among its population.

RANDOM FACTS
○ The annual Magal pilgrimage to the holy city of Touba attracts some two million people.
○ Dakar is one of West Africa's coolest spots, with average temperatures at around 26°C. In the north and east, it can get much, much hotter.
○ An estimated three million Senegalese live abroad.
○ Greater Dakar is estimated to have around three million inhabitants.

○ Renting an apartment in one of Dakar's chic neighbourhoods for a month could easily set you back US$3000.
○ A cleaner in Senegal might earn a monthly salary of around US$60.

MUSIC
Mbalax, the beat made famous by Senegalese icon Youssou N'Dour, is the heart and soul of Senegalese music – and its legs, thighs, hips and backside, too. Created from a mixture of Cuban beats and fiery *sabar* drumming in the mid-1970s, *mbalax* in its myriad transformations still dominates Senegal's dance floors and airwaves today – and if the gyrating bodies in Dakar's nightclubs are anything to go by, it will continue to do so for some years yet. Even the vibrant local hip-hop scene (think Daara J), the enduringly popular Afro-salsa led by Orchestra Baobab and the quieter, guitar-strumming folk and Afro-jazz troupes can't rival the immense full-body love the Senegalese have reserved for *mbalax*. If you're ever on an exploding Dakar dance floor, you'll understand.

URBAN SCENE
Senegal isn't a place for those in search of African stereotypes: if it's jungle, lions and elephants you're after, the country will disappoint. What it lacks in wildlife wonders, however, Senegal more than makes up in urban excitement. Dakar is one of Africa's most vibrant capitals, a noisy, bustling, and yes, polluted bubble of activity, where new fashion and music trends grow in a fertile soil of underground creativity and casual self-confidence. The two best places to discover the Dakar bustle are the heaving Dakar Plateau, with its ever-expanding markets, and the *quartier populaire* Médina, where tiny tailor's shops and boutiques stacked sky-high with goods compete

for space with clapboard housing and street stalls. The trade-off, of course, is having to negotiate the city's permanent gridlock and shake off overeager traders and smooth-talking hustlers.

IMPORT
↗ Cars (if they're less than five years old)
↗ Overland motorcyclists
↗ Former émigrés
↗ Dreadlock-shaking *djembe* amateurs
↗ French culture and cuisine
↗ Lions and elephants

EXPORT
↖ Some of West Africa's finest music
↖ Style
↖ The art of seduction
↖ Patchwork trousers
↖ Presidential poetry (Léopold Sédar Senghor)
↖ Hospitality
↖ Football players

ESSENTIAL EXPERIENCES

○ **Diving into the noisy, colourful chaos of Dakar's urban markets, clutching fistfuls of CFA francs tightly**

○ **Being buffeted by the salty winds of the Grande Côte and the sandy winds of the dunes of Lompoul**

○ **Catching *mbalax* fever on Dakar's glittering dance floors**

○ **Hopping from one beachside fishing village to the next along the Petite Côte**

○ **Enjoying the sweet solitude along the Senegal River route, passing crumbling French forts and subdued Sudanese-style mosques**

○ **Catching your breath as you gaze downwards at the dizzying drop of the Dindefelo waterfall**

○ **Steering a painted pirogue through the mangrove-lined estuaries and shimmering wetlands of the Siné-Saloum Delta**

○ **Resting your lazy bones on the breathtaking arch of Boucotte Beach in the Casamance, after a taste of Ziguinchor**

○ **Inhaling history in the streets of St-Louis**

ARIADNE VAN ZANDBERGEN // LONELY PLANET IMAGES

MAP REF // E5

BEST TIME TO VISIT **NOVEMBER TO APRIL**

⌃ INTO THE FRAY: PIROGUES SUPPLY FRESH FISH TO A BEACH MARKET ON THE PETITE CÔTE

HOMME : 500 F
ENFANT : 300 F
BARBE : 100 F

A GIRL SURROUNDED BY TOOLS OF THE BARBER TRADE, DAKAR ≫

ARIADNE VAN ZANDBERGEN // LONELY PLANET IMAGES

ALLEZ LES BLEUS, ST-LOUIS ≫

ALL AT SEA: PIROGUES HEAD OUT FROM ÎLE DE LA MADELEINE ≫

CAPE VERDE

TO VISIT THE HOMELAND OF SINGER CESÁRIA ÉVORA IS TO UNDERSTAND THE STRANGE, BITTERSWEET AMALGAM OF WEST AFRICAN RHYTHMS AND MOURNFUL PORTUGUESE MELODIES THAT ARE HER HAUNTING *MORNAS*.

CAPITAL CITY PRAIA   POPULATION 420,980   AREA 4030 SQ KM   OFFICIAL LANGUAGES PORTUGUESE, CRIOULO

LANDSCAPE

Cape Verde is made up of 10 major islands and five islets, all of volcanic origin. All are arid or semiarid, though the mountainous islands of Brava, Santiago, Fogo, Santo Antão and São Nicolau – which have peaks over 1000 metres – do catch enough moisture to support grasslands along with fairly intensive agriculture. By contrast, Maio, Boa Vista and Sal are flatter and almost entirely arid, with long, sandy beaches and moonlike interiors.

HISTORY IN A NUTSHELL

The Cape Verde islands were uninhabited when they were discovered by Portuguese mariners in 1456, but they proved to be the ideal staging ground and victualling station for Portugal's booming slave trade. However, in 1747, changing weather patterns, aggravated by deforestation and overgrazing, resulted in Cape Verde's first recorded drought. At the same time, Portugal's monopoly on the slave trade was beginning to slip, following challenges by Britain, France and the Netherlands, and so began a long period of colonial neglect that repeatedly resulted in mass starvation. Independence only came to the islands in 1974, after a bloody civil war led by leftist

intellectual Amilcar Cabral and waged by Cape Verde and its twin mainland colony Guinea-Bissau (though violence was largely limited to the latter). A one-party state was then established; however, the Partido Africano da Indepêndencia de Cabo Verde (PAICV) ruled moderately and peacefully conceded to demands for multi-party elections in 1991. By West African standards, the country enjoys remarkably high per capita income, life expectancy and literacy rates. Still, drought and lack of opportunity have resulted in mass emigration, particularly to the USA and Portugal, and currently there are more Cape Verdean citizens living abroad than in Cape Verde itself.

PEOPLE

Cape Verde's population is primarily of mixed European and African descent; most of the remainder are of purely African descent. About 40 per cent of the population lives on Santiago, with about half again in or around Praia, the nation's capital. Mindelo, on the island of São Vicente, is the second-largest city, with 50,000 residents. The rest of the nation lives largely in small towns, most of which are clustered in the agriculturally productive valleys of São Antão, São Nicolau, Santiago and Brava.

MARKETPLACE

Although much of the population lives in rural areas and survives on subsistence farming, the country must import as much as 80 per cent of its food. Industrial production is very limited. The fastest-growing sector is tourism, though the airport is another important source of foreign currency. With so many Cape Verdeans living abroad, 20 per cent of its GDP consists of foreign remittances.

TRADEMARKS

o Singer Cesária Évora
o The beaches of Sal and Boa Vista
o Hiking Santo Antão and São Nicolau
o Windsurfing in the trade winds
o Climbing Mt Fogo

NATURAL BEAUTY

The single most arresting sight in Cape Verde is Mt Fogo on the island of the same name. Its conical peak, clad in black cinder, tops out at 2829 metres. Santo Antão island in the northwest is a hiker's paradise, with dramatic canyons, high central peaks, and a dizzying variety of microclimates – including remarkably verdant valleys. Brava and São Nicolau are

similar. At the other extreme are the moonlike landscapes of Sal, Maio and Boa Vista islands, with endless beaches, shifting sand dunes and barren peaks.

RANDOM FACTS
○ England's Sir Francis Drake made devastating raids on the islands in 1585.
○ Today, more Cape Verdeans live abroad than in Cape Verde itself.
○ Many Cape Verdeans fled famine by joining American whaling fleets in the 19th century.

URBAN SCENE
While Praia has a fine natural harbour and a lively historic centre, it's best to move on from Cape Verde's picturesque capital once you've conducted your business. The smaller city of Mindelo is prettier and more sophisticated; besides cobblestone streets, candy-coloured colonial buildings and yachts bobbing in a peaceful harbour, it boasts bohemian cafés and a great music scene.

SURPRISES
○ While many African countries have struggled after independence, the standard of living for Cape Verdeans has dramatically improved. For example, life expectancy has leapt from 46 years to 70 years.

○ The town of Sinagoga on Santo Antão was founded by Jews fleeing the Inquisition; none remain now, but Jewish surnames like Benros, Ben David and Cohn occur throughout Cape Verde.

TOP FESTIVAL
From organised parades to free-for-all revelry, Mindelo's week-long pre-Lenten Carnival has its roots in Portuguese traditions, but takes its cues from the celebrations in Brazil. Neighbourhoods organise to produce florid floats and elaborately sexy costumes for one of Africa's great parties, and you're likely to hear samba alongside Cape Verde's own fantastic music. *Grogue*, the local version of rum, fuels the proceedings, which for many end only with sunrise on the town beach.

IMPORT
↗ Food
↗ Anything manufactured
↗ Portuguese beer
↗ Remittances from family members abroad

EXPORT
↖ Cesária Évora's music
↖ Suntans
↖ Shoes and clothing
↖ Transportation services
↖ Lobsters

↟ BOIL AND BUBBLE: A NATURAL SWIMMING POOL ON SAL ISLAND

ESSENTIAL EXPERIENCES

○ **Huffing to the top of stunning, cinder-clad Mt Fogo, the country's only active volcano and, at 2829 metres, its highest peak**

○ **Downing quantities of *grogue*, the rumlike national drink, before diving into Mindelo's Mardi Gras – one of Africa's great parties**

○ **Hiking over the pine-clad ridge of Santo Antão down into its spectacular canyons and valleys**

○ **Windsurfing off the beaches of Boa Vista, your sail filling with the same transatlantic winds that pushed Columbus to the New World**

○ **Watching traditional musicians wave loved ones goodbye with a *morna* or welcome them back with a *coladeira*, at Brava's little ferry port**

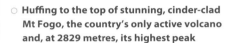

MAP REF // C5

BEST TIME TO VISIT **NOVEMBER TO MAY**

↟ A PRICKLY SPINE ALONG SANTO ANTÃO

A BROTHER AND SISTER MEET THE CAMERA'S GAZE ON SANTO ANTÃO »

LIVING ON THE EDGE, PONTA DO SOL »

MAGIC AND MONSTERS AT THE SÃO VICENTE CARNIVAL »

THE GAMBIA

A SLIVER IN THE SIDE OF SENEGAL, TINY GAMBIA ATTRACTS THOUSANDS OF TOURISTS TO LINGER ON ITS BEACH-LINED SHORES, OR HEAD UP COUNTRY TO SEE A STAGGERING NUMBER OF BIRD SPECIES.

CAPITAL CITY BANJUL   POPULATION 1.6 MILLION   AREA 11,300 SQ KM   OFFICIAL LANGUAGE ENGLISH

⌃ TANGLED TOGETHER: A FISHERMAN'S FAMILY MENDS NETS ON THE BEACH AT GUNJUR

LANDSCAPE

A quirk of colonial history, The Gambia is one of the world's unlikeliest countries. About 300 kilometres long, but averaging only 35 kilometres wide, The Gambia stretches only a few square kilometres north and south of the Gambia River, and is almost entirely surrounded by Senegal, bar some 80 kilometres of Atlantic coast that define its western edge. There isn't much space for exciting natural features: there are no hills or mountains, no deserts or imposing bush lands. Temperatures aren't quite as even as the land is flat, however – averaging around 25°C from December to April and 30°C from May to September.

HISTORY IN A NUTSHELL

Little is known about ancient history in The Gambia region, but the impressive Wassu Stone Circles in Eastern Gambia indicate that people settled here as early as AD 500. For centuries, the region formed part of West Africa's rising and falling precolonial empires. One of these was the Empire of Mali, ruled by the Malinke people – a branch of the Malinke settled in the region of The Gambia, and became one of the dominant ethnic groups. With colonial expansion, the Portuguese, French and British all tried to claim the region, and with the carving up of Africa in 1884–85, Britain was granted this tongue of land wedged into French territory. The Gambia finally shook off British colonial rule in 1965, though Queen Elizabeth remained titular head of state until 1970. Since the military coup on 22 July 1994, The Gambia has been ruled by Yahya Jammeh, and though the nation has not seen any major conflict in that time, it suffers from autocratic rule and restrictions on civil liberties and the press.

RANDOM FACTS

- The Gambia's famous beaches – the very ones that attract hundreds of thousands of tourists each year – are 'fake'. The original beaches had almost disappeared because of illegal sand mining: 'spraying' the beaches back on was a multi-million dollar project.
- The Gambia's two most iconic buildings, Banjul's Arch 22 and Yundum Airport, were actually designed by a Senegalese architect – the controversial Pierre Goudiaby.

PEOPLE

Comprising 42 per cent of the population, the Malinke are The Gambia's largest ethnic group, followed by the Fulani (18 per cent), Wolof (16 per cent), Jola (10 per cent) and Serahuli (nine per cent). Culturally, however, the Wolof are far more prominent than their humble population share suggests: the country is almost entirely surrounded by Senegal, and its strong Wolof culture spills across all borders. Around 90 per cent of Gambians are Muslim; the remaining 10 per cent is comprised of both Christians and those professing traditional beliefs.

MARKETPLACE

The Gambia's main source of revenue is the tourist industry; other important sources include groundnuts (peanuts) and the fishing industry. The apparent disovery of oil off The Gambia's shores in 2004 (proudly proclaimed by the president) so far hasn't turned it into one of the world's oil-rich nations – with a GDP per capita of US$1900, The Gambia is still one of the world's poorest countries (it's placed at 183 out of 232 nations).

TRADEMARKS

- Atlantic beaches
- Tourist-brochure smiles
- Exotic birds
- The Kunta Kinteh family, made famous through Alex Haley's book *Roots*

CELIA MANNINGS // ALAMY

SUE CUNNINGHAM PHOTOGRAPHIC // ALAMY

IN FULL VOICE: SINGING A SONG OF WELCOME

NATURAL BEAUTY

The Gambia is the country of the 'anti-superlative', claiming the titles for both smallest African nation and most understated capital. 'Smallest nature reserve' could be added to the list. The Abuko Nature Reserve near Banjul is a compact area with a stunning variety of mammals and birds – all easy to spot from well-placed hides. And there are plenty of other protected areas to cheer a nature lover's heart. Ornithologists are at risk of never wanting to return from the mangrove creeks and marsh plains of the Baobolong Wetlands or the savanna woodlands and tidal flats of Kiang West National Park.

URBAN SCENE

On a global index of odd capitals, Banjul would be a strong contender for one of the top spots, less because of what it is than what it's *not*. It's neither big and bustling, nor nauseating and noisy; there are no new buildings rising to the skies, no traffic clogs the streets and the city falls into a comatose state at 8pm every day. Despite this, Banjul has a charm all its own. There's an endearing intimacy to the crumbling colonial buildings and clapboard houses, the colourful scenes of Albert market and the pushing and shoving around the ferry terminal – an intimacy that's possibly unique to Banjul, the capital the world nearly forgot.

IMPORT
- ⤴ Binoculars
- ⤴ African-Americans in search of their roots
- ⤴ British pensioners
- ⤴ Reggae records
- ⤴ Youngster-hustling tourists

EXPORT
- ⤢ Tourist-hustling youngsters
- ⤢ Fish
- ⤢ *Djembe* drums
- ⤢ Tie-dye clothes
- ⤢ Exotic birds caught on film

MUSIC

The Malinke, The Gambia's largest ethnic group, are famous worldwide for their *griot* – a caste of musicians, praise-singers and historians. The *griot's* most famous instrument and African symbol, the kora (a type of harp or lute with 21 strings), is widely believed to have originated in the area of today's Gambia. To this day, some of West Africa's most prestigious families of kora players live here, including the descendants of renowned kora player Amadou Bansang Jobarteh.

While traditional music is alive and well in Africa's smallest nation, the popular scene isn't exactly thrilling – perhaps due to the lack of the kind of urban grit that usually drives the sounds of cities around the world. Tata Dindin Jobarth and Jalibah Kuyateh are among the biggest names of the 'modern *griot*'. The booming reggae rhythms spilling out onto every street should certainly clarify why the country is frequently dubbed 'Little Jamaica', however!

⤢ THE DIRTY WORK: GUTTING AND CLEANING FISH, GUNJUR

ESSENTIAL EXPERIENCES

- ○ Sipping cocktails and lounging on the beach at the resort hotels of Fajara, Kotu and Kololi
- ○ Trying to spot shimmering tail feathers in Abuko Nature Reserve
- ○ Steering a pirogue through the magnificent mangrove creeks of the Baobolong Wetlands
- ○ Weaving your way through the charming chaos of Serekunda market
- ○ Watching dozens of pirogues return from sea with their glistening catch at the tiny fishing village of Gunjur
- ○ Teasing the strings of the kora (an African harp-lute) with the famous griot families of Brikama
- ○ Strolling through the sleepy backstreets of Banjul

⤢ PLENTY OF ACTION OUTSIDE THE HUGE SEREKUNDA MARKET

⤢ POND LIFE IN TAIBATU

MAP REF // E6

A SIGN OF STYLE IN SEREKUNDA »

A BOY RIDES ON HIS DONKEY CART, BANJUL »

A MUSICIAN PLAYS A TRADITIONAL XYLOPHONE BY AN ANCIENT WASSU STONE CIRCLE »

GUINEA-BISSAU

BESIDES THE GUINEANS THEMSELVES – DIVERSE PEOPLES UNITED BY A TRULY REMARKABLE DEGREE OF NEIGHBOURLY GOODWILL – GUINEA-BISSAU'S BIGGEST DRAW IS THE ARQUIPÉLAGO DOS BIJAGÓS, WITH ITS TURQUOISE WATERS, POWDERY SAND BEACHES AND SOME OF THE WORLD'S BEST SPORT FISHING.

CAPITAL CITY **BISSAU** POPULATION **1.4 MILLION** AREA **36,120 SQ KM** OFFICIAL LANGUAGES **PORTUGUESE**

LANDSCAPE

Guinea-Bissau's tropical coast consists of estuaries, mangrove swamps and, in the south, rainforest. Inland, the landscape stays flat, and the highest ground, near the Guinean border, reaches only 300 metres. Going north and east from the coast, the land increasingly resembles the semiarid plains of the Sahel. Off the coast, the Arquipélago dos Bijagós is made up of dozens of low-lying islands with tall palm forests and mangrove swamps.

HISTORY IN A NUTSHELL

Parts of Guinea-Bissau were absorbed by the Empire of Mali, which flourished between the 13th and 15th centuries AD. In 1450 Portuguese navigators arrived, and were soon taking gold, ivory, pepper and, above all, slaves from the interior. Portugal's presence was limited to coastal trading, however, until the 20th century, when it decided to turn the country into one large, repressive peanut farm. Independence came in 1974 after a long, bloody civil war led by leftist intellectual Amílcar Cabral. The post-independence period has been marked by political corruption, coups and civil strife, including the 1998–2000 civil war and ongoing problems with Casamance separatists along the Senegalese border. Multi-party elections in 2005 were peaceful, nevertheless, and Guineans generally express cautious optimism about their future.

PEOPLE

Guinea-Bissau's 1.4 million citizens represent three major religions (Muslim, Christian and animist), 23 ethnic groups and more than 30 languages. The largest tribes include the Balante (30 per cent) in the coastal and southern regions and the Fulani (20 per cent) in the north.

MARKETPLACE

Most Guineans survive on subsistence farming and fishing. The 1998 civil war destroyed Guinea-Bissau's limited industrial infrastructure, and cashews are the country's only significant export, though there may be undiscovered oil reserves. Eighty per cent of the national budget comes from foreign aid.

TRADEMARKS

○ Arquipélago dos Bijagós
○ Cashews
○ Saltwater hippos
○ Sport fishing

CUISINE

Seafood is the glory of Guinean cuisine, especially the meaty *bica* (sea bream). Rice is the ubiquitous starch, supplemented with potatoes, yams, beans and *mandioca* (cassava). Common vegetables include okra, carrots and squash, with flavourings like onions and lime. Palm oil is another important staple. In rural areas, the meat in your meal may be *macaco* (monkey) – it pays to double check if chimp is not to your taste.

WILD THINGS

The Bijagós are home to a stunning variety of birds as well as the extremely rare saltwater hippos. Guinea-Bissau's wetlands and inland rivers harbour crocs, hippos, monkeys, flamingos and parrots, and the southern rainforests form Africa's westernmost chimpanzee habitat.

RANDOM FACTS

○ The Bijagós islands make up the only deltic archipelago on the Atlantic coast.
○ The country planned to merge with Cape Verde, but talks halted after Guinea-Bissau's 1980 coup.

CULTURE

While Guinea-Bissau's mainland peoples share much with the rest of West Africa, the matriarchal culture of the Bijagós islands is unique. A king and queen (who aren't husband and wife) serve as co-regents – the king managing the men's affairs and the queen managing the women's affairs. Women often serve as the chiefs of individual villages, and are also the sole homeowners – only fair since they're entirely responsible for home-building, from brick-making through to the end of construction.

TOP FESTIVAL

The pre-Lenten Carnival in the capital, Bissau, is by far the country's biggest party. The city's various neighbourhoods create elaborate masks and floats, and groups representing tribes and villages around the country descend on the capital. Palm wine is consumed in large quantities; music and dance rule the streets.

ESSENTIAL EXPERIENCES

○ **Discovering the stunning beaches and disarmingly friendly people of João Vieira Island**

○ **Stalking saltwater hippos after visiting the tombs of Bijagós kings and queens on Orango Island**

○ **Witnessing the quickly crumbling colonial grandeur of Bolama, the antique Portuguese capital**

○ **Disappearing into the sacred forests around Catió and Jemberem – the westernmost habitats of the African chimpanzee**

○ **Drinking through the blackouts in Bissau's lively cafés**

MAP REF // E6

BEST TIME TO VISIT **NOVEMBER TO FEBRUARY**

READY FOR OUR CLOSE-UP: THREE YOUNG GUINEAN BOYS »

A MANGO TREE PROVIDES MUCH-NEEDED SHADE TO THE VILLAGERS OF DEMBEL JUMPORA »

A BETTER SET OF WHEELS IN DOWNTOWN BISSAU »

TEXT TIM BEWER

GUINEA

THOUGH ITS PEOPLE HAVE LONG SUFFERED UNDER ONE OF AFRICA'S MOST CORRUPT AND COMPLACENT GOVERNMENTS, GUINEA'S STUNNING LANDSCAPE AND VIBRANT CULTURE ATTRACT INTREPID TRAVELLERS PREPARED TO ROUGH IT A BIT.

CAPITAL CITY CONAKRY   POPULATION 9.6 MILLION   AREA 245,000 SQ KM   OFFICIAL LANGUAGE FRENCH

≈ A PERPLEXED BABOON

LANDSCAPE

Guinea has four distinct geological regions, all of which receive considerable rain in season. From a narrow coastal plain the country rises into the Fouta Djalon plateau, where many peaks reach over 1000 metres, then drops to the northeastern dry lowlands and ends in the hilly Forest Region – which, due to excessive logging, no longer warrants its name. The once impressive biodiversity present in Guinea is now in rapid decline thanks to decades of unsustainable industry.

HISTORY IN A NUTSHELL

Samory Touré unsuccessfully rose up against French colonialists at the end of the 19th century; many decades later, one of his descendents, Sekou Touré, became the father of independence. In 1958, when Charles de Gaulle proposed that the French colonies in West Africa join a united Franco-African community, Touré famously declared his preference for 'freedom in poverty to prosperity in chains'. He got his wish. The French administrators pulled out and wealthy French citizens fled the country, leaving the local economy in a shambles. Touré was merciless against his opposition, among whom, in his paranoia, he eventually included the entire Fulani population.

Days after Touré's death in 1984, Lansana Conté took hold of the reins. Although some aspects of life have improved under his regime, the government has become increasingly repressive and at the time of writing, Conté was under pressure to resign.

PEOPLE

Guinea's three principal tribal groups – Fulani, Malinke and Susu – compose 90 per cent of Guinea's population. Eighty-five percent are Muslims, with the rest evenly split between Christianity and traditional animist beliefs. French is the official language, but all of Guinea's 18 tribal groups speak their own tongue.

MARKETPLACE

Despite a wealth of agricultural, hydropower and mineral resources – including nearly half of the world's bauxite reserves – Guinea is an economic basket case. At 25 per cent, the inflation rate is the third highest in the world and the country was ranked 156 out of 177 in the 2003 UN Human Development Index. The government's budget is US$590 million, about the same as the island of Jersey and 0.0005 per cent of France's budget. Most multilateral aid was cut off in 2003.

TRADEMARKS

○ Bauxite
○ Les Ballets Africains
○ Circus Baobab
○ Writer Camara Laye
○ Vine bridges

NATURAL BEAUTY

Most visitors to Guinea are here for the Fouta Djalon, a vast area of green rolling hills punctuated by peaks and canyons in the west of the country. Largely pastoral, with only scattered mud-hut villages beyond the main road, it's a beautiful area on the macro level and downright spectacular at certain sites. Even better, at its enormous waterfalls, and within its contorted slot canyons draped in jungle, you're far more likely to meet monkeys than other people.

RANDOM FACTS

○ Three major rivers – the Niger, Gambia and Senegal Rivers – begin their journey to the sea in Guinea's rainy highlands.
○ Scrap-metal sculpture is an emerging art form and growing industry in several towns in Guinea.

A PRIMARY-SCHOOL GIRL GAZES AT THE CAMERA ≫

NET WORTH: WOMEN FISHING IN THE NIGER RIVER ≫

URBAN SCENE

In some ways Kankan, Guinea's second city, feels more Malian than Guinean. The streets are shady and sandy and life seems to move a little slower here than in other cities its size. The Malian connection is even stronger culturally – Kankan is the spiritual capital of the Malinke tribe, who ruled much of West Africa in the 12th century when the Empire of Mali was at its peak. However, this is also a university town which draws people from across the nation, and while the nightlife doesn't swing anything like in does in Conakry, it's there if you want it.

WILD THINGS

A group of chimpanzees living in the forest near Bossou became famous in 2005, after Japanese primatologist Gaku Ohashi discovered that not only could they detect and destroy animal traps, but they were teaching this skill to other chimps.

≫ SEEING RED? TRADITIONALLY DRESSED DRUMMERS, CONAKRY

≫ WATER FALLS FROM ON HIGH IN A LUSH FOREST

FROM THE FOREST

When you see it, it's easy to understand why many people call the dark-dyed, intricately patterned fabric produced across southern Guinea 'mud-cloth'. In fact, in Guinea no dirt is involved in its production (unlike in Mali, for example). The earthy brown colour comes from kola nuts and tree bark, which is why Guineans call it 'forest-cloth'.

THREE-RING CINEMA

When French filmmaker Laurent Chevallier decided he wanted to make a documentary film about an African circus on tour, he ran into one big problem – there wasn't one. So, in 1998 he took directing to a new level and created one. The high-flying Circus Baobab have since toured the world to high acclaim. The film of the same name was released in 2001.

FUTURE DIRECTIONS

Guinea faces an uncertain future. In 2001 the constitution was changed to allow President Conté a third term, and, to no-one's surprise, he prevailed in the next election. Now a chain-smoking diabetic in his 70s, Conté can barely walk and has reportedly been on his death bed several times, but apparently has avoided making plans for his succession, nevertheless. No-one expects actual democracy to emerge after his death, but many observers fear that the transition will come violently. The political opposition has united to implore the ailing president, for the sake of the nation, to resign and allow a transitional government. His refusal, along with the fact that the economy is doing just as badly as his health, has prompted general strikes and violent demonstrations.

ESSENTIAL EXPERIENCES

- Hiking over the mountains and past the waterfalls of the Fouta Djalon
- Laughing at super-guide Hassan Bah's jokes and stories
- Watching local drum and dance troupes heat up the night
- Coming face to face with chimpanzees in the forests around Bossou
- Tracking elephants in the virgin rainforest of Forêt Classée de Ziama
- Lazing on the palm-fringed beaches of Sobané and Îles de Los

≫ FOOD'S UP! A WOMAN PREPARES A COLOURFUL MEAL

SENEGAL

MALI

GUINEA-BISSAU

- Koumbia
- Mali-ville
- Siguiri
- Boké
- Fouta Djalon
- Pita
- Dinguiraye
- Niani
- Kamsar
- Dabola
- Kouroussa
- Mandiana
- Boffa
- Mamou
- Kankan
- Kindia
- CONAKRY
- Gberia-Fotombu
- CÔTE D'IVOIRE
- Pamelap
- Forokonia
- Kérouané
- Sinko
- ATLANTIC OCEAN
- SIERRA LEONE
- Macenta
- Beyla

LIBERIA

- Bossou

MAP REF // F6

BEST TIME TO VISIT **NOVEMBER TO MAY**

DRAUGHTS AS A SPECTATOR SPORT, N'ZEREKORE »

A DANCING QUEEN FEELS THE BEAT »

SMILES AND SUSPICION IN A BAR IN CONAKRY »

TEXT TIM BEWER

SIERRA LEONE

AFTER YEARS OF VICIOUS CONFLICT, PEACE HAS BROKEN OUT ACROSS SIERRA LEONE AND THE STUNNING BEACHES AND WILD NATIONAL PARKS ARE WAITING FOR THE RETURN OF TRAVELLERS.

CAPITAL CITY **FREETOWN**   POPULATION **6 MILLION**   AREA **71,000 SQ KM**   OFFICIAL LANGUAGE **ENGLISH**

LANDSCAPE

Most of Sierra Leone is flat and low lying. However, the Freetown Peninsula is one of the few places in West Africa where peaks rise near the ocean, and the Loma Mountains in the northeast include Mt Bintumani (1945 metres), which is one of the highest mountains in West Africa. Rainforest is the natural vegetation for most of the country, though there are beaches and extensive mangrove swamps on the coast. Sierra Leone is one of West Africa's wettest and hottest places.

HISTORY IN A NUTSHELL

Though Sierra Leone was named by the Portuguese, the British were the first to control the area: in the 18th century, it became an important outpost of their slave trade. Starting in 1787, British philanthropists sent ex-slaves, mostly from North America, to the area, called a 'Province of Freedom'. The British declared it a colony in 1808, and when they abolished slavery soon after, British warships plied the West African coast intercepting slave ships and resettling those on board in the country. Independence came in 1961 and a tradition of coups and political violence followed. By 1991 the country had divided, with rebels exerting control in the east, where the richest diamond mines lie. Fighting grew increasingly vicious and indiscriminate, and in the resulting anarchy the rebels made hacking off people's limbs part of their strategy. Peace finally returned in 2001, with free and fair national elections the following year.

PEOPLE

The two largest tribal groups in Sierra Leone are the Temnes, who live mostly in the north, and the Mendes, who are predominantly from the south. The Krios, the descendents of the rescued and returned slaves, account for less than two per cent of the population, but their influence is far greater. There are also about 4000 Lebanese, and the profusion of aid workers has made Freetown a very multicultural city. Though English is the official language, Krio, an amalgamation of English and various African languages, is the lingua franca.

MARKETPLACE

Sierra Leone's economy has been improving, but it remains weak. The per capita GDP is just US$800 and the country ranked second to last in the United Nation's 2003 Human Development Index. Two thirds of the population live by subsistence farming. The annual government budget is US$351 million – a tenth of Ghana's and 0.00000037 per cent of the UK's – and 85 per cent of this comes from foreign aid. Diamond mining is the primary source of hard currency earnings.

TRADEMARKS

- Diamonds
- Palm-fringed beaches
- Chimpanzees
- Freetown's cotton tree
- Bunce Island
- Gara cloth

END OF THE ROAD

Sulima, at the mouth of the Moa River by the Liberian border, was once a busy seaport. These days it's just an overgrown village of mud-and-thatch houses and a handful of crumbling colonial buildings sleeping in the shade of palm trees. There isn't really anything to do other than wander the many miles of empty beach, but it's a great place to chill a while – and it's a much-needed rest after roughing it over the roads that lead here.

RANDOM FACTS

- The slaves who revolted on *La Amistad* had originally come from Sierra Leone.
- Every Easter Monday families gather together to fly kites.
- In October and November, humpback whale sightings off the Freetown Peninsula are common.

MONKEY SEE, MONKEY DO

Tiwai Island, a pristine plot in the Moa River, has one of the highest concentrations of primates in the world. It's common to see half of the 11 species, including diana monkeys and chimpanzees, in a short morning stroll.

ON FILM

The war spawned films like the harrowing *Cry Freetown* (1999), which features first-hand footage of the bloody battle for the capital. *The Refugee All Stars* (2004) is an inspiring documentary of the eponymous band; and the 2006 Hollywood blockbuster *The Blood Diamond* is about a poor farmer who gets between a diamond smuggler (played by Leonardo DiCaprio) and a diamond syndicate in Sierra Leone.

ESSENTIAL EXPERIENCES

- **Beach-bumming for a while on the Freetown Peninsula**
- **Primate watching at Tiwai Island Wildlife Sanctuary**
- **Tracking elephants and canoeing past hippos at Outamba-Kilimi National Park**
- **Dancing and drinking in Freetown's anything-goes nightclubs**
- **Bargaining in Freetown's many markets**
- **Exploring the Banana Islands and Turtle Islands**

MAP REF // E7

BEST TIME TO VISIT **NOVEMBER TO APRIL**

PUMPING IRON IN FREETOWN »

DIAMONDS IN THE ROUGH: A DEALERSHIP IN BO »

CHILDREN SIT DOWN AND TUNE IN

TEXT MARY FITZPATRICK

LANDSCAPE

Liberia's humid, palm-studded and heavily vegetated coastline is dotted with marshes and tidal lagoons, and cut by at least nine major rivers. Inland is a densely forested plateau rising to the low mountains of the Nimba Range. The country's rainforests – some of the region's most extensive – are part of the Guinean Forests of West Africa Hotspot, an exceptionally biodiverse area spanning 11 countries.

HISTORY IN A NUTSHELL

Liberia's polyglot mix of indigenous tribes, a small and rather insular 19th-century settler group of freed American slaves (Americo-Liberians) and rapacious outsiders greedy to get hold of the country's diamond reserves have made for a deadly combination. Since 1979 Liberia has been battered by a series of coups and brutal rebel wars and a string of failed peace accords. The intervention of the United Nations and the exodus in 2003 of warlord and former president Charles Taylor finally brought a respite. Since then the peace has held, and optimism – while cautious – is high, especially following the 2005 election of the widely respected Ellen Johnson-Sirleaf as president.

LIBERIA

TAKE A NEW LOOK AT LIBERIA – A LUSH, RAINFORESTED AND WAR-WRACKED COUNTRY WHERE AFRICA'S FIRST WOMAN PRESIDENT AND A FRAGILE BUT HOLDING PEACE ARE MAKING HEADLINES AND BOOSTING MORALE.

PEOPLE

Most Liberians belong to one of more than a dozen major tribal groups including the Kpelle, Bassa, Krahn and Mandingo. Americo-Liberians account for barely

CAPITAL CITY **MONROVIA**   POPULATION **3 MILLION**   AREA **111,370 SQ KM**   OFFICIAL LANGUAGE **ENGLISH**

⌃ A POSE WITH ATTITUDE

five per cent of the total population, although together with the sizable Lebanese community in Monrovia they wield a disproportionate share of economic power in the country.

MARKETPLACE

Liberia's economy is a shambles, and infrastructure is nonexistent outside Monrovia. Hope for the future lies in the country's reserves of timber, gold, diamonds and iron ore, plus increasing foreign aid and a tenuous peace that is finally giving the country enough breathing room to begin to pull itself up.

TRADEMARKS
- Rubber plantations
- Soccer great George Weah
- Rainforests
- Charles Taylor
- Gela and Gunyege masks
- Child soldiers

WILD THINGS

Liberia's rainforests are alive with hundreds of species of birds, who are kept company by other animals including forest elephants, pygmy hippos, antelopes, chimpanzees and even leopards. Sapo National Park – home to most of this wildlife and about 500 bird species – is slowly making a comeback. Thanks to the efforts of dedicated individuals in Liberia and other parts of the world, its infrastructure is in the process of being rehabilitated and the park should soon reopen to visitors.

NATURAL BEAUTY

Liberia is at its natural best along the coast – which is lined with tranquil white-sand coves and long beaches – and in the bird-filled rainforests of Sapo National Park. Listen in the mornings for the distinctive call of the pepperbird, which is also one of Liberia's national emblems.

URBAN SCENE

Yes, it's war-devastated and bullet-scarred, but look past the building shells and you will see Monrovia's unmistakable pep and determination to rebuild. The capital of Liberia is a down-to-earth, friendly place, with a small-town feel and a lively restaurant scene. In the central area around Benson and Randall Streets, traders, streetside tailors and vendors all jostle for space, while the sprawling and chaotic Waterside Market has almost everything anyone could need for sale, including a wonderful selection of colourful imported textiles.

RANDOM FACTS
- Monrovia is one of Africa's two wettest capitals (Freetown in Sierra Leone is the other), with rainfall averaging 4500 millimetres annually.
- Firestone, once the world's largest rubber plantation, employed more than 10 per cent of Liberia's labour force in its heyday, and Liberia was once known as the Firestone Republic.
- The Masonic Order was once a symbol of Americo-Liberian solidarity, and five presidents were grand masters. Today the order is banned in the country.

CULTURE

Secret societies, which are called *poro* for men and *sande* for women, have long played a central role in growing up in Liberia. These societies still serve as important repositories for traditional knowledge and a means of passing on general life skills. In the countryside, initiates can be identified by their white-painted faces and bodies and their shaved heads. There is a strict pecking order at work within the societies, and *zoes* (*poro* society leaders) wield significant political influence.

ESSENTIAL EXPERIENCES

- **Strolling through central Monrovia, seeing what sidewalk vendors have on offer, and getting a feel for the beat on the street**
- **Relaxing on surf-pounded, palm-fringed Silver Beach, just outside the capital**
- **Chatting with Liberians over a plate of *fufu* with sauce and a cold Club beer**
- **Cheering on the Liberia Lone Stars at a soccer match**
- **Spotting forest elephants, pygmy hippos and other wildlife in Sapo National Park, one of the last remaining rainforests in West Africa**

THE TWO-TONE GAZE OF A KISSI BOY »

MAP REF // G7

BEST TIME TO VISIT **NOVEMBER TO APRIL**

JUBILANT SUPPORTERS OF THE SUCCESSFUL PRESIDENTIAL CANDIDATE, ELLEN JOHNSON-SIRLEAF »

TEXT TIM BEWER

CÔTE D'IVOIRE

A SURPRISINGLY DIVERSE COUNTRY BOTH ECOLOGICALLY AND CULTURALLY, CÔTE D'IVOIRE WAS ONCE THE ECONOMIC MIRACLE OF WEST AFRICA BUT HAS SEEN FEW VISITORS SINCE IT HAS BEEN DEVASTATED BY WAR.

CAPITAL CITY YAMOUSSOUKRO   POPULATION 17.6 MILLION   AREA 322,460 SQ KM   OFFICIAL LANGUAGE FRENCH

≈ SHELLS AND STRIPES IN PAYS YACOUBA

LANDSCAPE

Southern Côte d'Ivoire once had the largest forests in West Africa, but very little of them remains. The drier north is savanna land. A coastal lagoon stretches from the Ghanaian border across half the country, and in the west, around Man, several mountains rise over 1000 metres. Wildlife has taken a hit with the conversion to cropland, though the birdlife remains rich. During the last three decades of the 20th century, agricultural lands expanded from a little over three million hectares to eight million hectares, at the expense of almost half of the country's rainforest and woodland.

HISTORY IN A NUTSHELL

Most of Côte d'Ivoire's major tribal groups, including the Baoulé, Senoufo, and Malinke, arrived between 400 and 200 years ago. The Portuguese were the first Europeans to drop anchor, but it was the French who colonised the country, defeating the illustrious Samory Touré in the process. They built a formidable export economy with coffee, cocoa, banana and palm tree plantations (for palm oil), only to hand the reins to Félix Houphouët-Boigny in 1960, who ruled with a one-party system for 33 mostly prosperous and peaceful years before dying at age 88.

After Houphouët-Boigny's death, the economy stumbled and xenophobia flared (25 per cent of the population are foreigners), eventually leading to the 2002 civil war that has divided the country. Though there have been positive signs recently, the years of peace deals brokered and broken have sapped most Ivorians of their hope.

TRADEMARKS

- Basilique de Notre Dame de la Paix
- Korhogo Cloth
- Masks
- Abidjan's outdoor laundry
- Hôtel Ivoire
- Musician Alpha Blondy
- Child jugglers
- Stilt dancers
- Cocoa

PEOPLE

Côte d'Ivoire has over 60 tribal groups, which can be divided into four principal groups. The largest group are the Akan (which include the Baoulé, the largest tribe), accounting for 42 per cent of the indigenous population. The others are the Mande (27 per cent), the Voltaiques (17 per cent) and the Krou (15 per cent).

A large majority of the 14,000 French that were living in the country have fled the fighting. Muslims make up about 40 per cent of the population, and mostly live in the north, and the 35 per cent who are Christian are mainly in the south.

MARKETPLACE

Despite the conflict, Côte d'Ivoire remains a world leader in the production of coffee, palm oil and cocoa beans – the last-mentioned counts for 90 per cent of foreign exchange earnings – though farmers earn much less than they once did, due to transport and export difficulties. Though no-one is currently keeping statistics, unemployment is high and average incomes are low. The country ranked 163 out of 177 in the 2004 UN Human Development Index. The government's budget is US$2.8 billion: that's about twice Burkina Faso's, but only 20 per cent of Nigeria's, by comparison.

RANDOM FACTS

- The annual maintenance bill for the Basilique de Notre Dame de la Paix is about US$1.5 million.
- The national football team, the Elephants, qualified for their first ever World Cup in 2006.

A FLOCK FROM THE CELESTIAL CHURCH OF CHRIST »

WORSHIPPERS GATHER AT A MOSQUE FOR FRIDAY PRAYERS, ODIENNE »

URBAN SCENE

It's been ages since Abidjan wore the 'Paris of West Africa' label, but this city still astounds. The shimmering skyscrapers of Le Plateau so defy African stereotypes that many visitors do a double take on first sight. But beyond the Paris-worthy bistros and boutiques are vibrant (and these days, unfortunately, pretty dangerous) neighbourhoods where the close-knit culture of village life remains largely intact.

THE NEXT BEST THING TO BEING THERE

A trio of insightful books peek into Ivorian village life. In *Nine Hills to Nambonkaha*, Sarah Erdman, a Peace Corps health worker who arrived in a Senoufo village in 1998 about the same time AIDS did, discusses the changes and challenges the disease brings. *In the Shadow of the Sacred Grove* (Carol Spindell) and *Parallel Worlds* (Alma Gottlieb and Philip Graham) date back to around 1980, but still ring true today.

TOP FESTIVAL

The Fêtes des Masques (Mask Festival) held in the villages around Man is one of the most famous celebrations in West Africa, but unfortunately the war has dampened the dancing. To fill the void, villagers near Sassandra, in conjunction with the Best of Africa beach resort, have created the biannual Trepoint Mask Festival, which they hope will grow into something big.

ECOTOURISM

Côte d'Ivoire's dismal environmental record got much worse with the war, but Taï National Park has largely escaped the destruction. The 454,000-hectare World Heritage Site protects one of West Africa's largest remaining patches of virgin rainforest. While the war has taken a toll, the World Wildlife Fund and other outside agencies have kept the antipoaching patrols active and visits are still possible.

WILD THINGS

The country's last few hundred elephants are in serious danger. Côte d'Ivoire chooses not to enforce the UN Convention on International Trade in Endangered Species, and ivory carvings are openly sold in Abidjan markets. Add rampant deforestation and a local taste for elephant steak, and the future looks bleak for them.

DANCE FEVER

After the discovery of bird flu in Côte d'Ivoire, there was an outbreak of wild shaking, clucking and arm-flapping – not on the farm, but on the dance floor. Mimicking the moves of DJ Lewis, dancers in Abidjan made the Dead Chicken Dance 2006's biggest dance craze. While some club-goers laughed, it was a gimmick that proved… well, infectious.

FRANCES LINZEE GORDON // LONELY PLANET IMAGES

≫ A CRUMBLING COLONIAL BUILDING IN GRAND BASSAM

≫ THE GLASS ARMOUR OF THE BAI DES SIRENS COAST RESORT

YANN ARTHUS-BERTRAND // CORBIS

ESSENTIAL EXPERIENCES

○ **Meeting the chimpanzees resident in Taï National Park**

○ **Getting an eyeful of Yamoussoukro's colossal basilica**

○ **Taking in an exhilarating live performance of music and masked dance in the villages around Man**

○ **Watching the skilled craftspeople at work in Korhogo and the surrounding artisans' villages**

○ **Soaking up the sun at rainforest-clad West Coast beaches, such as those around Grand-Béréby and Sassandra**

○ **Exploring the faded colonial charm of Grand Bassam**

MAP REF // G7

BEST TIME TO VISIT **NOVEMBER TO FEBRUARY**

≫ A SMALL VILLAGE ENCASED IN FOREST NEAR GUIGLO

CHARLES & JOSETTE LENARS // CORBIS

FASCINATING RHYTHM: DRUMMERS FOR THE SENOUFO PANTHER DANCE ⌃

LITTLE BOY BLUE

THE STREETS OF OUR TOWN: VILLAGERS MOVE AMONG THE GRASS HUTS OF BIANKOUMA ⌃

MALI

MALI IS WEST AFRICA IN MICROCOSM: THE TRACKLESS SANDS OF THE SAHARA AND THE FASCINATING CITIES AND CULTURES OF THE NIGER RIVERBANK, ALL SET TO A SOUNDTRACK OF THE WORLD-FAMOUS MALIAN MUSIC.

CAPITAL CITY BAMAKO   POPULATION 11.7 MILLION   AREA 1.2 MILLION SQ KM   OFFICIAL LANGUAGES FRENCH, BAMBARA

LANDSCAPE

The Sahara, in the north, covers 60 per cent of Malian territory, but the Niger River is Africa's third-longest and cuts through the heart of Mali for 1626 kilometres, even venturing into the desert briefly. En route, the river pauses in the Inland Delta, Africa's largest. Further south, Mali is pure Sahel, its plains picked clean by desert winds from the north; the country's far south, however, is green and rich in agricultural possibility.

HISTORY IN A NUTSHELL

Mali looms large in African history and once stood at the centre of the gold-rich empires of Ghana, Mali and Songhaï. In 1324 King Kankan Musa set out on his pilgrimage to Mecca carrying enough gold to cause the world gold price to collapse. By the time he returned home, Mali was known to the world as a land of incomparable riches and Timbuktu had lodged in the West's imagination. After Moroccan forces swept away Mali's riches in the late 16th century, Mali slid into a decline that French colonial rule did little to arrest. Mali became independent in 1960, suffered from military governments and Cold War meddling, before yielding to the pull of

democracy in 1992. A rebellion by the Tuareg paralysed Mali throughout the 1990s, although the country is now at peace once again.

PEOPLE

Mali's largest ethnic group is the Bambara (33 per cent). Other important groups include the Fulani (17 per cent), Senoufo (12 per cent), Dogon (seven per cent), Songhaï (six per cent), Tuareg (six per cent) and Bobo (2.5 per cent), and there are also groups of Bozo (the fishing nomads of the Niger), Soninke and Malinke. Almost 90 per cent of Malians are Muslim.

TRADEMARKS

- o Timbuktu
- o Africa's best-known musicians
- o Baobab trees in abundance
- o Intriguing Dogon rituals unlike any others
- o Salt caravans plying the desert wastes
- o Ceremonial wooden masks and statues

MARKETPLACE

Mali's significant natural resources include cotton (Mali is Africa's largest producer and cotton accounts for half of Malian exports) and, increasingly, gold.

Despite the potential for wealth, more than 90 per cent of Malians survive on less than US$2 a day, compared to 85 per cent in neighbouring Niger and just 15 per cent in Algeria to the north.

NATURAL BEAUTY

The Sahara, which dominates the northern half of Mali, is a surprisingly diverse world of sand seas, plains devoid of all life and palm-fringed oases. The Niger River charts a course up the middle of the country through every conceivable type of terrain, from the lush reed gardens of the inland delta to towering sand dunes that turn pink with the setting sun. Perhaps most dramatic of all, however, are the towering cliffs of the Bandiagara Escarpment, which run like a spine through central Mali.

RANDOM FACTS

- o During its 16th-century heyday, 25,000 students and scholars attended Timbuktu's university.
- o The famous saying that 'the death of an old man is like the burning down of a library' was coined by Mali's greatest writer, Amadou Hampaté Bâ.
- o Salt from Mali's deserts was once so highly prized that it traded ounce for ounce with gold.

TWO STILT DANCERS PERCH ON A STONE WALL, DOGON COUNTRY

≫ AN ELDER IN FRONT OF THE DOGON *TOGU-NA* (TRADITIONAL MEETING PLACE OF THE ELDERS) ON THE BANDIAGARA ESCARPMENT

MATT FLETCHER // LONELY PLANET IMAGES

≫ ROCK PAINTINGS BY DOGON BOYS DURING THEIR CIRCUMCISION RITUALS ON THE CLIFFS ABOVE SONGO

≫ SITTING IN A DOORWAY OF DYINGEREY BER MOSQUE, TIMBUKTU

KICKING UP DUST AT THE ANNUAL FULANI CATTLE CROSSING FESTIVAL, NIGER RIVER, DIAFARABE »

EACH YEAR THE GREAT MOSQUE OF DJENNÉ IS GIVEN A NEW LAYER OF CLAY TO REPLACE WHAT THE RAINS HAVE WASHED AWAY »

WOMEN MAKE A STRIPY STATEMENT »

DAVID ELSE // LONELY PLANET IMAGES

CHRIS CALDICOTT // AXIOM

YADID LEVY // ALAMY

CLIVE SHIRLEY // PANOS

URBAN SCENE

Bamako would never win a beauty contest but few other cities in the world can match its intoxicating nightlife or its nightly promise of world-famous musicians playing in your friendly neighbourhood bar. On any weekend night, chances are that you'll be able to find Salif Keita, Toumani Diabate and Oumou Sangare playing somewhere in town. Throw in a world-class museum, clamorous markets that devour entire city blocks and top-flight restaurants and it's a city that's easy to love.

IN ART

○ *The Epic of Sundiata* – the 13th-century founding myth of the Empire of Mali

○ *The Fortunes of Wangrin* by Amadou Hampaté Bâ – a masterful novel by Mali's greatest modern writer

○ *Yeelen* (1987), directed by Souleymane Cissé – an outstanding Malian film which won the Special Jury Prize at the Cannes Film Festival in 1987

○ *In the Heart of the Moon* – a landmark musical collaboration between the desert blues of Ali Farka Touré and the kora of Toumani Diabaté

WILD THINGS

Most of West Africa's wildlife may have gone the way of the dodo, but the animal kingdom's most prodigious feeder – the elephant – somehow manages to survive on the meagre resources of the Sahel, roaming the Gourma region between the Niger River and the Burkina Faso border. Mali's elephants spend the rainy season in the verdant south and migrate north to spend November to January at desert watering holes: an annual round-trip of more than 1000 kilometres.

SALT & GOLD

The coexistence of Mali's culturally distinct peoples has always depended upon their wary separation, and nothing expresses their historical relationships quite like the fascinating ancient practice of silent trading. Long ago, desert nomads travelled to the banks of the Niger, left their cargoes of salt and returned to the desert. Traders from the south would then arrive by river, leave a quantity of gold beside the salt that corresponded to their estimate of its value, and return home. The nomads came back: if they accepted the price, they took the gold and left the salt; if not, they left and waited for the traders to add more gold. The process was repeated until they considered that they were being offered a fair price. Trade was completed without the two groups ever meeting, each group dependent upon the honesty and goodwill of the other.

SURPRISES

○ Elephants in the desert
○ Timbuktu does actually exist

MYTHS & LEGENDS

The Dogon people believe that the earth was created by a divine male being called Amma, who moulded the earth into the shape of a woman. Amma later created a man and a woman who gave birth to eight children, who are regarded as the ancestors of all Dogon. The stars were also the work of Amma, and Sirius, the Dog Star (which was also revered by the ancient Egyptians), was central to the Dogon's understanding of the universe. The Dogon can predict Sirius' periodic appearances and have always claimed that Sirius is in fact three stars – the third star was only discovered by astronomers in 1995 using a powerful radio telescope.

MUSIC

Griot (also called *jalis*) are a powerful hereditary caste of musicians who once served as praise-singers and storytellers to the traditional chiefs and kings of Mali's past (as they did to many traditional rulers throughout West Africa). The kings may have gone, but many of Mali's modern singers are members of the *griot* caste and a significant proportion of their songs draw on ancient Malian myths.

TOP FESTIVAL

Every January, caravans of musicians converge on Essakane, 50 kilometres from Timbuktu, for the three-day Festival in the Desert. Featuring everything from the electric guitars and desert blues of the Tuareg group Tinariwen to the master musicians of Mali's Bambara south, the festival hit the big time in 2003, when former Led Zeppelin frontman Robert Plant turned up.

CLIVE SHIRLEY // PANOS

ESSENTIAL EXPERIENCES

○ **Following in the footsteps of the great explorers in the legendary city of Timbuktu (Tombouctou)**

○ **Marvelling at the Great Mosque of Djenné, the largest adobe building in the world, during the colourful Monday market**

○ **Trekking down off the escarpment and into the fantastical Dogon Country**

○ **Taking a slow boat up the Niger River from Mopti, the river's busiest port**

○ **Dancing the night away to the live performances of some of the finest musicians in Africa**

⩘ A DRY DESTINATION: TUAREG TRADERS AND THEIR CAMELS OUTSIDE THE ANCIENT CITY OF TIMBUKTU

FROM THE TRAVELLER

This picture was taken on a trip to Dogon Country. Dogon belief holds that foxes have the ability to predict the future. When a person has a question, they visit one of the village 'diviners'. There is a spot outside the village, where the diviner creates symbolic marks, arranges sticks, and scatters peanuts about the design. During the night a fox will come and eat the peanuts, leaving a telling trail. The diviner interprets the fox's footprints across the design to make predictions.

JUDITH FENSON // USA

MAP REF // H5

BEST TIME TO VISIT **OCTOBER TO FEBRUARY**

TUAREG WOMEN SERENELY SIPPING TEA »

A PIROGUE CUTS THROUGH THE NIGER RIVER, GAO »

TEXT ANTHONY HAM

BURKINA FASO

FEW PEOPLE OUTSIDE AFRICA KNOW IT EXISTS, BUT BURKINA FASO ROUTINELY WINS HEARTS WITH ITS LAID-BACK CITIES, VIBRANT MARKETS AND THE EASY SMILES OF ITS DIVERSE PEOPLES.

CAPITAL CITY **OUAGADOUGOU**   POPULATION **13.9 MILLION**   AREA **274,200 SQ KM**   OFFICIAL LANGUAGE **FRENCH**

⌃ THE SPINY EXTERIOR OF THE GRANDE MOSQUÉE, BOBO-DIOULASSO

LANDSCAPE

Landlocked Burkina Faso has three of West Africa's signature landscapes, with arid desert plains in the far north, surprisingly green woodland in the southwest and the Sahel covering the rest – a vast laterite plateau that forms the transition zone between the Sahara and the savanna lands of the south.

HISTORY IN A NUTSHELL

Burkina Faso's early history belongs to the Bobo, Lobi and Gourounsi, but they came to play second kora to the highly organised Mossi kingdoms in the late 15th century. French colonial rule in Burkina Faso (from the late 19th century to independence in 1960) was characterised by neglect and the country's early post-colonial history is a familiar story of coups, counter-coups and general instability. From 1983 to 1987, however, the charismatic revolutionary Thomas Sankara held sway. The man who overthrew him, Blaise Compaoré, remains in power to this day.

PEOPLE

The Mossi (48 per cent of the population) are Burkina Faso's dominant ethnic group, but there are also 60 other groups, including the Bobo (seven per cent), Lobi (seven per cent) and Gourounsi (five per cent).

The seminomadic Fulani (eight per cent) roam the country's north and beyond. Half of Burkinabés are Muslim; a further 40 per cent profess traditional animist beliefs.

MARKETPLACE

With few natural resources, Burkina Faso is the world's third-poorest country and most of its vital signs are weak: almost half of Burkinabés subsist on less than US$1 a day, just 13 per cent of the adult population can read and write and life expectancy is a short breath over 47. By comparison, in Africa's richest country, Libya, adult literacy is 81 per cent and life expectancy is 73 years – a contrast that gives considerable pause for thought. Some 80 per cent of the population lives on the land although just 13 per cent of the land is suitable for crops.

TRADEMARKS

- The absence of police corruption
- Fespaco, Africa's premier film festival
- Thorn-bush and baobab-strewn Sahelian landscapes
- Frenetic music heavy on the drums
- Lyrical African names like Ouagadougou, Bobo-Dioulasso and Rambo that roll around in the mouth in a very African way

NATURAL BEAUTY

The country's southwest is home to lush forests, rocky outcrops that spring from the earth like apparitions, waterfalls amid mango trees and lakes inhabited by hippos or chicken-eating sacred fish. And with the merest suggestion of rain the whole landscape transforms into a world of green.

RANDOM FACTS

- 'Burkina Faso' means 'Land of the Honest Men' or 'Land of the Incorruptible'.
- Burkinabé filmmaker Idrissa Ouédraogo won the 1990 Grand Prix at Cannes for his film *Tilä*.

URBAN SCENE

Bobo-Dioulasso has that special something that calls travellers to rest from the rigours of life on the African road – its quiet tree-lined streets make you want to slow down and live life at the more civilised African pace. There's a sense that Bobo is growing old gracefully, especially in the picturesque old quarter of Kibidwe or around the Great Mosque, which resembles a timeworn fossil. The town springs to life, however, in its sprawling market, where all the treasure, kitsch and aromatic spices of Africa congregate under one roof.

A *DOBA* (FAMILY ALTAR) TAKES PRIDE OF PLACE IN A BOBO VILLAGE

I always feel awkward taking pictures of people because I know I wouldn't like someone to take a picture of me doing everyday things that are normal in my life, so I try not to do it. But as I was sheltering from the heat under a tree in Bobo-Dioulasso, I couldn't resist taking a picture of these women also resting before walking back to their homes.

ELENA RADINA // ITALY

KING OF THE MOSSI

The emperors (Moro-Naba) of the Mossi people still play an important role in the life of the nation. Burkina Faso's government routinely consults the Moro-Naba of Ouagadougou (the 37th ruler of his dynasty), and every Friday he acts out *la cérémonie du Nabayius Gou*. With Mossi dignitaries arrayed before him, the Moro-Naba appears in ceremonial red (which represents war), disappears, then returns in white (signifying peace). The ceremony commemorates a legend in which the Moro-Naba was preparing for war, only for his advisers to dissuade him. Afterward, the Moro-Naba hears the grievances of his people and gives judgements, just as he and his predecessors have done for centuries.

THE CHE GUEVARA OF AFRICA

Thomas Sankara, or 'Thom Sank' as he is still affectionately called, was known throughout the region as the Che Guevara of Africa for his revolutionary ways and rakish charm. On coming to power in 1983, he promptly ditched the presidential limousine in favour of a dinky little Renault 5, cut his salary by 25 per cent and declared war on official corruption and disease, vaccinating 60 per cent of the country's children in one remarkable 15-day burst. He also oversaw the construction of 350 village schools in just four years. In 1987, partly because of the company he kept (Cuba's Fidel Castro was a friend), Thom Sank was deposed and shot.

TOP FESTIVAL

Every odd year, in late February or early March, Ouagadougou hosts the Pan-African Film Festival (Fespaco), a nine-day celebration of African film. International celebrities fight for festival tickets with ordinary Burkinabés (who love nothing more than a trip to the cinema), and the continent's directors vie for the coveted Étalon D'Or de Yennenga, the Fespaco equivalent of an Oscar.

FUTURE DIRECTIONS

On one level, Burkina Faso's future promises to hold more of the same. In November 2005 President Compaoré was re-elected for a third term, despite a constitutional amendment in 2000 limiting presidents to two terms. On another level, however, changes are afoot. Vast swaths of central Ouagadougou have been bulldozed. Where once there were vibrant inner-city neighbourhoods, now there are open fields waiting for development. The plan is to transform the city into a high-rise commercial centre that some foresee will be 'the new Wall Street of Africa'.

- Bargaining amid the colour of Gorom Gorom's Thursday market, when the whole region comes to town
- Acquainting yourself with the Africa of old at the beautiful Great Mosque and old quarter of Bobo-Dioulasso
- Discovering that there's more to Ouagadougou than Africa's most evocative name in the city's great restaurants and dance-crazy nightlife
- Searching for hippos in the otherworldly terrain of the Sindou Peaks
- Finding exquisite mud-brick architecture in the unlikely village of Bani, home to seven intricate adobe mosques

⌃ A FARMER AND HIS TRUSTY STEED RETURN FROM THE MARKET

⌃ ELEPHANTS COOL OFF IN A POND NEAR BOROMO

MALI

Gorom-Gorom
• Djibo   • Dori   NIGER

• Ouahigouya

• Yako   • Kaya

Dédougou •
Koudougou •   ✪OUAGADOUGOU
                        • Fada
                          N'Gourma
Sindou   • Bobo-Dioulasso
Peaks   • Léo   • Pô
  • Karfiguaéla
  Banfora •
         • Gaoua   GHANA
                                        BENIN

CÔTE D'IVOIRE   TOGO

MAP REF // H6

LEAN, GREEN MACHINES: TAXIS PARKED OUTSIDE THE COVERED CENTRAL MARKET IN OUAGADOUGOU ≫

CHILDREN OF THE SAHEL CARRYING FOOD ≫

THE STUPENDOUSLY COLOURFUL MARKET OF GOROM-GOROM IN THE SAHEL ≫

TEXT MICHAEL GROSBERG

GHANA

CONSIDERED WEST AFRICA'S MOST WELCOMING COUNTRY, GHANA OFFERS SUN AND SAND, VITAL MODERN AND TRADITIONAL EXPRESSIONS OF CULTURE AND A LESSON IN THE FAULT LINES CREATED WHEN FAR-FLUNG VILLAGES COME UP AGAINST THE FORCES OF MODERNISATION.

CAPITAL CITY **ACCRA**   POPULATION **22.4 MILLION**   AREA **239,460 SQ KM**   OFFICIAL LANGUAGE **ENGLISH**

≪ HARD-HITTING MESSAGE: A BOXER TRAINING AT A GYM IN ACCRA, WHERE POSTERS ENCOURAGE SEXUAL HEALTH

LANDSCAPE

Ghana is generally flat: in fact, the whole country lies below 1000 metres. The northern two thirds are a low plateau. The country's major asset is 500 kilometres of coastline, stretching from Côte d'Ivoire to Togo. Dominating its eastern flank is Lake Volta, the world's largest artificial lake. Wherever you go, it's hot year-round, with maximum temperatures above 30°C. In the humid southern coastal region, the rainy seasons are from April to June, and during September and October. The harmattan wind which blows in from the Sahara from December to March makes things dusty and hazy.

HISTORY IN A NUTSHELL

Though Ghana has been inhabited since at least 4000 BC, it wasn't until the 13th century that a number of kingdoms fuelled by gold came to the notice of the rest of the world. The most prominent of these was the kingdom of the Ashanti, an expanding empire that by the 18th century was often in conflict with the European traders on the coast. Despite this, slaves soon became the region's principal export, attracting the Dutch, British and Danes. Slavery was finally outlawed in the early 19th century. By this stage, the British controlled much of the country,

following a series of wars with the Ashanti. Economically, the British didn't do so badly in Ghana: by World War I the Gold Coast, as it was then known, was the most prosperous colony in Africa.

In 1957 Ghana became the first independent sub-Saharan African country, under the leadership of Kwame Nkrumah. He was driven from power only nine years later, however, and it wasn't until Jerry Rawlings, an air force lieutenant, restored some stability a number of coups later that the country began to rebound. Rawlings and his party ruled until 2000, when Ghanaians wary of continued corruption and cronyism gave the opposition party a chance to correct course and steer the country forward.

PEOPLE

Ghana is one of the most densely populated countries in West Africa. The major tribal groups are the Akan (44 per cent), the Dagomba (16 per cent), the Ewe (13 per cent) and the Ga (eight per cent). Almost 70 per cent of Ghanaians are Christian; 15 per cent are Muslim, mostly concentrated in the north, and traditional religions are practised as well. English is the official language but there are at least 75 local languages and dialects, the most widely spoken of which is Twi.

MARKETPLACE

Compared to other countries in the region, Ghana has a diverse and vibrant economy. However, the estimated per capita income in 2002 was a mere US$290. The bulk of the country's labour force is employed in agriculture (much of it subsistence farming), which accounts for 37 per cent of its GDP and 35 per cent of its export earnings. A good proportion of the economy is being propped up by foreign investment in the mining industry (which includes gold, manganese, diamonds and bauxite), and large-scale international financial and technical assistance – there are over a thousand local and international NGOs in the country. Attempts to diversify the economy and reduce Ghana's dependence on gold and cocoa have led to increased exports of timber, shea-nut butter, tobacco, cotton and pineapples.

TRADEMARKS

○ Kofi Annan, UN Secretary General (1997 - 2007)
○ Kente cloth
○ Hiplife music
○ Pan-African politics
○ Friendly people
○ Coastal castles/slave forts

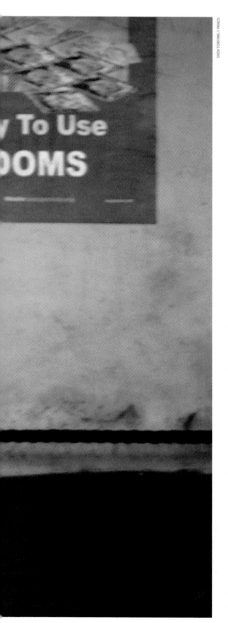

THE SERIOUS BUSINESS OF DRUMMING AT A KROBO FESTIVAL ⌃

This is the resting place of the Okomfe Anokye Sword. The sword resides in a white 'well', inside a small visitors' center, where I found these two lovely schoolgirls 'on duty' to answer questions. I asked if I could take their picture, they agreed, and then instinctively held hands. It's such a lovely gesture of friendship, one I saw often in West Africa.

RINA KOR // USA

RANDOM FACTS

○ Oddly enough, one of the most popular TV shows in the country is *The Promise*, a soap opera from the Philippines.
○ Artisans in Teshie build coffins to match the occupation of their eternal residents – lobsters for fishermen, Mercedes for drivers, guns for soldiers, and so on.

SEATS OF TRADITION

There's an Ashanti saying: 'There are no secrets between a man and his stool.' The stool – an elaborately carved seat on a central support – is an everyday household object, of course, but it also has a special place in Ghanaian culture. The Golden Stool, according to Ashanti legend, descended from heaven to mark the spot where the kingdom should be established. It's considered to embody the soul of the nation, and is not, of course, for everyday use: in fact it's not permitted to touch the ground. The British recognised its importance early on and demanded it be handed over to them, but never realised the stool they were given was a fake. The decorative carvings on stools are also significant: designs featuring leopards and elephants were historically reserved for the elite or royalty, and are still considered powerful symbols of authority for chiefs. When a chief dies his people say, 'The stool has fallen'. Stools are also usually the first gift from father to son and husband-to-be to bride-to-be; women's stools are different from men's.

IMPORT

↗ Rita Marley, musician and wife of reggae legend Bob Marley
↗ Missionaries
↗ Peace Corps volunteers
↗ Old Peugeots
↗ Nigerian movies

EXPORT

↖ Gold
↖ Hybrid musical genres
↖ Cocoa
↖ Regional confidence
↖ Textile designs

TOP FESTIVAL

The Aboakyer (Deer Hunt Festival) has been celebrated for more than 300 years on the first weekend in May. The festival is centred on a competitive hunt in which two Asafo (companies of men) hunt an antelope in order to sacrifice it to the tribal god Penkye Otu. The captains of each Asafo carry swords and before starting out the young men purify themselves, washing at the beach. The first man to capture an antelope alive rushes with his company to the *omanhene*'s (village chief) dais, and they sing and dance and taunt their opponents. The following day both Asafo assemble before the Penkye Otu deity's shrine to question the oracle, who forecasts either rain or drought, prosperity or war, depending on certain signs. The antelope is then sacrificed, cooked and eaten. At the conclusion of the two-day festival – and the meal – the priest takes a little of the hot soup in his hands and pours it on the Penkye Otu statue.

SURPRISES

○ There are around 500 internet cafés in the capital, Accra.
○ Almost half the residents of Kumasi are Muslim and speak Hausa.
○ The University of Legon in Accra is the oldest in sub-Saharan Africa.

ESSENTIAL EXPERIENCES

○ **Staring eye to eye or at least eye to knee with a lumbering elephant in Mole National Park**

○ **Revelling in the shade provided by hundreds of fluttering bats in the crystal-clear pool at the foot of Wli Falls**

○ **Wandering endlessly in circles in Kejetia market in Kumasi – West Africa's largest**

○ **Touring the suffocating chambers of Cape Coast Castle, a sombre and moving reminder of the slave trade**

○ **Dining alfresco on lobster at Busua beach**

MAP REF // H7

MARGARET COURTNEY-CLARKE // CORBIS

BEST TIME TO VISIT **NOVEMBER TO MARCH**

⌃ A COCOA FARMER CARRIES THE PRECIOUS BEANS HOME

ELLERINGMANN // LAIF / AURORA // IPN

MICHAEL MACINTYRE // EYE UBIQUITOUS / HUTCHISON

NOW SHOWING: THE PROPRIETOR OF A CINEMA IN ACCRA ≫

LOOKING BACK AT AN ANCESTOR-WORSHIP CEREMONY ≫

A BOY HAS SOME QUIET TIME SITTING IN A PAINTED *GRUNNE* HUT ≫

TEXT JAMES BAINBRIDGE

TOGO

POLITICAL CORRUPTION HAS BROUGHT TINY TOGO TO ITS KNEES, BUT IT'S STILL EASY TO SEE WHY THE COUNTRY WAS ONCE CONSIDERED THE PEARL OF WEST AFRICA.

CAPITAL CITY LOMÉ   **POPULATION** 5.5 MILLION   **AREA** 56,790 SQ KM   **OFFICIAL LANGUAGE** FRENCH

LANDSCAPE

Woodlands and waterfalls, such as the dramatic Akloa Falls, are plentiful as far north as the national icon of the Aledjo Fault, where the Route Internationale winds through a chasm in the cliff. Further north, savanna takes over and temperatures rise the closer you get to the Sahel with its harmattan onslaughts. The country is relatively dry – Lomé only receives up to about 220 millimetres of rainfall, compared to over 300 millimetres in Porto Novo, the capital of neighbouring Benin. Apart from the hippos in the River Oti, Togo is short on wild animals, which were scared away by farmers and rioters during the 1990s. The Swiss Fondation Franz Weber is repopulating Fazao-Malfakassa National Park with elephants by encouraging them back across the borders of neighbouring countries.

HISTORY IN A NUTSHELL

Togo was forgotten by both West Africa and the rest of the world until the area's incarnation as the 'Slave Coast', when slave-traders used Togo as a conduit – and a hunting ground. The Germans 'protected' the country they called Togoland from 1884 until the Allies ousted them in World War I. France and Britain then shared Togoland between them; the British incorporated the western third of the country into the Gold Coast (now Ghana). In 1963 Togo became the first African country to have a coup following independence, and its fortunes only worsened during Gnassingbé Eyadéma's 38 years of dictatorship. When he died in 2005, his son Faure Gnassingbé seized power, but then relented and held elections – though they were most likely rigged. Hundreds were killed in riots and some 40,000 fled the country. However, Gnassingbé junior is gradually winning over the Togolese people, who admit that he's an improvement on his father. Gnassingbé is working with opposition leaders, and the refugees are starting to return home.

PEOPLE

With some 40 ethnic groups, Togo has a patchwork population even by African standards. The most significant groups – and languages – are the southern Ewe and Faure Gnassingbé's Kabyé clan, who are concentrated around Kara and in top government jobs in Lomé. Other major northern groups are the Kotokoli and the Tamberma – the latter are famous for their fortified compounds near Kandé. A number of groups, including the Mina and Guin, consider themselves Ewe, though they're not ethnically part of that tribe. Fifty-nine per cent of the population hold indigenous beliefs such as animism and voodoo, particularly in the southeast, though Christianity (29 per cent) and Islam (12 per cent) are on the rise in the south and north respectively.

MARKETPLACE

With foreign debt of over US$2 billion and over 30 per cent of its population living below the poverty line, Togo desperately needs international aid and commerce, but this has dried up in response to the country's human rights record. The government is now working with the World Bank and the IMF to reform the economy and encourage foreign investment. Togo's principal exports are phosphate (it's the world's fourth-largest producer), cotton, coffee and cocoa.

TRADEMARKS

o Riots and refugees
o Emmanuel Adebayor
o Tamberma compounds
o Lomé boulevards
o Voodoo skulduggery

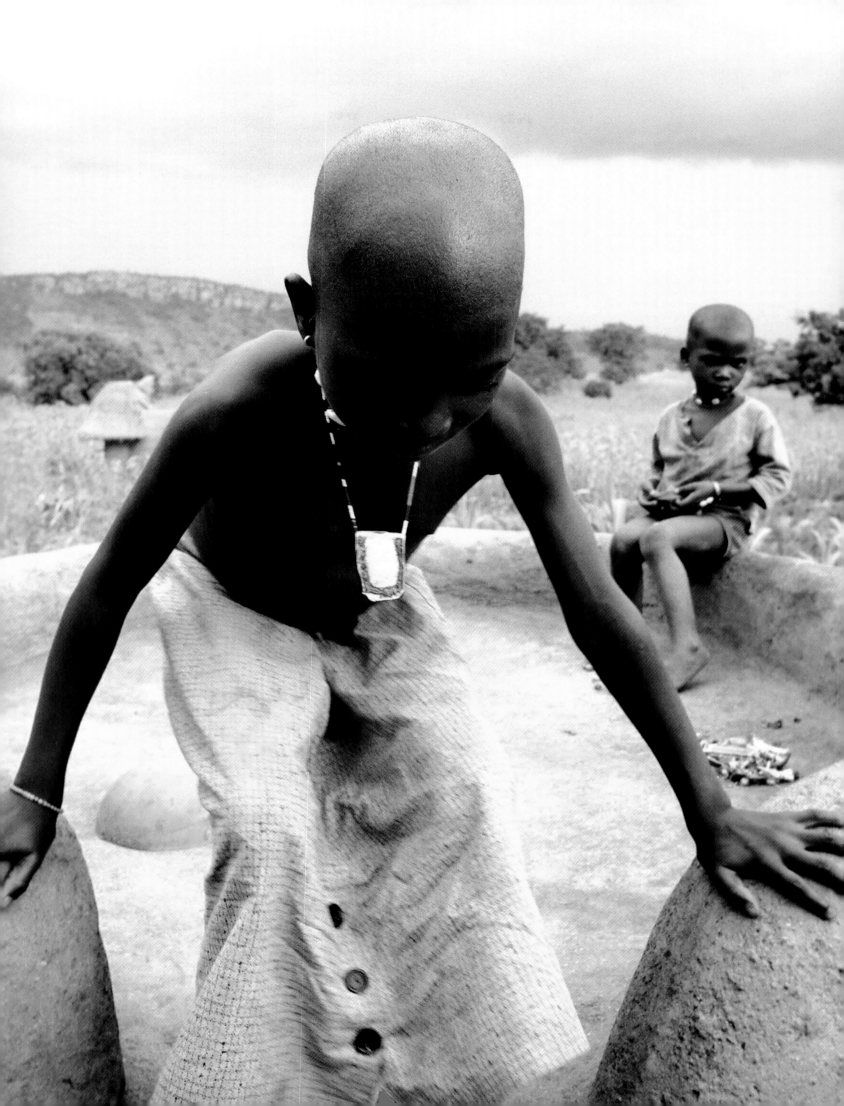

○ Pope John Paul II visited Lake Togo in 1985, following a reported sighting of the Virgin Mary walking on its water.
○ The lake also gave Togo its name, which derives from the Ewe word *togodo*, meaning 'behind the lake'.
○ On the menu in many restaurants, *agouti* are large rodents called 'grasscutters' in English.

NATURAL BEAUTY

In Togo's coffee and cocoa triangle west of Atakpamé, waterfalls crash through the undergrowth, 700-metre-plus hills offer views into Ghana, and iridescent butterflies flutter in the forests around the French-style Château Viale. Though they are mostly devoid of animals, national parks such as Malfakassa Zone de Chasse and the pointedly misnamed Fosse aux Lions (Pit of Lions) boast woodland, savanna, cliffs and more waterfalls.

URBAN SCENE

With its broad boulevards sweeping down to the beach, Lomé is what Paris might be if the French capital was transported to the tropics and overrun by civil unrest for 40 years. The city centre is no place for the faint-hearted after dark, but for the daring it's well worth sitting at one of Boulevard du 13 Janvier's open-air bars and watching the hustlers and prostitutes ply their trades.

REPRESENTATIONS

○ *Hustling is Not Stealing: Stories of an African Bar Girl*, by John M Chernoff, could be Africa's answer to cult black American fiction, transcribing the wild tales and wry observations of protagonist Hawa as she works it to survive in the discos of 1970s Lomé.
○ *Do They Hear You When You Cry?* is Fauziya Kassindja's account of her brave flight from polygamy and impending female genital mutilation to Germany and the USA, where she spent years in detention centres and prisons.

MYTHS & LEGENDS

In one Togolese folk tale, three brothers leave home to seek their fortunes. They bag themselves a mirror, a pair of sandals and a calabash respectively, all with magical powers. When they meet again, the first son looks into his mirror and sees their father is ill. The second uses his sandals to quickly transport them to the grave of their father, who has died. The third cures the dead man by pouring medicine from his calabash onto the grave. The revived father applauds his sons for displaying a quality that is not always evident in Togo – unity.

THE BEAUTIFUL GAME

Perhaps the only thing every Togolese agrees on is their love of national soccer team Les Eperviers (the Sparrow Hawks). When the team qualified for the 2006 World Cup (despite losing to the undistinguished Equatorial Guinea team in a qualifier), striker Emmanuel Adebayor solidified his position as a national icon, and Lomé went postal. Crowds surged into the city centre in the heavy rain, holding aloft Adebayor fetish dolls wearing the Les Eperviers team colours. The team's odds to win the World Cup were 500 to 1, however, and its campaign started badly. After the Togolese Football Association refused the players' pay demands (one of which was €155,000 each to play in the tournament), they boycotted training sessions. In response, their German coach Otto Pfister temporarily resigned. Though these early problems were overcome and Les Eperviers played valiantly, they were knocked out in the first round of the tournament after losing to South Korea, Switzerland and their former colonial masters France.

ESSENTIAL EXPERIENCES

○ **Stashing your valuables and hitting the bars on Lomé's Boulevard du 13 Janvier**

○ **Climbing beneath the cocoa trees to reach the peak of Mt Agou for views of Lake Volta in Ghana**

○ **Feeling a palpable sense of history in Aného's dilapidated colonial buildings and its creole population, descended from repatriated slaves**

○ **Spending a day spotting turreted clay compounds in the Tamberma Valley and finishing the expedition in a *tchoukoutou* (fermented millet) den at Nadoba market**

○ **Stocking up on snakes' heads, thunderstones and other voodoo essentials at Lomé Marché des Féticheurs**

⌃ GRACEFUL AS A GAZELLE: A HAT WORN DURING INITIATION RITES

⌃ YOUNG BOYS SHARE THE MUSIC

BURKINA FASO

● Dapaong

Kandé ●
Niamtougou ● ● Pagouda
● Kara
Bassar ● ● Bafilo
Sokodé ●
GHANA   BENIN
● Sotouboua

Badou ●
● Atakpamé

Kpalimé ●   ● Notsé
● Tabligo
Lake   ● Vogan
Togo ● Aného
LOMÉ ✪
ATLANTIC OCEAN

MAP REF // I7

BEST TIME TO VISIT **NOVEMBER TO FEBRUARY**

PHILIPPE LISSAC // PANOS

CRAIG PERSHOUSE // LONELY PLANET IMAGES

SCHOOLGIRLS IN LOMÉ »

FIERCE DOGS' HEADS FOR SALE AT A FETISH MARKET »

VOODOO INITIATES TALK SHOP, LOMÉ »

BENIN

ONCE A MIGHTY SLAVE-TRADING KINGDOM, BENIN IS ALSO THE BIRTHPLACE OF VOODOO – AN INTRIGUING COUNTRY AND A FINE PLACE TO SINK A FEW BOTTLES OF LA BÉNINOISE BEER ON THE BEACH.

CAPITAL CITY **PORTO NOVO**   POPULATION **7.8 MILLION**   AREA **112,620 SQ KM**   OFFICIAL LANGUAGE **FRENCH**

≪ STILTS TENUOUSLY SUPPORT HOUSES IN THE WETLANDS, PORTO NOVO

LANDSCAPE

Benin's byways give an overwhelming impression of dusty flatlands, but this long, thin country actually has various landscapes, from the equatorial to the Sahel. In the south, where a coastal sand bar has created a string of lagoons, are beach towns like Grand Popo, with a palm-dotted tropical feel. North of the Atakora mountains (rising to a whopping 658 metres), fat mango trees offer welcome shade in an arid, harmattan-blown area where temperatures top 45°C. Elephants, crocodiles, lions and other big cats can be spotted in the two northern wildlife parks – the renowned Pendjari and the developing Parc Régional du W, a 10,240-square-kilometre Unesco-recognised biosphere that crosses into Burkina Faso and Niger.

HISTORY IN A NUTSHELL

For one of the 20 least developed nations in the world, Benin has a surprisingly extravagant history of monarchs trying to outdo each other's palaces and temples. The 17th-century king Akaba named the empire 'Dahomey' when he defeated his enemy Dan, sliced open his belly (ho in Fon) and planted a tree inside (mey). Life was a frenzy of slave-trading and human sacrifice for Akaba's successors – Ghézo, for example, had a throne mounted on the skulls of his enemies. France brought all this to an end in the late 19th century, when it defeated the final king Béhanzin and turned Abomey into its colonial administrative centre. The French nicknamed Dahomey 'the West African Latin quarter' for its intellectualism, but the country unravelled after independence in 1960. The next decade saw five coups, nine governments and five changes of constitution. Mathieu Kérékou seized power in 1972 and changed the country's name to Benin in 1975 during a revolutionary Marxist phase. He ruled almost uninterrupted until 2006, when he was replaced by former West African Development Bank head Yayi Boni.

PEOPLE

Benin has over 20 different ethnic groups, dominated by the southern Fon (40 per cent) and Yoruba (12 per cent). These coexist peacefully, if a touch icily, with their northern neighbours the Bariba (nine per cent); the Betamaribé (eight per cent); and the nomadic Fulani (six per cent), originally from Niger. In Porto Novo and Ouidah there are also Afro-Brazilians descended from repatriated slaves. Christianity (30 per cent) is popular in the south and Islam (20 per cent) in the north, but 50 per cent of Beninese also practise traditional religions such as voodoo and animism.

TRADEMARKS

- Route des Esclaves (Slave Road), Ouidah
- Mashed yam
- Ganvié stilt village
- Gory fetish markets
- The Temple des Pythons in Ouidah

MARKETPLACE

Benin's economy grew some five per cent between 2000 and 2006, but this has been offset by population growth of 2.8 per cent. Over 30 per cent of the population lives below the poverty line. The country's US$1.6-billion-plus foreign debt was reduced as part of the G8 package in 2005, but it continues to struggle due to depressed cotton prices and corruption, the latter caused chiefly by Nigeria's trade protection restricting imports from Benin. The country's main exports are cotton, crude oil, palm products and cocoa.

RANDOM FACTS

- Mathieu Kérékou named Benin after the ancient Nigerian kingdom.
- Twins are revered in the voodoo religion.
- King Ghézo had over 200 wives and an army of female warriors.

FISHERMEN UP TO THEIR NECKS IN NETS ≫

WORKERS SIT ATOP A HILL OF RAW COTTON OUTSIDE THE SONAPRA COTTON GINNERY, PARAKOU ≫

TALE OF TWO CAPITALS

Benin's commercial capital, Cotonou, is a polluted example of urban Africa that lives up to its name, which means 'mouth of the river of death' in Fon – a reference to Dahomey's slave-trading ways. The official capital, Porto Novo, is far more appealing: offices in peeling colonial buildings roll over hills bordering a lagoon. The sleepy town's attractions include the somewhat disjointed Musée da Silva, which begins with an 1870s Afro-Brazilian house and culminates with the museum owner's moth-eaten Rolls Royce, slowly leaking oil onto the garage floor.

GRISLY READ

The Viceroy of Ouidah, by fey English travel writer Bruce Chatwin, is the semifictional biography of Don Francisco Felix de Souza, a Brazilian mulatto enlisted by the Portuguese to set up their Beninese slaving operation. De Souza had a tempestuous relationship with the Dahomeyan kings, who variously formed blood pacts with him and tortured him. In the book, Chatwin (who witnessed the 1972 coup that installed Kérékou) evokes the *Ozymandias*-like irony in Benin's fall from cruel empire to obscure African republic.

IMPORT

↗ European slave-traders
↗ Creoles from the Americas
↗ Afro-Brazilian architecture
↗ Communism
↗ Travel writer Bruce Chatwin
↗ Togolese refugees
↘ Nigerian gangsters
↗ French tourists

EXPORT

↖ Voodoo
↖ Fear of the Dahomeyan kings
↖ Chanteuse Angélique Kidjo
↖ Appliqué banners
↖ Nigerian narcotics
↖ Dazed-looking French tourists

VOODOO HOEDOWN

The whole of Benin explodes with voodoo festivals on 10 January, the National Voodoo Holiday, but the celebrations in Ouidah, the religion's historic centre, are the most flamboyant in the country. Don't believe the versions of voodoo you've seen on the silver screen, though – there's no *Live and Let Die*–style orgy of shrieking witch doctors rising from the grave. The supreme voodoo priest just sacrifices a goat on the beach to honour the spirits, then there's traditional dancing, singing and drumming, and the consumption of large amounts of *sodabe* (moonshine).

SURPRISES

○ Voodoo was outlawed by Kérékou's Marxist government, which considered it inimical to a rational and socialist work ethic.
○ Benin bronzes, made using the *cire perdue* (lost wax) method, originate from Benin City in Nigeria.

⌃ A WOMAN IN TROPICAL COLOURS

ESSENTIAL EXPERIENCES

○ **Feeling the Atlantic breeze as you consider Ouidah's sombre Point of No Return, the last glimpse of the motherland for plantation-bound slaves**

○ **Discovering the temples and palaces quietly decaying along Abomey's rutted backstreets**

○ **Taking care not to touch the shell-masked Egungun spirit and investing in a charm for safe travel in a voodoo fishing village on Lake Ahémé**

○ **Stepping quickly under the slits from which arrows are fired in a clay and straw fortress in the Atakora Mountains**

○ **Drifting through the Lake Nokoué stilt villages in a pirogue, wondering what possessed the Tofino people to move to a crocodile-infested lake**

⌃ VOODOO BELIEVERS AT A TEMPLE CEREMONY, OUIDAH

⌃ THE DOORS OF THE MUSEUM OF ETHNOGRAPHY, PORTO NOVO

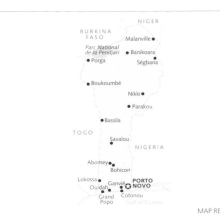

NIGER
BURKINA FASO
Malanville
Parc National de la Pendjari
Banikoara
Porga
Ségbana
Boukoumbé
Nikki
Parakou
Bassila
TOGO
Savalou
NIGERIA
Abomey
Bohicon
Lokossa
Ganvié
PORTO NOVO
Ouidah
Cotonou
Grand Popo
Gulf of Guinea

MAP REF // I6

BEST TIME TO VISIT NOVEMBER TO FEBRUARY

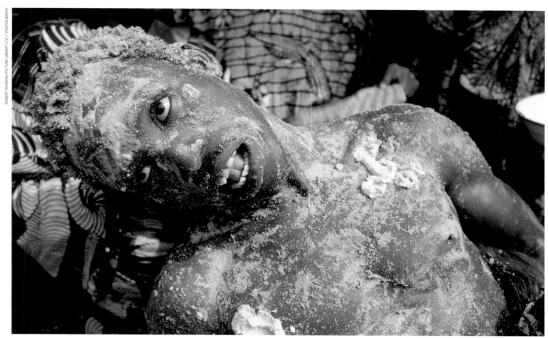

ROBERT HARDING PICTURE LIBRARY LTD // PHOTOLIBRARY

ENCHANTÉ: A MAN IN A TRANCE DURING A VOODOO CEREMONY, ABOMEY ≫

VICTOR ENGLEBERT // PHOTOGRAPHERS DIRECT

A BIRD'S BLESSING: A SOMBA GIRL IS INITIATED INTO ADULTHOOD ≫

AN OPEN-DOOR POLICY IN PORTO NOVO ≫

TEXT MATT PHILLIPS

NIGER

ECONOMIC INDICES MAY SHOW THAT NIGER IS THE WORLD'S POOREST NATION, BUT THOSE WHO TRAVEL THE COUNTRY, INTERACT WITH ITS PEOPLE AND WITNESS ITS SUBLIME SAHARAN LANDSCAPES WILL RANK IT AMONG THE RICHEST.

CAPITAL CITY NIAMEY   POPULATION 12.5 MILLION   AREA 1.2 MILLION SQ KM   OFFICIAL LANGUAGE FRENCH

LANDSCAPE

Today, two thirds of Niger is desolate desert; the remainder is Sahel (the semidesert zone south of the Sahara). The most notable landscapes are northern Niger's Aïr Mountains and Ténéré Desert, and the Niger River, which flows through 300 kilometres of the country's southwest. Temperatures between March and June can reach 45°C or more, especially in the north. With such harsh conditions, it's no surprise biodiversity isn't Niger's strong point.

HISTORY IN A NUTSHELL

Lying at the crossroads of the lucrative trans-Saharan trade in gold, salt and slaves, Niger's arid landscape supported some of West Africa's great empires between the 10th and 19th centuries. The French strolled into the picture late in the 19th century, but met stronger-than-expected local resistance. Decidedly unamused, the reinforcements quickly laid waste to much of southern Niger. The subsequent French rule wasn't much kinder. Niger eventually gained independence in 1960, though its first 40 years were frenetic: full of bloody coups, military juntas, mock one-party elections, deadly famines and short-lived uranium booms. Niger turned the corner in 1999, however, and its democracy is now an example to all of Africa.

PEOPLE

More than 90 per cent of Niger's population lives in the south, mostly in the southwest. The south is dominated by the Hausa, who make up 56 per cent of the nation's people, and the Songhaï-Djerma, who are centred on the Niger River and comprise 22 per cent. The next largest groups are the traditionally nomadic Fulani (8.5 per cent) and the Tuareg (eight per cent), both living in Niger's north, and the Kanuri (over four per cent), located between Zinder and Chad. The remainder is the Gourmantché in the south and the Toubou and Arabs in the north.

MARKETPLACE

To state the obvious, Niger's economy is truly struggling. Niger is ranked last on the UN's Human Development Index, Human Poverty Index and Gender-Related Development Index. The economy centres on subsistence crops, pastoralism (cattle and goats) and uranium mining. Niger relies on foreign sources for over 40 per cent of its US$320 million annual budget.

TRADEMARKS

o Desert Tuareg nomads
o Cure Salée (Salt Cure festival)
o Agadez' pyramidal mud mosque
o The Aïr Mountains
o The Ténéré Desert

NATURAL BEAUTY

The northern third of Niger, its most barren part, has two of Africa's most beautiful environments. The dark volcanic masses of the Aïr Mountains rise dramatically from the Sahara and culminate in grand peaks, the highest at 2022 metres. In some areas, amazing deep-blue marble outcrops poke from rich red sands, and east of the Aïr Mountains, the Ténéré, one of the world's most legendary deserts, has some of the Sahara's most extraordinarily beautiful sand dunes.

RANDOM FACTS

o An ounce of salt was as valuable as an ounce of gold in Niger's markets of old.
o The heat can be so intense that rain evaporates before reaching the ground.
o Big is beautiful. At Niamey's Hangandi festival, the heaviest woman always wins the beauty contest.

A WODAABÉ MAN WEARS MAKE-UP TO ENHANCE HIS FEATURES WHILE COMPETING FOR A WIFE »

I took this photo of a girl in Zinder, Niger last year. Zinder was one of the happy surprises in a trip of nearly three months' duration – great people and a town full of interestingly decorated facades, not to mention the Sultan of Zinder's palace. This sort of defiant pose is more commonly seen in adolescent boys than girls, so it is unusual for that reason.

CHRISTOPHER KEAN // USA

URBAN SCENE

Agadez, on the frontier of the Aïr Mountains and the Ténéré Desert, is Niger's most fascinating city. When you're standing in the porcupine shadow of the Grande Mosquée or weaving through the sandy streets and distinctive mud-brick architecture, it's not hard to imagine what it was like at its zenith four centuries ago. Back then, its 30,000-strong population flourished on the caravans (azalai) plying between Gao in Mali and Tripoli in present-day Libya. Some azalai had as many as 20,000 camels laden with gold, salt and slaves.

IMPORT
↗ NGOs
↗ Saharan explorer Heinrich Barth
↗ Four-wheel drives
↗ Harmattan winds
↗ Mining equipment
↗ Sympathy

EXPORT
↖ Uranium
↖ Livestock
↖ Four-wheel drive names (Volkswagen Touareg, for example)
↖ Afro-pop band Mamar Kassey
↖ Harmattan winds
↖ Pride

≫ TUAREG MEN SHOOTING THE BREEZE

TOP FESTIVAL

One of the most famous annual celebrations in West Africa is the Cure Salée (Salt Cure). It's held in the vicinity of In-Gall after the rains in August or September, when hundreds of Wodaabé nomads arrive to have their herds feed on the area's mineral salt-rich pastures. The Cure Salée's main event is the Gerewol festival, where men don make-up and compete in a beauty contest to woo potential brides. Eventually, the (less elaborately dressed) women timidly make their choices. If a marriage proposal results, the man takes a calabash full of milk to the woman's parents. If they accept, he brings them the bride price – three cattle, which are slaughtered for the festivities that follow. Rivalry between suitors can be fierce, and to show their virility they take part in the Soro, an event where they stand smiling while others try to knock them over with huge sticks.

SURPRISES
○ The massively publicised 2005 starvation crisis was not caused by a lack of food, but rather by food prices increasing beyond what millions of Nigeriens could afford.
○ Slavery was officially outlawed in May 2003, but human rights groups believe at least 43,000 Nigeriens still live in subjugation.

ESSENTIAL EXPERIENCES

○ **Making tracks with camel companions through red sands and blue rocks in the mystical Aïr Mountains or buckling up and tackling the Ténéré Desert**

○ **Spiralling up and squeezing out onto the spiky summit of the mud mosque in Agadez, to take in its captivating views over the surrounding Sahara**

○ **Wandering through the banco (mud) houses in the Birni quartier of Zinder and soaking up the Hausa history**

○ **Savouring the Sunday-market smells in Ayorou, then taking a boat on the Niger River to visit bellowing hippos**

○ **Walking in silence with the last wild herd of giraffes in West Africa, near Kouré**

○ **Taking a serious four-wheel drive expedition to the remote Djado Plateau and visiting the honeycombed ruins of a medieval citadel**

LIBYA
ALGERIA
MALI
TÉNÉRÉ DESERT
Aïr Mountains
• Agadez
Tahoua •
⊙ NIAMEY   Maradi •   • Zinder   Diff •   CHAD
Dosso •
BURKINA FASO   • Gaya
BENIN   NIGERIA   CAMEROON

ERIC L WHEATER // LONELY PLANET IMAGES

MAP REF // K5

BEST TIME TO VISIT **NOVEMBER TO FEBRUARY**

≫ LOCAL MERCHANTS WITH WIND IN THEIR SAILS ON THE NIGER RIVER

ALVARO LEIVA // MARKA

GIRLS PUT THEIR BACK INTO POUNDING GRAIN IN THE VILLAGE OF MADOUFA »

MAKING A BIG ENTRANCE: A TUAREG MAN AT HIS HOUSE, AGADEZ »

GRANARIES LIKE MASSIVE BEEHIVES, NEAR TAHOUA »

NIGERIA

THE POWERHOUSE OF WEST AFRICA, NIGERIA IS A COUNTRY OF EXTREMES, AND ITS CRUMBLING INFRASTRUCTURE AND DIVERSE POPULATION MAKE IT A CHAOTIC AND EXUBERANT COUNTRY TO VISIT.

CAPITAL CITY **ABUJA**   POPULATION **131.8 MILLION**   AREA **923,770 SQ KM**   OFFICIAL LANGUAGES **ENGLISH, HAUSA, IGBO, YORUBA**

≫ TAKING IT EASY IN THE CITY OF ZARIA

LANDSCAPE
Northern Nigeria borders the Sahel, and its dry and dusty environment puts visitors in mind of camel caravans. Further south the humidity and vegetation increases until you reach the steamy Atlantic coast and the tangle of mangroves and waterways of the Niger Delta. Mostly flat, Nigeria only rises significantly in the east, in the hills and mountains of Gashaka Gumpti National Park and the Cross River region.

HISTORY IN A NUTSHELL
By rights, Nigeria should be two countries. The north developed as a series of Muslim city-states, linked to the outside world by the Saharan trade route. The coast attracted European traders, who swapped Christianity and guns for slaves, but the scramble for Africa led the British to seize control completely and unite north and south. Independence led immediately to strife, culminating in the bloody Biafran war for secession in the southeast, followed by a parade of military dictators more interested in lining their pockets than governing. Democracy of sorts finally arrived in the 1990s, although Nigeria continues to give the impression of a very fine balancing act – ostensibly doing well, but always one step from disaster.

PEOPLE
Nigeria is the most populous nation on the continent: every fifth African is a Nigerian. Three ethnic groups dominate the country – the Muslim Hausa in the north and the Yoruba and Igbo in the Christian south. Ethnic and religious tensions are never far from the surface and are manipulated by unscrupulous politicians; communal violence is a sad feature of Nigerian life.

MARKETPLACE
In a word: oil. The black gold has been the blessing and curse of Nigeria. Since independence, the profits from the oil fields of the Niger Delta have been siphoned off to enrich a self-serving elite, with the poor majority rarely benefiting from trickle-down economics. Corruption has flourished, while the infrastructure that holds Nigeria together has been allowed to largely collapse.

TRADEMARKS
○ Oil
○ Afro-beat
○ Lagos' urban sprawl
○ Writers Chinua Achebe and Wole Soyinka
○ Email scams

RANDOM FACTS
○ A 2005 survey declared Nigerians to be the 'happiest people on earth' .
○ Nearly US$400 billion of oil wealth was embezzled from Nigeria between independence in 1960 and the year 2000.
○ 'Nollywood', Nigeria's film industry, is the third-biggest in the world (after Bollywood and Hollywood); a typical film costs just US$20,000 to produce.
○ The 10th-century Sungbo's Eredo, a 160-kilometre-long earthen rampart and ditch, is the largest man-made structure in Africa, and once surrounded the ancient kingdom of Ijebu.

URBAN SCENE
Lagos, Nigeria's former capital, is the largest city in Africa, and is predicted to be the biggest city in the world by 2025. A scary, violent reputation precedes it, but it isn't always justified. Lagos is Nigeria's main port and commercial centre – and it's the African New York, the cultural centre of the region, with a thriving arts and music scene and some of the best clubs on the continent. The traffic is just as bad as in New York, too – Lagos single-handedly redefines the term 'traffic jam'.

GETTING DOWN AT A CONCERT OF FUJI MUSIC IN LAGOS »

This picture was taken while crossing into Cameroon from Nigeria at Ekok, where traders from Cameroon cross into Nigeria to buy cheap goods to resell in their local markets. I was astounded how these overloaded vehicles traversed the pothole-strewn road, and even more amazed that I never saw one flipped over on the journey from the border.

STUART WHITEFORD // CANADA

ON PAPER

Nigeria seems to have more writers than the rest of Africa put together. Chinua Achebe's *Things Fall Apart* is *the* classic novel of colonialism, and Wole Soyinka's canon earned him the Nobel Prize in Literature. Modern writers at the top of their game include Ben Okri *(The Famished Road)*, Chimamanda Ngozi Adichie *(Purple Hibiscus)* and Helon Habila *(Waiting for an Angel)*.

SURPRISES

It's divided sharply between a Muslim north and Christian south, but Nigeria is probably the most openly religious country in Africa. Everything stops in the south for church, with everyone in their Sunday best. Evangelical churches, in particular, are booming, advertised by huge billboards along the highways, all

≈ A BIRD'S-EYE VIEW OF KANO

promising salvation and miracles. In the north, Islamic Sharia law thrives, with alcohol frequently banned and women increasingly veiled. Religion is a major flash point in Nigerian society.

CUISINE

For a Nigerian, food is known as 'chop'. Dishes are hot and peppery, usually consisting of a meat sauce mopped up with a hearty portion of starch such as cassava or pounded yam. Vegetarians have a hard time in Nigeria – *isiewu*, or goat's head soup, is the closest thing to a national dish, with cow-leg soup or *jollof rice* with chicken almost as popular. Spicy meals can be washed down with 'pure water', which is sold on the streets in plastic bags.

MUSIC

Nigeria's Fela Kuti was one of Africa's musical superstars, and fused African rhythms with jazz and soul to create the Afro-beat genre. A thorn in the side of successive military dictators for his politics, Kuti died of AIDS in 1997 but his son Femi Kuti carries the musical flame. *Juju* and *fuji* are other popular music styles (listen for King Sunny Ade and Ayinde Barrister); younger musicians are increasingly incorporating elements of hip-hop into traditional grooves.

TOP FESTIVAL

The Kano Durbar, which marks the end of Ramadan, is one of Nigeria's great spectacles. The Emir of Kano is accompanied to his palace by throngs of horsemen who are decked out in ceremonial armour and plumed helmets; one of these horsemen shades his ruler with a heavily brocaded silver parasol. At the palace, singing and drumming accompany further celebrations, and the whole event is topped off with massed cavalry charges.

ESSENTIAL EXPERIENCES

○ **Club-hopping until the early hours of the morning in Lagos**

○ **Exploring Saharan trade routes in Kano's old city**

○ **Soaking in the warm springs of Yankari National Park**

○ **Holding on tight to your motorcycle taxi as it weaves through traffic**

○ **Washing down a bowl of goat's head soup with a cold Star beer**

MAP REF // J6

BEST TIME TO VISIT **NOVEMBER TO MARCH**

≈ AN ISLAND IN A SEA OF BOWLS AT A MARKET IN KANO

THE UNIVERSAL SCHOOLYARD GAME IN ABUJA »

PARTICIPANTS IN THE ARGUNGU FISHING FESTIVAL »

MEN FROM THE IFIE-KPORO COMMUNITY PLAY POOL »

CAMEROON

THE CROSSROADS OF WEST AND CENTRAL AFRICA, CAMEROON IS ALMOST DIZZYING IN ITS DIVERSITY, WITH WICKED WILDLIFE AND MELODIOUS MUSIC IN A LANDSCAPE THAT SWEEPS FROM ROCKY MOUNTAINS TO LUSH RAINFOREST.

CAPITAL CITY YAOUNDÉ   POPULATION 17.3 MILLION   AREA 475,440 SQ KM   OFFICIAL LANGUAGES FRENCH, ENGLISH

⌃ WHICHEVER WAY THE WIND BLOWS, REY BOUBA

LANDSCAPE

Cameroon's landscape has a bit of everything: mountains, desert, forest, savanna and coast. Much of its coastal region is thick with some of the lushest rainforest in Africa, which stretches as far as the Congo Basin. In contrast, the Mandara Mountains are barren but beautiful – often punctuated with stunning crater lakes – and form a natural border with Nigeria down to the Atlantic coast. They culminate in Mt Cameroon, which at 4095 metres is the highest peak in West Africa.

HISTORY IN A NUTSHELL

Cameroon stood on the fringes of medieval Africa, its lush forests documented mainly in the oral histories of Pygmy tribes such as the Baka. In the 15th century, however, the Muslim Fulani people arrived in the north, at roughly the same time as European traders started to explore the coast. Colonialism, from the late 19th century onward, saw the country divided between the British and French (with a brief period of German rule to begin with), but at independence in 1960 the two colonies were stitched together – they continue to compete politically in modern Cameroon. While it was a one-party state for most of this time, Cameroon now functions technically as a democracy,

although its political environment is far from free and the country's Anglophone minority complains of persistent discrimination.

PEOPLE

Around 280 ethno-linguistic groups call Cameroon home; the major tribes include the Bamileke and Fulani. Amid this unruly jigsaw, there are two main divisions – language and religion. The southwest of the nation is English-speaking (making up around 20 per cent of the population), while the rest of the population is Francophone, with French the main language of business and politics. The country also has a roughly equal north–south split between Islam and Christianity.

MARKETPLACE

Riotously fertile and well-watered, Cameroon is one of the major exporters of agricultural produce in the region, and a major exporter of timber, exploiting the hard woods of its rainforests. The country's geographic location also works well for it: it earns hard currency as the port for the landlocked nations of Chad and the Central African Republic, and receives transit fees from Chad's oil pipeline, which terminates on the coast.

TRADEMARKS

- ○ Football
- ○ Mt Cameroon
- ○ Rainforest
- ○ Smoked fish
- ○ Waza National Park

NATURAL BEAUTY

The western mountain chain is one of Cameroon's most beautiful areas. In the south, volcanic Mt Cameroon seems to rise almost straight from the sea and peters out into a chain of green hills and massifs punctuated with sublime crater lakes – the Ring Road area is perhaps the most picturesque. Further north, the Mandara Mountains are a total contrast, drier and dotted with rocky escarpments – it's hard to believe you're still in the same country.

RANDOM FACTS

- ○ The 'Race of Hope' is an annual 40-kilometre sprint up Mt Cameroon – the record time is under four and a half hours.
- ○ Korup National Park is believed to hold the oldest rainforest in Africa.
- ○ In Rhumsiki in the Mandara Mountains, the local witch doctor tells fortunes using a bucket of crabs.

WASHED UP IN A FISHING BOAT

STRAW-HATTED DWELLINGS IN A REMOTE VILLAGE IN THE MANDARA MOUNTAINS ⌃

WILD THINGS

Cameroon has an embarrassment of wildlife riches. Waza National Park hosts healthy populations of elephants, antelopes and big cats, and some excellent bird-watching to boot. The southern rainforests are also home to forest elephants, lowland gorillas, chimpanzees and drills – Africa's most endangered species of primate.

SPORT

Football is the one thing capable of uniting Cameroon, and is followed with almost as much fervour as a religion. The country paved the way for African football on the global stage at the 1990 World Cup when they reached the quarter finals, led by the illustrious Roger Milla. Cameroon also holds a fine record in the African Cup of Nations, winning it four times. The golden boy of Cameroonian – and African – football at the time of writing is the striker Samuel Eto'o.

CUISINE

As in much of the region, Cameroonian food is heavy on starch, with yam, plantain or manioc to soak up a peppery sauce. Where Cameroon really excels is fish, which is usually cooked over coals by women. When eating out it's common practice to order your fish and then retire to a nearby bar to sink a beer and wait for your meal to be delivered to your table. Grilled meats are just as ubiquitous, but are cooked by men.

MUSIC

Music is everywhere in Cameroon, and the country grooves to *makossa*, an infectious blend of highlife, Congolese and soul styles. Its undisputed king is still Manu Dibango, whose hit *Soul Makossa* was a worldwide smash in the 1970s; Mona Bile and the band Petits-Pays are almost as big. *Makossa's* main rival for popularity is *bikutsi*, with its martial rhythms and often sexually charged lyrics – listen out for Les Têtes Brûlées.

ECOTOURISM

Slow moves are being made to develop tourism sustainably in Cameroon. The Mt Cameroon Ecotourism Organisation is pioneering community-led tourism on the mountain, while the nearby Limbe Wildlife Centre leads the way on educating locals about wildlife conservation, particularly regarding the devastation caused by Cameroon's bushmeat trade. The Korup and Campo-Ma'an National Parks have great potential as rainforest eco-destinations, but await further investments in infrastructure.

△ SURFING WITHOUT WAVES ON TARA BEACH, KRIBI

△ GIRL MAKES CAREFUL PROGRESS OVER A ROPE BRIDGE

△ SEAT OF POWER: A VILLAGE LEADER, MANDARA MOUNTAINS

ESSENTIAL EXPERIENCES

○ Trekking the green slopes of Mt Cameroon, West Africa's highest mountain

○ Chilling on the palm-fringed beaches of Kribi

○ Getting off the beaten track in the beautiful and hilly Ring Road area

○ Elephant-spotting at the waterholes of Waza National Park

○ Hiking through the rugged landscapes of the Mandara Mountains

CHAD

Kousséri
Mandara • Waza National
Mountains   Park
• Maroua
NIGERIA

Garoua •
• Lagdo

Missaje • • Banyo • Meiganga
• Kumbo
Bamenda   CENTRAL
Ekok •   AFRICAN
            • Yoko   REPUBLIC
Baro •
          Bertoua
Mt Cameroon Obala • Mbama • Kenzou
• Douala
YAOUNDÉ ✪
          • Mbalmayo
EQUATORIAL • Kribi   • Olounou   Mambele
GUINEA • Campo
    GABON CONGO

MAP REF // K7

BEST TIME TO VISIT NOVEMBER TO MARCH; JULY TO OCTOBER ARE THE RAINIEST MONTHS

BABY ON BOARD: A KOMA DOBE WOMAN AND HER CHILD IN THE ALANTIKA MOUNTAINS »

THE DECORATED FACE OF A FULANI WOMAN »

A HORSEMAN IN THE FANTASIA AT GAROUA »

CENTRAL AFRICA

SEPARATING EAST FROM WEST AND NORTH FROM SOUTH IS CENTRAL AFRICA, THE HEART OF THIS COLOSSAL CONTINENT. ITS BEAT IS FRENETIC, SULTRY AND PRECARIOUS – PUTTING A FINGER ON IT CAN BE AS FRUITFUL AS IT IS FRIGHTFUL. THOSE WHO VENTURE INTO ITS VIRGIN RAINFORESTS CAN FIND HEAVEN AT THE SIGHT OF GORILLAS OR DISCOVER HELL AT THE WRONG END OF A GUERRILLA'S AK-47.

Wars have been raging on and off in Central Africa for decades, and the recent war in the Democratic Republic of Congo (DRC) alone cost nearly four million lives. The Republic of Congo (Congo), the Central African Republic (CAR), Chad and Sudan have also been entrenched in bloody internal conflicts. Sadly, outside forces are often responsible for fuelling these civil wars. The DRC's 1998–2003 conflict, for example, involved no fewer than nine African nations and 20 armed groups. Some of the foreign leaders joined the fray simply in hopes of grabbing a piece of the wealth associated with the DRC's vast natural resources.

Although things are far from settled in many areas, they are currently far from their worst. Fragile peace deals and ceasefires are now being maintained, at least nominally, in the DRC, Congo and southern Sudan. Gabon, one of Africa's richest nations, also continues to be one of its most safe and stable – a Central African bright spot indeed.

Equatorial Guinea and São Tomé and Príncipe are also calm, though new-found oil money is starting to gently rock their political boats.

Look behind the conflicts, however, and you have an African wonderland. Dense jungles host the likes of gorillas, bonobos (pygmy chimps: humanity's closest relatives), elephants, hippos, giraffes, sitatungas, African civets, buffaloes, red river hogs, leopards, lions, cheetahs, wild dogs, spotted-necked otters, and insanely diverse birdlife – and let's not forget about the pythons. Islands off the coast boast turquoise waters, deserted paradisal beaches and more giant turtles than you can shake a stick at. Spread through it all, paying no attention to political boundaries, is a fascinating mix of cultures, ranging from Pygmies to Saharan nomads.

The dominant geographical feature of Central Africa is the behemoth basin of the Congo River and its tributaries. The drainage area covers much of the DRC, CAR and Congo, and totals an astounding 3.7 million square kilometres – only the Amazon basin is bigger. It's this fertile basin that supports the world's second-largest rainforest and all its accompanying wildlife. The Congo River is no less important to Africans, who cling to its fertile shores, draw life from its waters and use its surface as a frenetic transportation network.

The Sahara and the Rift Valley are the two other important players in the landscape of Central Africa. The Sahara sweeps across northern Chad and Sudan, while the Rift has produced a series of deep lakes, towering mountains and active volcanoes along the eastern edge of the DRC.

With its ample, unspoiled assets coupled with enduring security problems, Central Africa has its fair share of angels and demons – all that makes Africa what it is today.

TEXT: MATT PHILLIPS

MAURITANIA

CAPE
VERDE

SENEGAL

THE GAMBIA

GUINEA-
BISSAU

GUINEA

SIERRA
LEONE

LIBERIA

MALI

BURKINA
FASO

CÔTE
D'IVOIRE

GHANA

BENIN

TOGO

NIGER

NIGERIA

LIBYA

EGYPT

Tibesti

CHAD

Lake
Chad

Abéché •

• Mongo

N'DJAMÉNA ✪

Am Timan •

Sarh •
Moundou •

CENTRAL
AFRICAN
REPUBLIC

• Bouar

Berbérati •   • Bambari

CAMEROON   BANGUI ✪

Darfur

Marra
Mountains

SUDAN

Omdurman •

KHARTOUM ✪

El-Fasher •

Nyala •

Sudd

Malakal •
• Wau

Nubian
Desert

Atbara •

Port
Sudan •

Kassala •

Wad Medani •

Gedaref •

El-Obeid •

ERITREA

DJIBOUTI

ETHIOPIA

Juba •   Elemi
Triangle

Gulf of Guinea

MALABO ✪

EQUATORIAL GUINEA

SÃO TOMÉ & PRÍNCIPE

SÃO
TOMÉ

• Bata • Oyem

✪ LIBREVILLE

GABON   CONGO

Port
Gentil •

Franceville •

Luobomo •

Point Noire •   ✪ BRAZZAVILLE

✪ KINSHASA

Cabinda
(Angola)

Matadi •

DEMOCRATIC
REPUBLIC OF CONGO
(ZAÏRE)

• Kisangani

• Mbandaka

Congo
Basin

• Kikwit

Kananga •

Tshikapa •   Mbuji-
Mayi •

UGANDA

RWANDA

BURUNDI

Lake
Turkana

Lake
Victoria

KENYA

SOMALIA

INDIAN
OCEAN

SOUTH
ATLANTIC
OCEAN

ANGOLA

ZAMBIA

Kolwezi •

Lubumbashi •

Likasi •

TANZANIA

Kalémie •

Lake
Malawi

MALAWI

COMOROS

Mayotte
(France)

SEYCHELLES

TEXT VANESSA WRUBLE

EQUATORIAL GUINEA

A PINT-SIZED NATION OF VIRGIN FORESTS, REMARKABLE WILDS AND TRADITIONAL VILLAGES, AND A SPANISH-INFLUENCED ISLAND FULL OF EXPATS MINING THE BOUNTIFUL OIL RESERVES (AND POLITICIANS ENJOYING THE PROFITS).

CAPITAL MALABO   **POPULATION** 540,110   **AREA** 28,050 SQ KM   **OFFICIAL LANGUAGES** SPANISH, FRENCH

LANDSCAPE

This mostly unexplored nation-in-miniature is composed of two separate landmasses – the mainland of Rio Muni, and Bioko Island – plus a series of even smaller islands off the coast. Rio Muni has lush forests that are full of wildlife, as well as stretches of white beaches and, to the south, a series of rivers and estuaries. Bioko Island, which is actually closer to Cameroon, is of volcanic origin, with a steep rocky coast and a mountainous, wooded interior. It's always hot and humid and is often rainy, even in the dry season.

HISTORY IN A NUTSHELL

Portuguese explorer Fernando Pó is credited with the Western world's discovery (and subsequent colonisation) of Bioko Island in 1470. In 1778 the country was traded with Spain in exchange for land in Latin America. Independence came in 1959 with President Francisco Macías Nguema, who killed, tortured and stole his way into being 'President for Life'. He was overthrown and executed in 1979 by his nephew, Teodoro Obiang Nguema Mbasogo, who remains president to this day. His human rights record is a bit better than his uncle's.

PEOPLE

The original inhabitants of mainland Equatorial Guinea were Pygmies, but Bantu peoples migrated into the area during the 12th and 13th centuries and the descendants of these people remain today. Bioko Island is inhabited primarily by the Bubi tribe, while the Fang now dominate the mainland. Owing to 400 years of Spanish occupation, the majority of the population is Roman Catholic; traditional animist beliefs are still strong, however, and are often intermingled with Catholicism.

MARKETPLACE

Equatorial Guinea has always relied on cocoa production and timber exports for cash, but the discovery of oil on Bioho Island in the mid-1990s has made the land quite wealthy – though not much of the windfall gets into the people's hands. Agriculture, fishing and logging make up the rest of the GDP.

RANDOM FACTS

- At the Sydney Olympics, Equatorial Guinean Eric Moussambani won a wildcard to compete in the 100 metres freestyle. He'd only been swimming for eight months and had never seen an Olympic-size pool. Though he finished over a minute behind his competitors, he instantly became a media sensation and is still held up as an icon of determination.
- In 2004 American-based Riggs Bank (now part of the PNC Financial Services Group) was shown to have helped Equatorial Guinean politicians siphon hundreds of millions of dollars of state oil revenue into private accounts. The money was spent on massive mansions, land purchases and sending the politicians' children to colleges in the US.
- Bioko Island was originally called Formosa, meaning 'the beautiful' in Portuguese.

WILD THINGS

The 'wilds' of Equatorial Guinea are still wild enough to shelter gorillas, elephants, monkeys, sea turtles, leopards, manatees, tropical birds, snakes, crocodiles and a host of plant species – many still undiscovered.

SURPRISES

- Recent oil discoveries have given Equatorial Guinea the world's second-highest per-capita income
- In the interior villages, sorcerers and harp players are still highly respected community members.
- In 2004 Margaret Thatcher's son was given a $500,000 fine and a four-year suspended jail sentence for helping to plot the overthrow of President Obiang.

MYTHS & LEGENDS

The legend of how the Bubi tribe came to Bioko Island is passed down from generation to generation. The Bubi tribe of Bioko Island had lived and prospered for years on the coast of mainland Africa. But soon other tribes came, oppressing the Bubi and forcing them into slavery. Every day they looked out to sea, to the island beyond, to where the peaks of the mountains spoke of the freedom of that land. In secret they worked: cutting huge trees, carving boats, storing provisions. One night they all stole away, using great palm leaves as their sails. They soon reached freedom, and it was in this way that the Bubi came to live on Bioko Island.

TRADEMARKS

- Being small
- Corrupt officials
- New-found oil
- Virgin rainforest
- Being confused for Guinea and Guinea-Bissau

ESSENTIAL EXPERIENCES

- **Gasping at the unnatural wonder of the oil rigs as you touch down in Malabo**
- **Piercing the border by pirogue across the Mouni River to the southern frontier village of Cogo**
- **Whispering through forest walks in search of gorillas, elephants and chimps in Monte Alen National Park**
- **Delighting in the utterly deserted white-sand beaches of untouched, barely inhabited Corisco Island**

MAP REF // K8

BEST TIME TO VISIT BIOKO ISLAND: DECEMBER TO FEBRUARY; MAINLAND: MAY TO SEPTEMBER

ALL ABOARD! CHILDREN AT EBEBIYN RECLAIM THE RUSTING SHELL OF A CAR AS THEIR PLAYTHING »

TEENAGE FOOTBALL FEVER COOLS ITS HEELS IN THE GULF OF GUINEA SURF »

TRADITIONAL RURAL DWELLINGS FORM A BACKDROP FOR THIS PASSER-BY »

SÃO TOMÉ & PRÍNCIPE

SÃO TOMÉ AND PRÍNCIPE, ONE OF AFRICA'S SMALLEST AND MOST OBSCURE NATIONS, IS A SET OF TINY, TRANQUIL AND LITTLE-VISITED ISLANDS ON THE CUSP OF HITTING THE ECONOMIC BIG TIME.

CAPITAL SÃO TOMÉ   **POPULATION** 193,410   **AREA** 1000 SQ KM   **OFFICIAL LANGUAGE** PORTUGUESE

LANDSCAPE

São Tomé and Príncipe's position near the equator makes for steamy, obscenely rich forest which peters out onto undisturbed sandy beaches. In fact, in contrast to many African countries, São Tomé's biggest problem is re-forestation. Nature has reclaimed many of the roads, railway tracks and plantation buildings of the Portuguese colonial era, making the south of São Tomé and most of Príncipe essentially unreachable.

HISTORY IN A NUTSHELL

Portuguese settlers 'discovered' uninhabited São Tomé in 1470. It soon became a centre for the production of sugar, and later of coffee and cocoa as well, and a hub for the shipment of slaves. Those brought from Angola and Mozambique and forced to work on the islands were 'freed' when Portugal abolished slavery in 1875, but continued poor conditions led to a series of marches and riots over the years, culminating in Portuguese landowners fleeing as the islands declared independence in 1975. With virtually no skilled labour on the islands, a 90 per cent illiteracy rate and many abandoned cocoa plantations, the economy collapsed soon afterward. The majority of the population today live in dire poverty. There is potential for economic improvement, however, partly from increased tourism, but mainly from the huge oil reserves that were discovered in the Gulf of Guinea in the 1990s.

PEOPLE

There is no indigenous population in São Tomé and Príncipe – everybody is of immigrant descent. The main groups include *angolares* (descendants of slaves from Angola), *forros* (descendants of Portuguese settlers) and *serviçais* (from Cape Verde and Mozambique). The official language is Portuguese, but there are also three local creole dialects: São Tomense, Principense and Angolar.

MARKETPLACE

Foreign aid accounts for a vast amount of the country's GDP. Though tourism is very much encouraged, realistically, the only thing that's likely to get São Tomé out of its current economic rut is revenue from the recently discovered offshore oil reserves.

TRADEMARKS

○ Roads and railway tracks petering out into the dense jungle
○ Battered yellow taxis looking for trade in quiet São Tomé town
○ Gossip in every backstreet bar and café about what oil money will do to São Tomé
○ Women barbecuing freshly caught fish on the main waterfront in São Tomé town, for the benefit of passing locals
○ Children running wild in the myriad colonial-era plantation buildings and hospitals that litter the island

URBAN SCENE

The town of São Tomé must be the quietest capital city in Africa. Paint peels away from decaying colonial townhouses; bored guards push flies away from their eyes outside the presidential palace – and the narrow winding streets never seem to properly wake up from their dusty slumber.

RANDOM FACTS

○ There was a military coup d'état in São Tomé in July 2003, but it took less than a week to restore order.
○ Santo António town, on Príncipe island, is thought to be the smallest place on earth to have the status of a capital city – it has a population of only 1600.
○ The lyrics of the national anthem ('Independência Total', meaning 'Total Independence') were written by Alda Neves da Graça do Espírito Santo, the country's national poet and a prominent dissident in the colonial years.
○ São Tomé now produces no more than 4500 tonnes of cocoa per year.

CUISINE

The national dish of *calulu* is a delight – a fiery, slow-cooked stew made using smoked fish, prawns, palm oil, aubergine and spices. The half-dozen different types of banana are all worth experimenting with, too, as is the national practice of tapping palm trees for palm wine.

ESSENTIAL EXPERIENCES

○ **Sampling the locally produced chocolate – rated by many as the very best on earth**
○ **Roaming the crumbling remains of the giant Agostinho Neto roça, a Portuguese colonial cocoa plantation and the most stunning structure on São Tomé**
○ **Bartering with local fishermen on the beach in São Tomé town in the late afternoon, as the catch of the day comes in**
○ **Taking serenity to a new level at the Bom Bom luxury resort on Príncipe**
○ **Hiring a local guide to take you to the top of the 2000-metre-high Pico São Tomé, for incredible views over some of the most pristine ancient forest in Africa**

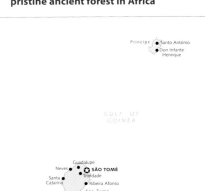

MAP REF // J8

BEST TIME TO VISIT JUNE TO SEPTEMBER

THE CARCASSES OF SALTED FISH DRY OUT UNDER WATCHFUL EYES, PORTO ALEGRE »

YELLOW-TAXI PARKING LOT IN SÃO TOMÉ »

HANGING OUT FOR A REFRESHING PICK-ME-UP AT BAR PEPE, SÃO TOMÉ »

TEXT VANESSA WRUBLE

GABON

IN THIS GLORIOUS COUNTRY, WITH ITS ABUNDANT BIODIVERSITY AND STUNNING NATURAL BEAUTY, MASSIVE CONSERVATION EFFORTS AND MASSIVE EXPLOITATION OF NATURAL RESOURCES COEXIST.

CAPITAL CITY **LIBREVILLE**   POPULATION **1.4 MILLION**   AREA 267,670 SQ KM   OFFICIAL LANGUAGE **FRENCH**

⌃ UP CLOSE AND PERSONAL: A FEMALE CHIMP GAZES INTO THE CAMERA LENS

LANDSCAPE

Gabon is a land of astonishing landscapes and insane biodiversity, much of which is still undiscovered. Almost 75 per cent of Gabon is covered in dense tropical rainforest, but it also has white-sand beaches, cloud-tipped mountains and inselbergs (isolated rock domes overlooking the surrounding forest canopy), rocky plateaus and canyons (including the famous Cirque de Lékoni), open, hilly savannas, rushing rivers and hidden lagoons – all of which shelter an amazing array of flora and fauna. The equator cuts straight across the country, so it's warm, warm, warm all year and scorching during the rainy season, which lasts intermittently from September to May.

HISTORY IN A NUTSHELL

Inhabited for at least 400,000 years, Gabon has West Central Africa's oldest archaeological relics. In and around Lopé are some 1200 rock carvings, made by the iron-working cultures who also created the savanna by burning and felling the forest for agriculture. The Portuguese arrived in 1472, followed by the British, Dutch and French, all seeking ivory, slaves and wood. Ultimately the French took control, and by 1894 Gabon was a territory of French Equatorial Africa. Independence came in1960, with Léon M'Ba as president for the first seven years. After his death, vice president Albert Bernard Bongo (now El Hadj Omar Bongo Ondima) took the reins. He remains president today, making him one of the world's longest-serving heads of state.

RANDOM FACTS

○ President Bongo is said to have changed his religion – and his name – so Gabon could join the other oil-bearing Muslim nations in OPEC and garner support from them for costly projects like the Trans-Gabon Railway.
○ Gabon's forest elephants munch on hallucinogenic iboga, and the gorillas crunch kola nuts for energy.
○ In the Ivindo River near Makokou, there are electric fish that emit signals from their tails – these allow them to sense their surroundings and communicate with other fish.

PEOPLE

The forest-dwelling Pygmies were the earliest of Gabon's present-day inhabitants to arrive, but between the 16th and 18th centuries much of the land was taken by Bantu tribes, primarily the Fang. They are still the most numerous tribe in Gabon, but many other (often closely related) tribes are represented, and 41 different tribal languages are still spoken. While missionary influence is palpable – over half the population is Christian – traditional animist beliefs are still strong among churchgoers and Bwiti societies.

MARKETPLACE

Gabon is often hailed as an African success story, as its per capita income is almost four times that of most of its sub-Saharan neighbours. In part, this is due to a small population, abundant natural and mineral resources and considerable foreign support. Most of the country's wealth, however, comes from the oil discovered in the 1970s. Despite the fact that this massive revenue has lined the elite's pockets, rather than those of the populace, Gabon has escaped the desperate poverty of many of its neighbours.

TRADEMARKS

○ Virgin rainforests
○ President Bongo
○ Gorillas
○ Petroleum
○ Bushmeat
○ Hallucinogenic plants
○ Ebola

GABONESE WOMEN SHARE A BELLYLAUGH ≫

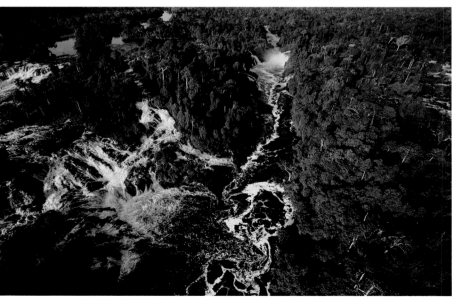

AERIAL VIEW OF THE WATERY MAELSTROM AT KONGOU FALLS ≫

WILD THINGS

Gabon is wild: wandering through its amazing landscapes and seascapes are gorillas, chimpanzees, mandrills, forest elephants, buffalos, crocodiles, antelopes, hippos, humpback and killer whales, all kinds of monkeys, leopards, red river hogs, sea turtles and a rainbow of rare birds (to name just a few).

CULTURE

Ancestral forest spirits, sorcerers, vampires and mermaids all play a big role in the traditions and the Bwiti culture, one of Gabon's three official religions. It has two to three million followers in Africa – and more than a few in Western societies, due to the increasing popularity of the sacred iboga plant. Used in ancient initiation rites, the hallucinogenic root bark of iboga is said to induce spiritual enlightenment; those who eat it are able to commune with the ancestors, gain protection from evil spirits and have complex visual insights into the world. Ibogaine, a chemical compound in iboga, is being tested in the West as a potential treatment for drug addicts.

IMPORT

↗ Most of its meat and produce
↗ Secondhand Toyotas
↗ Immigrant workers
↗ Wildlife enthusiasts and conservation nuts
↗ Nobel Peace Prize winner and Lambaréné hospital founder Albert Schweitzer
↗ The Ivorian dance craze *Coupé Décalé*

EXPORT

↖ Timber
↖ Petroleum
↖ Manganese
↖ Iron ore
↖ Illegal ivory
↖ Bushmeat
↖ Animist spirituality

≫ A FISHERMAN DISPLAYS THE CATCH OF THE DAY

MYTHS & LEGENDS

Stories of many creatures abound in the Gabonese tribal cultures, but the tortoise – slow, smart, patient and sometimes vengeful – is perhaps the most popular. In one story that's often told to children, a baboon invites a tortoise to a dinner party. The tortoise, who is unable to climb, waits patiently as the other animals celebrate the feast in the baboon's treetop house. Finally the other animals leave, passing the tortoise on the way out and explaining that the fiesta is finished. The tortoise, in turn, invites all the animals for a party, but insists that they all wash their hands before eating. When the baboon arrives, the tortoise asks him to wash his hands again, and makes sure he can only do so at a river that lies beyond a scorched field. Each time the baboon returns, the burnt grasses make his hands dirty again, and he spends the entire night going back and forth to the river – missing out on the party altogether, as the tortoise intended.

A CONSERVATION COUP

In 2002 President Bongo made history: he set aside 10 per cent of Gabon to create 13 national parks protecting a variety of different ecosystems. Gabon has since been hailed as a model of conservation, and many international groups have flocked to the parks to help build a robust ecotourism industry. Bongo, knowing that timber and petroleum are not sustainable, hopes this will become the country's new source of revenue.

ESSENTIAL EXPERIENCES

○ **Gulping Régab beer and eating brochettes on the streets of Libreville**

○ **Tracking the vibrant mandrill troupes of Lopé Reserve**

○ **Lounging on the observation platform above the gorillas, elephants and antelopes of Langoue Bai**

○ **Gaping at the beaches full of elephants, buffalos and surfing hippos in Petit Loango National Park**

○ **Body-surfing the waves at Mayumba while watching humpback whales breach in the distance**

○ **Tripping out on ancient ceremonies at a Bwiti initiation near Mimongo**

MAP REF // K8

BEST TIME TO VISIT **MAY TO AUGUST**

≫ ANYONE FOR COFFEE? A BOY SHOWS OFF THE LOCAL HARVEST

PETRODOLLARS PUMP UP THE VOLUME ON MODERN ARCHITECTURE IN GABON'S CAPITAL, LIBREVILLE ≫

THIS WOMAN HAS CARTAGE ALL SEWN UP ≫

GABON'S FOREST ELEPHANTS ENJOY VENTURING ONTO THE BEACHFRONT AT PETIT LOANGO NATIONAL PARK ≫

TEXT BRENDAN SAINSBURY

REPUBLIC OF CONGO

NOT TO BE CONFUSED WITH THE INFAMOUS DEMOCRATIC REPUBLIC OF CONGO ACROSS THE RIVER, THE REPUBLIC OF CONGO IS A SMALLER, FRIENDLIER AND MARGINALLY MORE PEACEFUL COUNTRY THAN ITS NEIGHBOUR.

CAPITAL CITY BRAZZAVILLE   **POPULATION** 3.7 MILLION   **AREA** 342,000 SQ KM   **OFFICIAL LANGUAGE** FRENCH

LANDSCAPE

The Republic of Congo is said to be one of Africa's most urbanised countries: over 70 per cent of its population resides either in the cities of Brazzaville and Pointe-Noire or is clustered along the railway line in between. Geographically the state can be split into the western coastal plain, southern basin, central plateau and northern basin areas. Tropical rainforest and woodland, mainly in the sparsely populated northeast, cover some 62 per cent of the land, and 169 kilometres of Atlantic coastline hosts the economically important oil industry.

RANDOM FACTS
- Built by the French between 1924 and 1934, the 530 kilometre Congo-Ocean Railway runs from Brazzaville to Pointe-Noire on the Atlantic coast, bypassing the unnavigable rapids on the lower Congo River.
- Between 1940 and 1943, during the Nazi occupation of Europe, Brazzaville was the symbolic capital of Free France.
- Congo boasts approximately 80 per cent of the world's lowland gorillas and wild chimpanzees.

HISTORY IN A NUTSHELL

The Kongo, Loango and Tio peoples competed for power in the pre-colonial Congo area, until Frenchman Pierre Savorgnan de Brazza signed a treaty with the local rulers in 1880, ushering in 80 years of French colonial rule. The country became part of French Equatorial Africa in 1910. The relatively peaceful transition to independence in 1960 was followed by two decades of iron-fisted Marxist-Leninist rule. In 1992 the one-party state was renounced and diminutive professor Pascal Lissouba elected, but he was deposed in 1997 amid escalating unrest. Elections in 2002 installed Denis Sassou-Nguesso as president and brought a shaky cease-fire.

PEOPLE

Among the Congo's diverse ethnic groups the Kongo tribe predominates, with over 48 per cent of the population. Other key groups are the Sangha (20 per cent), the Teke (17 per cent) and the M'Bochi (12 per cent). As well as French, the lingua francas Lingala and Monokutuba and many other local languages and dialects are spoken. Fifty per cent of the population is nominally Christian.

MARKETPLACE

Oil has dominated the country's economy since it replaced lumber as Congo's premier natural resource in the 1960s and '70s. Bad management, falling oil prices and ongoing internal conflict saw a sharp economic slump in the mid-1990s, and with the political crisis still largely unresolved, the country has struggled to stimulate recovery and reduce widespread poverty.

TRADEMARKS
- Lowland gorillas
- The oil industry
- The expansive Congo River
- Brazzaville Beach

WILD THINGS

Congo's 13,600-square-kilometre Odzala National Park has one of Africa's oldest and least-known tropical ecosystems. Beneath a jungle canopy of 40-metre-high trees, mammals like elephants, buffaloes and indigenous red river hogs roam through almost-virgin undergrowth. But the real draw cards are the lowland gorillas and chimpanzees that gather at Odzala's unique 'salines' (clearings). Since 2002 Ecofac, a European Union–funded conservation project, has been fighting to save the gorillas in the wake of two massive outbreaks of the Ebola virus.

IMPORT
- Pope John Paul II (on a brief 1980 visit)
- Daring French architects
- The Free French
- Gorilla watchers
- Construction materials

EXPORT
- Oil
- Timber
- Traditional fabrics and handicrafts

SURPRISES
- Congo has an adult literacy rate of 83 per cent.
- Despite its image as a jungle country, Congo has some impressive Afro-European fusion architecture, as seen in the buildings of Roger Erell in Brazzaville – a haul that includes St Anne's Basilica, the Case de Gaulle and the Lycée Savorgnan de Brazza.

ESSENTIAL EXPERIENCES

- **Surfing on the Atlantic beaches of Pointe-Noire**
- **Espying lowland gorillas, African forest elephants and lions in the gigantic Odzala National Park**
- **Lapping up Congolese culture in the low-key capital Brazzaville**
- **Watching water hyacinths floating serenely down the Congo River**
- **Browsing Brazzaville's colourful markets, including the Marché Total and the Marché de Moungali**

MAP REF // L8

BEST TIME TO VISIT MAY TO SEPTEMBER

GREY HAZE: A TRIBAL MAN EXHALES A LONG PLUME OF SMOKE

A CANOE CUTS ACROSS A CONGOLESE RIVER HEMMED IN BY DENSE RAINFOREST

A TAME CHIMP BEING PREPARED FOR RERELEASE INTO THE WILD SHARES AN INTIMATE MOMENT WITH HIS KEEPER

JOSE AZEL // CORBIS

MICHAEL NICHOLS // GETTY

LATOUR STEPHANIE // CORBIS

TEXT BRENDAN SAINSBURY

DEMOCRATIC REPUBLIC OF CONGO

AFRICA'S 'HEART OF DARKNESS', THE DEMOCRATIC REPUBLIC OF CONGO HAS LONG BEEN CONSIDERED A BASKET CASE. SHOULD IT SUCCEED IN BUILDING A LASTING PEACE, ITS POTENTIAL IS ALMOST LIMITLESS.

CAPITAL CITY KINSHASA   POPULATION 62.7 MILLION   AREA 2.3 MILLION SQ KM   OFFICIAL LANGUAGE FRENCH

≋ A BOY CLAMBERS OVER FISH TRAPS LOWERED INTO THE CONGO RIVER NEAR THE TOWN OF KISANGANI

LANDSCAPE

Carpeted by vast swaths of rainforest and bisected by the Congo River, the Democratic Republic of Congo (DRC) straddles the equator like a lumbering giant. To the west, the country's eponymous river gushes to the foaming Livingstone Falls before emptying into the Atlantic. In the east are more precipitous landscapes: a series of volcanoes and the Great Lakes merge into East Africa's famous Rift Valley. Tectonic activity has also endowed the eastern DRC with immense mineral riches, including copper, diamonds and uranium.

HISTORY IN A NUTSHELL

Formerly the preserve of the powerful Kongo tribe, the modern DRC's official borders were carved out by European nations at the Berlin Conference in 1885. The country (inappropriately named the Congo Free State) was acquired by the ruthless King Léopold II of Belgium as a personal fiefdom, and quickly descended into chaos and cruelty. In 1908 well-documented human rights abuses finally impelled the Belgian government to intervene and annex the territory, bringing stability. Independence came in 1960, followed by over 30 years of dictatorial one-party rule under the watchful eye of maverick megalomaniac President Mobutu Sese Seko. The post-Mobuto DRC has not been much better, sadly – since Mobutu was deposed by Laurent Kabila in 1997 the country has been embroiled in an on-off guerrilla war initially sparked by fleeing Hutus from Rwanda.

RANDOM FACTS

○ In October 1974 in Kinshasa, Muhammad Ali fought George Foreman for the world heavyweight boxing crown in a fight that became known as 'The Rumble in the Jungle'. The match was sponsored by none other than President Mobutu Sese Seko, in an attempt to raise the country's profile.
○ The DRC provided the uranium for the American-made atomic bombs that were dropped on Hiroshima and Nagasaki at the end of World War II.
○ The Second Congo War (1998–2003), sometimes referred to as 'Africa's World War', involved nine African nations and 20 armed groups, and led to the death of 3.8 million people.

PEOPLE

The racially complex DRC is home to over 250 individual ethnic groups and more than 700 different languages and dialects. The most numerous indigenous peoples are the Kongo, Luba and Mongo, who make up over 40 per cent of the population, while the most-spoken national languages, aside from French, are Lingala, Kikongo, Swahili and Tshiluba. Approximately 80 per cent of the population is either Protestant or Roman Catholic, despite widespread animist beliefs.

MARKETPLACE

Loaded with potential but with not much to show for it, the DRC's economy has suffered dramatically in recent years from the seemingly endless cycle of war, corruption, nepotism and large-scale government incompetence. Ongoing problems include inflation, reduced national output and increased external debt. Despite the rich seam of mineral wealth, most of the population continues to live in a state of abject poverty thanks to regular military skirmishes, government instability and a lack of foreign investment.

TRADEMARKS

○ War
○ Government corruption on a spectacular scale
○ Mountain gorillas
○ Impenetrable jungle
○ Kleptocracy

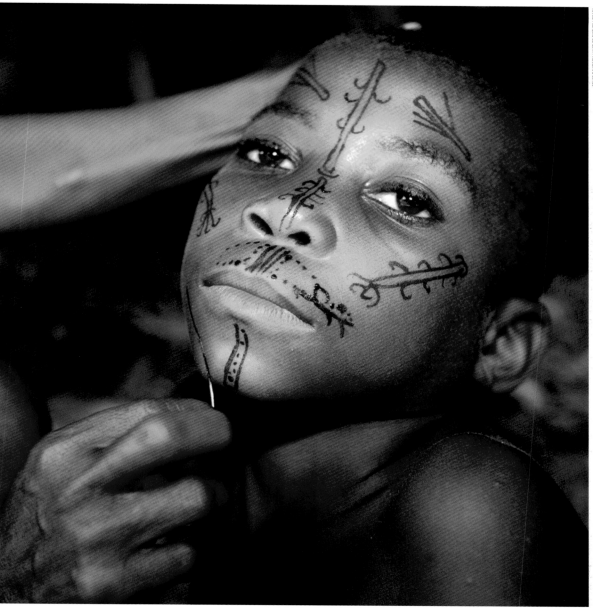

BAMBUTI PYGMY BOY BEING PAINTED WITH A MIXTURE OF CHARCOAL AND PLANT JUICES, EPULU ITURI RESERVE »

BELIEFS

Kimbanguism is Africa's most popular form of 'indigenous' Christianity. The movement is named after its mentor and founder Simon Kimbangu, who allegedly had a vision of Jesus Christ near Kinshasa in 1921, telling him to reconvert his people into 'native' Christians. Though he was initially sceptical of the vision, Kimbangu supposedly then developed miraculous healing powers, and before long had acquired followers. He was later excommunicated by the Protestant and Catholic churches and imprisoned by the Belgian authorities for 'inciting revolution', but the cult that developed around him grew quickly among the anticolonial movement and was finally given official status by President Mobutu in the 1960s. Today, Kimbanguism has followers in nine different African countries.

CULTURE

During the Mobutu era, Western-style clothing was banned under a government-sponsored 'authenticity' campaign. Most men resorted to wearing a Congolese version of the Mao jacket, known in-country as an *abacost* – a word derived from the French phrase *à bas le costume* (down with the suit).

IMPORT

↗ United Nations peacekeeping troops
↗ Che Guevara and his band of Cuban guerrillas
↗ Muhammad Ali
↗ Rwandan refugees
↗ Foreign armies

EXPORT

↖ Diamonds
↖ Copper
↖ Retired megalomaniacs
↖ *Soukous* music, an African variant of rumba

MUSIC

Soukous, derived in the 1930s and '40s from Cuban rumba, is a uniquely Congolese mix of West African highlife music and congas, maracas, acoustic bass and electric guitar. By the 1950s *soukous* had developed a big-band format featuring trumpets, saxophones and clarinets, and was spearheaded by such icons as Franco Luambo and his TPOK Jazz orchestra. More recent artists such as Papa Wemba – Africa's Elvis Presley – have fused *soukous* with Congolese folk music and soul, and taken it to even greater heights.

SURPRISES

○ Joseph Conrad wrote his seminal novella *Heart of Darkness* based on his personal experiences as a sea captain on the Congo River in the 1890s. During one trip upriver he apparently witnessed such shocking levels of colonial barbarity that he quit his post on the spot.
○ Nicknamed 'the Sorcerer of the Guitar', DRC-born François Luambo Makiadi – better known to the world as 'Franco' – is considered one of *the* major figures of 20th-century African music.

↟ FEW CONGOLESE HAVE ESCAPED THE COUNTRY'S INFAMOUS CONFLICTS

↟ EARNING HER DAILY BREAD: A KINSHASA STREET HAWKER

↟ VILLAGE ON STILTS ON AN ISLAND IN THE CONGO RIVER

ESSENTIAL EXPERIENCES

○ **Viewing mountain gorillas at Virungas National Park, one of the DRC's five Unesco World Heritage Sites**

○ **Playing with bonobos (pygmy chimps) at the out-of-town Chutes de Lukia lake area**

○ **Testing the vibe in chaotic Kinshasa, a city once dubbed Kin La Belle (Beautiful Kinshasa), and checking out the Grand Marché, Académie des Beaux-Arts (art gallery) and the tomb of former president Laurent Kabila**

○ **Taking a pirogue from the fish market of Kinkole and picnicking on the sandbanks of the Congo River**

○ **Casting an eye over an impressive collection of 100-year-old trees at the botanical gardens in Kisanto**

MAP REF // M9

BEST TIME TO VISIT **DECEMBER TO FEBRUARY**

A YOUNG GIRL SITS UNDER A DRIER IN A HAIRDRESSING SALON HOUSED IN A WOODEN SHACK »

PULSATING CONGOLESE MUSIC SETS KINSHASA'S NIGHTLIFE ALIGHT »

CHILDREN OF THE YAKA ETHNIC GROUP PREPARE TO DANCE AS PART OF NATIONAL DAY CELEBRATIONS IN KINSHASA »

TEXT TONY WHEELER

CENTRAL AFRICAN REPUBLIC

ITS JUNGLE, PYGMIES, ELEPHANTS AND GORILLAS MAY BE CLASSIC AFRICA, BUT THE CENTRAL AFRICAN REPUBLIC HAS ALSO SUFFERED UNDER MISMANAGEMENT, LOST OPPORTUNITIES, A SAD HISTORY AND LARGER-THAN-LIFE TYRANTS.

CAPITAL CITY BANGUI   POPULATION 4.3 MILLION   AREA 622,980 SQ KM   OFFICIAL LANGUAGE FRENCH

LANDSCAPE

The Central African Republic (CAR) is a 600- to 700-metre-high plateau of jungle and savanna, numerous rivers and a scattering of hills in the northeast and southwest (Mt Ngaoui, at 1420 metres, is the highest).

HISTORY IN A NUTSHELL

Like many other nations in the region, the CAR has been repeatedly devastated: first by the slave trade, then by colonialism and finally by post-independence chaos. The French arrived in the 1880s and left in 1960; within two years the CAR was a one-party state. In 1977 dictator Jean-Bédel Bokassa renamed the country the CAE (Central African Empire). Two years later he was out, and two decades of chaos followed. A 2005 election may have brought some stability.

PEOPLE

The country has numerous tribal groups; 33 per cent of the population are Baya (in the west), 27 per cent are Banda (in the centre and east), and some four per cent are Aka pygmy people (the plural is BaAka). French is the official language, but almost everyone speaks Sangho: a rare occurrence in Africa. Half of the population is Christian (Catholics and Protestants with animistic influences), 15 per cent are Muslim and the remaining 35 per cent profess indigenous beliefs.

MARKETPLACE

Adding to years of governmental chaos, the CAR's landlocked situation and dire transport facilities compound its economic difficulties. Seventy per cent of the population depends upon subsistence agriculture, and the UN Human Development Index ranks the CAR in the world's bottom 10, although the government's annual budget is a mystery. Timber and diamonds, the main exports, are often smuggled out. France is the principal source of foreign aid.

TRADEMARKS

○ Winding rivers
○ Lowland gorillas
○ Forest elephants
○ Butterflies
○ BaAka – Pygmies

RANDOM FACTS

○ Bangui is the only town of any size; after the jungles of central Africa it even seems like a big city.
○ During the colonial period, cotton, tobacco and coffee were produced and exported by French companies who conscripted the local population to work in conditions of near-slavery.
○ Diamonds, the CAR's top commodity, are mostly smuggled. There's also gold and uranium.
○ The number-one import is probably chaos – with Chad, Sudan and the DRC for neighbours, it's not surprising that trouble spills across the borders.

MUSIC

In many African tribes music is reserved for men, and is often further restricted to those from specific castes, but among the BaAka, everyone is a musician. Singing, clapping and stamping accompany almost every activity, and the songs are often decidedly bawdy!

SURPRISES

○ Africa's worst post-independence ruler? It's a toss-up between Uganda's Idi Amin and the CAR's Jean-Bédel Bokassa. Being 'president' of the 'republic' wasn't enough for Bokassa; in 1977 he converted the CAR to the CAE, Central African Empire, with guess who as emperor? France footed most of the US$20 million coronation bill. When he was finally booted out in 1986, Bokassa was convicted of treason, murder and cannibalism.
○ During the colonial period, the CAR was one of Africa's prime big-game hunting destinations. Even as late as the 1970s, the French president of the day (Valéry Giscard d'Estaing), regularly went hunting in the country, and it's said he had a personal financial interest in the hunting grounds.

WILD THINGS

Despite threats like poaching, the CAR has probably the highest density of lowland gorillas and forest elephants in Africa; it's also the world's best place for butterflies. But there's a real danger that lack of governmental control will lead to disastrous exploitation of the jungle timber and wildlife.

For obvious reasons, the country's huge ecotourism potential is virtually untapped.

CUISINE

Gozo (manioc paste) and ngunza (manioc leaf salad) are two widely popular local dishes. Along the Oubangui River, Nile perch (capitaine) is another local delicacy. Banana and palm wine are widely brewed.

ESSENTIAL EXPERIENCES

○ **Visiting the Chutes de Boali during the rainy season, when the dam controllers let water flow over the falls**

○ **Tracking lowland gorillas and forest elephants in the Dzanga Sangha Reserve**

○ **Joining the BaAka (a Pygmy tribe) on a hunting trip from M'Baïki or Bayanga**

○ **Hoping that the St Floris and Bamingui-Bangoran Parks are recovering from years of uncontrolled poaching**

○ **Catching a boat up or down the mighty Oubangui from Zinga**

MAP REF // M7

BEST TIME TO VISIT NOVEMBER TO APRIL

A BUTTERFLY-CATCHER SHOWS OFF HIS TECHNICOLOR HAUL »

THE BOALI FALLS, NORTHWEST OF THE CAPITAL BANGUI, TUMBLE OVER A 50-METRE-HIGH CLIFF »

WOMEN OF THE SANGO TRIBE KNOW THE BEST MEANS OF CARRYING SUPPLIES »

LANDSCAPE

Chad spans some of Africa's most important geographic zones, from the Sahara in the north, through the central semiarid Sahel and the savanna lands of the south. The lake that gave Chad its name recedes further north each year – it may no longer be within Chad's borders by the time you read this! The Chari and Logone rivers are more enduring, flowing deep into southern Chad.

HISTORY IN A NUTSHELL

Archaeologists believe Chad may be the cradle of humankind, after the 2002 discovery of Toumaï, a seven-million-year-old human-like skull. In the Middle Ages, Chad was ruled by the Kanem and Bornu empires, whose domain stretched from the shores of Lake Chad to the deep Sahara. After these empires fell, Chad was a virtual backwater, ruled by local tribes and far from the centres of regional power. The French conquered Chad in the 19th century, did nothing to develop the country for much of the 20th century and then proceeded to prop up Chad's corrupt and repressive post-independence rulers. For good measure, the French often fought battles with the Libyan army on Chadian soil. Power has alternated between southern Christian and northern Muslim rulers, but since independence in 1960, it has never changed hands by democratic means. Chadians say that power comes from the east, as most

CHAD

A BYWORD FOR DEEPEST AFRICA, CHAD HAS A TROUBLED PAST, AN UNCERTAIN PRESENT AND A LANDSCAPE, WILDLIFE AND CULTURES THAT DESERVE FAR BETTER.

CAPITAL CITY **N'DJAMÉNA**   POPULATION **9.9 MILLION**   AREA **1.3 MILLION SQ KM**   OFFICIAL LANGUAGES **FRENCH, ARABIC**

WHO SAID RELIGION AND COMMERCE DON'T MIX? MERCHANTS IN THE OLD MARKET OF FAYA-LARGEAU READ THE QURAN

presidents have fallen to a rebel army from that lawless part of the country. It remains to be seen whether the same fate awaits President Idriss Déby.

TRADEMARKS
- Civil war
- Lake Chad
- The north–south divide
- Remote mud-brick villages
- Unpaved roads

PEOPLE
Around 200 ethnic groups rub shoulders in Chad, with the main fault line running between the southern Bagirmi and Sara (30 per cent) and the northern Sudanic Arabs (26 per cent) and Toubou (seven per cent). Chad's religious map has the same divide: Muslims in the north are 51 per cent of the population and Christians in the south 35 per cent.

RANDOM FACTS
- Lake Chad disappeared completely in 1984 during a devastating Sahel-wide drought.
- Chad has one billion barrels of known oil reserves.
- The Gala Brewery in Moundou hasn't closed during any of Chad's civil wars.

MARKETPLACE
Once dominated by cotton, Chad's economy was saved by the 1990s discovery of oil in the Doba Basin. A deal between the government, the World Bank and foreign oil companies aimed to ensure oil revenue goes to easing the poverty of many Chadians (GDP per capita is US$1500), but so far results are mixed.

NATURAL BEAUTY
Desert aficionados swear by the Tibesti Mountains, the ultimate moonscape of monoliths in the most incredible shapes rising from orange sand. Sculpted by wind and water, they were once surrounded by a vast inland sea and sheltered the great mammals of Africa that are now depicted on the mountain walls. They're considered the Sahara's most inaccessible but greatest prize. The lesser-known but similarly beautiful Ennedi mountain range is easier to reach.

WILD THINGS
Zakouma National Park, once emptied of wildlife by war, is now a wildlife success story. Restocked with animals from the neighbouring Central African Republic (CAR), the EU-funded park employs locals as guides and hosts epic herds of elephants, giraffe, lions, antelopes and weird-and-wonderful birdlife.

IMPORT
- Rebel groups from Sudan
- Armies from Libya and France
- Western oil companies
- Thor Heyerdahl, who built his reed boat *Ra* on the shores of Lake Chad (with Chadian help) and later sailed *Ra II* across the Atlantic
- All things French (a quarter of Chad's imports)

EXPORT
- Oil
- Cotton
- Gala beer – *le goût du bonheur* (the taste of happiness)
- Wildlife, which flees across the border into Sudan or the CAR whenever hostilities resume
- Former dictator Hissène Habré, in exile in Senegal and perhaps soon to be tried in Belgium for crimes against humanity

ESSENTIAL EXPERIENCES
- Searching for iconic African wildlife in the remote Zakouma National Park
- Watching the sunset over the Chari River from war-scarred N'Djaména
- Strolling the streets of sleepy Sarh, with its unmistakeably Central African air
- Mounting a deep-desert expedition into the astonishing Tibesti Mountains of Chad's far north, and taking in Emi Koussi (the Sahara's highest peak)
- Nursing a beer in a riverside bar on the Logone, in the city of Moundou
- Pushing the frontiers and travelling to the remote desert town of Abéché

N'DJAMÉNA JOCKEYS GEE UP THEIR MOUNTS »

MAP REF // M5

BEST TIME TO VISIT **DECEMBER TO MID-FEBRUARY**

THE GUELTA D'ARCHEI PROVIDES WADING BLISS FOR CAMELS; ASTONISHINGLY, THE CANYON IS ALSO HOME TO AN ISOLATED POPULATION OF CROCODILES »

TEXT PAUL CLAMMER

SUDAN

IT'S DOMINATED BY THE MIGHTY NILE AND REACHES FROM THE SAHARA'S EXPANSES TO LUSH EQUATORIAL FOREST, BUT SUDAN'S NAME IS MORE CLOSELY ASSOCIATED WITH CIVIL WAR AND FAMINE THAN WITH NATURAL WONDERS.

CAPITAL CITY **KHARTOUM**   POPULATION **41.2 MILLION**   AREA **2.5 MILLION SQ KM**   OFFICIAL LANGUAGES **ARABIC, ENGLISH**

⌃ DINKA HERDERS BLEND INTO THE TREES NEAR DIEM ROM; THE FOREST ALSO PROVIDES SHELTER FROM MARAUDING GOVERNMENT TROOPS

LANDSCAPE

The landscape of Sudan is very big and very flat. In the equatorial south of the country, hardwood forests and Nile floodplains gradually give way to the watery maze of the Sudd, Africa's biggest marsh – it's the size of France. From here, the White Nile flows through increasingly dry land until it is joined by the Blue Nile at Khartoum and reaches the stony deserts of the north.

HISTORY IN A NUTSHELL

Modern Sudan is a victim of colonial borders, both ancient and modern. The Egyptian pharaohs raided the country for its natural resources, and so did the Arabs in the Middle Ages. Victorian Britain divided and ruled, splitting the country into the educated Arab north and the undeveloped black south: a painful division that within years of independence (established in 1956) sparked the civil war which has been burning on and off ever since. Hard to govern, Sudan has nevertheless occasionally played the regional power, from the kingdom of Meroe that kicked the pharaohs back to Egypt to the Mahdist rebellion that gave a bloody nose to 19th-century Britain. The present troubles in Darfur indicate that a Sudanese resurgence in this century may still be some time away, however.

PEOPLE

Over a hundred languages are spoken in Sudan, a testament to its ethnic diversity. The country is 70 per cent Muslim, with Arabs, Nubians and the Beja making up the majority of the northern population. The south is black Africa, dominated by the pastoral Dinka and Nuer tribes and the Azande, who mainly follow traditional religions. Christians represent around five per cent of the population.

MARKETPLACE

Throughout history, Sudan has been a provider of raw materials to outside powers – slaves, gold, wood and cotton. Agriculture is still the major employer, but Khartoum now earns most of its hard currency from oil exports. Unfortunately, the oil fields lie on the border between north and south Sudan, and were a major trigger in the southern civil war.

TRADEMARKS

- The confluence of the Blue and White Niles
- Quiet but warm hospitality
- Villages and palm groves strung along the Nile
- *Bokasi* pick-up trucks as public transport
- Empty desert
- The Sudd swamp

NATURAL BEAUTY

The flat emptiness of Sudan's northern deserts is punctuated with the shock of the wide Nile and tiny Nubian villages. The Nile is at its most impressive at its confluence in Khartoum, but the Blue and White branches are actually different shades of brown. Several mountain groups rise from the plains – the granite Taka peaks at Kassala, and in the west the Nuba Mountains and Jebel Marra range. Off the Red Sea coast lie the hidden beauties of coral reefs.

RANDOM FACTS

- Sudan has more pyramids than Egypt.
- At its height, the kingdom of Meroe stretched from Sudan to Lebanon and Syria.
- The streets of modern Khartoum were laid out by the British as a series of interlocking Union Jacks.
- The Sudanese claim that the Mahdist rebellion was the world's first Islamic anticolonial movement.

WILD THINGS

It's half a century too late to hit Sudan for a safari. Its wildlife once rivalled Kenya's and South Africa's, but decades of war have largely put paid to that. Wildlife does still thrive in the Sudd, most notably million-strong herds of Nile Lechwe antelopes.

CONICAL *QUBBAS* (ISLAMIC RELIQUARIES) FRINGED BY GRAVEYARDS PUNCTUATE SUDAN'S EMPTINESS »

A MONDARI WOMAN JUGGLES A SMILE AND A SILVER-STEMMED PIPE »

CULTURE

Cattle are crucial to the identity of the Dinka and Nuer tribes, as well as being a source of wealth. Young boys live in cattle camps to tend the herd, and will even decorate and sing to their favourite cow. It doesn't save the cattle from the knife, however – they are sacrificed at religious and family celebrations.

MONUMENTS

Though it doesn't have the fame of its neighbour Egypt, Sudan has antiquities that rival anything further north. The kingdom of Meroe took its inspiration and gods from ancient Egypt and added some African twists of its own – wide-hipped queens and plenty of elephants. Even better, at the Sudanese ancient sites – the temples of Naqa and Soleb, say, or the steep-sided pyramids of Meroe and Nuri – there's not a tourist tout for miles.

ON PAPER

Sudan has one of Africa's greatest living writers in the shape of Tayeb Salih. His books *Season of Migration to the North* and *The Wedding of Zein* paint delicate portraits of village life along the Nile in the north of the country.

CUISINE

Breakfast is the most important meal of the day in Sudan. It's taken around the middle of the morning, and all work stops to enable people to tuck into big bowls of *fuul* (stewed beans) or *adis* (lentils). The former is enlivened with oil, salads, cheese and egg, and mopped up with a piece of flat bread. It's all washed down with sweet black tea or coffee spiced with cardamom.

FUTURE DIRECTIONS

Sudan entered the 21st century seemingly on the verge of peace – the civil war in the south had finally been settled with a peace treaty. However, war and ethnic cleansing then immediately broke out in the western Darfur provinces. The international community has proved largely ineffective at tackling the crisis, and the Sudanese government has continually deferred action while continuing to support its militia proxies. Ceasefires and peace deals come and go with depressing regularity – and are often violated before the ink has dried. Sudan's unhappy present looks set to continue for the immediate future.

⌃ AZANDE CHILDREN CARRY HONEY THROUGH THE GRASS

⌃ ACTORS PERFORM A PLAY ABOUT FEMALE GENITAL MUTILATION

ESSENTIAL EXPERIENCES

○ **Exploring the ruined pyramids of Meroe and enjoying having the sights and the desert all to yourself**

○ **Watching the dizzying religious spectacle of Omdurman's whirling dervishes at Friday's sunset prayers**

○ **Village-hopping along the Nile, squeezed into a bumpy pick-up truck with a dozen Nubians heading to market**

○ **Rock scrambling on the otherworldly Taka Mountains outside Kassala**

○ **Swimming with manta rays and hammerheads in the Red Sea**

○ **Pondering the opening of the south to travel, and whether the river barges south to Juba will ever sail again**

MAP REF // 06

BEST TIME TO VISIT **OCTOBER TO MARCH**

⌃ AN ITALIAN CHURCH ON THE ROAD TO YEI, SOUTHERN SUDAN

WHITE MAY BE THE DRESS CODE FOR MUSLIM MEN, BUT THE SUDANESE ARE CERTAINLY NOT COLOUR-SHY (GATEWAY AT OLD DONGOLA) «

MAGNET FOR THE FAITHFUL: A MOSQUE CAPPED WITH SILVER «

THE RUINS OF THE KHATMIYYA MOSQUE AT KASSALA IN EASTERN SUDAN NESTLE BELOW HUMPED HILLS «

EAST AFRICA

IF YOU ASK SOMEONE TO CLOSE THEIR EYES AND DREAM AN AFRICAN DREAM, THEIR THOUGHTS WILL USUALLY LAND THEM SQUARELY IN EAST AFRICA. CONSIDERING ITS PLETHORA OF WILDLIFE, ITS STAGGERING NATURAL LANDSCAPES AND ITS PEOPLES' DIVERSITY, THAT FACT SHOULD COME AS LITTLE SURPRISE.

East Africa is the original home of the safari (*safari* is Swahili for 'journey') and there are dozens of wildlife parks and reserves across its breadth that are unrivalled elsewhere on the planet. Rumble over the grassy plains in a classic open-topped Land Rover while tracking the Big Five (lion, leopard, elephant, rhino and buffalo) in Kenya and Tanzania; have close encounters with a rare silverback gorilla in the jungles of Rwanda and Uganda; or get up close and personal with the aquatic life of the Indian Ocean's archipelagos. You can see every African animal you've ever dreamed of and many more that you've never heard of before.

The soils beneath East Africa have contained some of the oldest hominid remains ever discovered, leading some scholars to call the region the 'cradle of humanity'. Today, East Africa contains a vast array of purely African societies, as well as countless others, like those on Zanzibar, that have been influenced over the centuries by the Middle East, India and Europe. And like most regions with

newly delineated borders, many of East Africa's cultures straddle political boundaries. The most widespread language is Swahili, which is spoken by almost 50 million people across eight nations. That said, Swahili is only the first language of five million people, or two per cent of East Africa's population – a testament to the hundreds of other local languages that survive here.

Much of East Africa's astounding physical beauty exists not because Mother Nature has painstakingly pieced the region together, but because she's tried to rip it apart. East Africa's famous battle scar, the Rift Valley, is the area's largest and most spectacular geographical feature.

The western section of the Rift crosses Uganda, Rwanda, Burundi and Tanzania. It is edged by some of Africa's tallest peaks, including the Rwenzori Range and the Virunga volcanoes, and houses some of the deepest lakes on the planet – Lake Tanganyika reaches a depth of 1470 metres in sections. The eastern limb of the Rift stretches from

Eritrea and Djibouti through Ethiopia, Kenya and Tanzania. Serrated escarpments, splintered volcanoes and the continent's two largest mountains (Mt Kilimanjaro and Mt Kenya) tower over this eastern section, which is carpeted with ochre soils, grassy plains and shallow soda lakes. Between the Rift's two limbs is Lake Victoria, the region's second-largest geographical feature. Its 68,000-square-kilometre surface covers sections of Kenya, Tanzania and Uganda, and helps feed the world's longest river, the Nile.

Where there are highs there are usually lows, however, and East Africa is no exception – AIDS, drought, poverty and corruption continue to be major issues. While many of the region's nations have happily put their civil wars and genocides behind them, Somalia's current state of affairs, sadly, ensures bloodshed will be part of East Africa's future too.

TEXT: MATT PHILLIPS

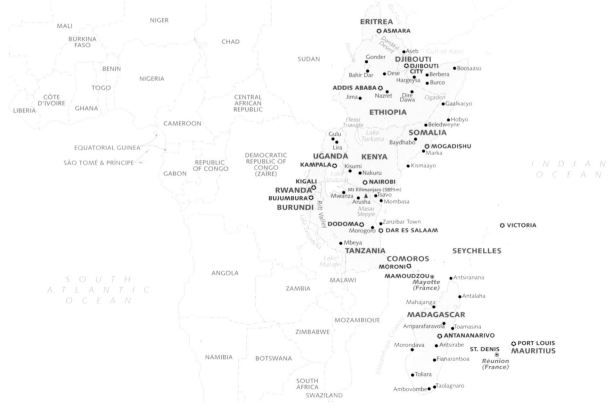

ETHIOPIA

IF ETHIOPIA'S HISTORICAL AND NATURAL TREASURES RECEIVED AS MUCH AIRTIME AS THE INDELIBLE IMAGES OF PAST FAMINES AND WAR, ETHIOPIA WOULD BE MENTIONED IN THE SAME BREATH AS EGYPT, MOROCCO AND TANZANIA AS ONE OF AFRICA'S MOST CAPTIVATING COUNTRIES.

CAPITAL CITY ADDIS ABABA   **POPULATION** 74.8 MILLION   **AREA** 1.1 MILLION SQ KM   **OFFICIAL LANGUAGES** AMHARIC, TIGRINYA, SOMALI, ARABIC, OROMIGA, GUARAGIGNA

LANDSCAPE

With the Simien and Bale mountains climbing over 4000 metres and the Danakil Depression diving below sea level, Ethiopia's landscapes cover a glorious gamut. The highlands, which have been exquisitely carved by the hands of time, offer some of the continent's most dramatic chasms. Flowing from the highlands are four large river systems, the most famous being the Blue Nile. Africa's renowned Rift has bisected southern Ethiopia and left several lovely lakes in its wake. Rifting continues in the Danakil Depression, where the wafer-thin crust parts to put the earth's insides on permanent display.

HISTORY IN A NUTSHELL

While Lucy, the representative of Ethiopia's most ancient citizens, *Ardipithecus ramidus* (they're possibly our oldest upright ancestors), awaited discovery in the ground, a mysteriously short-lived civilisation with Arabian influences blossomed in Ethiopia around 1500 BC. Next, between the 4th and 2nd century BC, the Aksumite civilisation rose and dominated the region until the 7th century AD – their remarkable obelisks and tombs survive today. In the 4th century Christianity took hold and, despite devastating holy wars with invading Muslims and onslaughts by the Oromo (a tribe from northern Kenya) over the centuries, it continues to dominate Ethiopian society.

Emperor Menelik stunned the world by thrashing Italy's colonial army in 1896, thus saving Ethiopia from colonialism. The following century witnessed a brief Italian occupation during the 1930s, communists overthrowing (and murdering) the last of Ethiopia's Solomonic emperors (Haile Selassie) in the mid-1970s, and a decade-long civil war that ended in 1991. In 1998, only seven years after shedding its socialist shackles, Ethiopia briefly went to war with Eritrea; much to Ethiopia's detriment, they continue to squabble today.

PEOPLE

Religion is the most important aspect of Ethiopian life. Forty-five per cent of Ethiopians are Ethiopian Orthodox Christian, 35 per cent are Muslim and 11 per cent follow traditional animist beliefs. Ethiopia has almost 75 million citizens: an astounding figure considering the population was just 15 million in 1935. Most belong to one of eight main ethnic groups: Oromo (40 per cent), Amhara (21 per cent), Tigrayan (11 per cent), Sidama (nine per cent), Somali (six per cent), Afar (four per cent), Gurage (two per cent) and Harari (one per cent). The Orthodox Amharas have traditionally dominated the country and imposed their language and culture on society, leading to resentment from other groups. Today there are similar feelings towards the Orthodox Tigrayans, who have dominated the government since 1991.

MARKETPLACE

With 80 per cent of the country working in agriculture, it unsurprisingly accounts for half the nation's GDP and 60 per cent of its exports. Ethiopia's two biggest exports are currently coffee and qat (a mildly intoxicating leaf that's illegal in many nations but embraced in others), which bring in US$335 million and US$99 million per year respectively. The Eritrean tensions hinder economic growth, however, as does the land tenure system, under which the government owns all land and provides citizens with long-term leases. Also, although the country is incredibly fertile, it's prone to drought – and with almost the entire nation relying on their crops for sustenance, the consequences are dire.

HEADWEAR WITH SOME SERIOUS HARDWARE: A MURSI GIRL IN SOUTH OMO »

∧ THE OTHERWORLDLY DANAKIL DEPRESSION

FRANCES LINZEE GORDON // LONELY PLANET IMAGES

∧ THE KNIGHTS OF THE ROUND TABLE, ABYSSINIAN STYLE, AT THE FESTIVAL OF TIMKAT

∧ A CONTEMPLATIVE MOMENT OUTSIDE THE ENTOTO MARYAM CHURCH

BET GIYORGIS (ST GEORGE'S CHURCH) IS CARVED OUT OF A SOLID ROCK TERRACE »

TALK TO THE HAND: A MURSI MOTHER AND CHILD IN JINKA »

FROM THE TRAVELLER

The Christianity of Ethiopia is often described as closest to the type that was practised in the times of Jesus. Ceremonies involve drums and worship takes place in churches hewn from rock. I felt like an intruder when visiting the famous subterranean complexes in the town of Lalibela as ceremonies still take place daily. For a small contribution, this priest held his cross for my camera.

THORNTON // USA

TRADEMARKS

○ Famine
○ Emperor Haile Selassie
○ Lalibela's rock-hewn churches
○ Mursi lip-stretchers
○ Aksum's stelae
○ Haile Gebreselassie

NATURAL BEAUTY

Venturing into the Danakil Depression is an exercise in insanity (daytime temperatures can exceed 50°C), but it will give you a lesson in the beauty of bleakness that you'll never forget. And in the pre-dawn darkness, a peek into Irt'ale's permanent cauldron of lava will turn all that bleakness into brilliance.

RANDOM FACTS

○ After rudely nicking an Aksumite stele in 1937 and dragging their diplomatic feet for decades, Italy had to fork out US$7.7 million for its return over 67 years later.
○ The missing body of Emperor Haile Selassie was found buried under the president's personal office toilet in 1992, 17 years after his murder.
○ Ethiopians fear moving air – it sounds odd, until you try and open a window on a sweltering bus

URBAN SCENE

The centuries-old walls of the ancient section of Islamic Harar, built to protect it from the attacks of the invading Oromo tribe, still enclose a square kilometre packed with fascination. Floating through the old city's myriad crooked alleyways, innumerable mosques, shrines and architectural gems are the perpetual aroma of coffee and the silhouettes of the alluring Adare women. Equally transfixing, though just outside the city's walls, are the men who continue the tradition of feeding the hyenas by hand (and occasionally by mouth!).

SURPRISES

○ When the Ethiopian People's Revolutionary Democratic Front tanks rolled into Addis Ababa in 1991, they were navigating with the map in Lonely Planet's *Africa on a Shoestring*.
○ A total of only two per cent of Aksum's ruins have been excavated.
○ Ethiopia is one of Africa's most fertile countries.

WILD THINGS

Isolated as it is from the rest of Africa by its fortress-like mountains, Ethiopia's wildlife has evolved to be unique; there are 89 species here that are seen nowhere else on earth. What's even more remarkable is that it's fairly easy to observe them, even the highly endangered Ethiopian wolf, walia ibex and mountain nyala. The birdlife is prolific – at last count 842 species have been identified, of which 21 are endemic.

IMPORT

↗ Live Aid money
↗ Christianity
↗ Islam
↗ Mussolini's vengeance
↗ One long-overdue stele
↗ Unesco World Heritage designations – seven at last count

EXPORT

↖ Coffee and lots of it
↖ Enough qat to stone a small country
↖ World-record runners
↖ The inspiration for Rastafarianism
↖ An unwarranted reputation as a barren wasteland

MYTHS & LEGENDS

At least 1000 years before Starbucks frothed its first cappuccino in 1971, Kaldi, an astute Ethiopian herder, noticed his goats behaved rather excitedly after eating a certain plant. He followed suit and sure enough, he became a hyper herder! He rushed his news to the nearest monastery, only to be reprimanded for 'partaking in the Devil's fruit'. However, the monks quickly came around after smelling the aroma wafting from the fire in which they'd thrown Kaldi's beloved beans. Soon they were shipping beans to monasteries everywhere. Surely something that helped them pray into the early hours must be God's work, not the Devil's! The name of Kaldi's kingdom stuck to this elixir of wakefulness. And to what kingdom did he belong? Kafa, of course!

CUISINE

Ethiopia's cuisine is much like Ethiopia: completely different from the rest of Africa. Plates, bowls and even utensils are replaced by *injera*, a savoury pancake of huge proportions. Atop its rubbery expanse can sit anything from spicy meat stews to colourful dollops of boiled veggies to cubes of raw beef. And despite preconceptions, most Ethiopians do not habitually go hungry.

ESSENTIAL EXPERIENCES

○ Sharing an Abyssinian abyss with enigmatic 'bleeding heart baboons' while trekking in the Simien Mountains

○ Flirting with gravity at Abuna Yemata Guh, Tigray's most precariously positioned rock-hewn church

○ Stepping down into a mesmerising medieval world frozen in stone at Lalibela, one of the continent's true marvels

○ Witnessing some of Africa's most colourful tribes in the Omo Valley and seeing lip-stretching, bull-jumping and body-painting

○ Discovering the entrancing history of the old walled city of Harar while wandering through its alleyways and shrines

○ Observing the fabled remains of 'Africa's Camelot' in Gonder, tickled by the last shivers of sunlight

⌃ IT TAKES WORK TO LOOK THIS GOOD – GELADA BABOONS GROOMING

BEST TIME TO VISIT **OCTOBER TO JANUARY**

MAP REF // Q7

FRANCES LINZEE GORDON // LONELY PLANET IMAGES

SUNDOWNERS AT THE SUNRISE RESTAURANT, DELANTA PLATEAU »

A PRAYER GATHERING IN A CAVE NEAR BET GIYORGIS »

TEXT MATT PHILLIPS

DJIBOUTI

WITH ROBUST RED SEA REEFS, A COLOURFUL AND COSMOPOLITAN CAPITAL CITY, ARAB-INFLUENCED VILLAGES AND AN INTERIOR THAT'S BOTH AN APOCALYPTIC WASTELAND AND A GEOLOGICAL WONDERLAND, DJIBOUTI IS NO ORDINARY AFRICAN NATION.

CAPITAL CITY **DJIBOUTI CITY**   POPULATION **486,530**   AREA **23,000 SQ KM**   OFFICIAL LANGUAGES **FRENCH, ARABIC**

⌃ COLOURFUL DJIBOUTI PERSONIFIED IN AN AFAR WOMAN AND HER FAMILY

LANDSCAPE

Although Djibouti's north is scattered with mountains ranging up to 2063 metres, and its 350 kilometres of coastline are lined with white sandy beaches and coral reefs, the country is dominated by a desolate volcanic desert. Fumaroles spew steam from the desert's insides; rocks are strewn across the wasteland like marbles on the baking asphalt of a playground. Much of the desert is actually below sea level, and Lac Assal, at -155 metres, ranks as the world's third-lowest point. Most of Djibouti's lakes are saline and host incredible crystal formations: Lac Assal's shore is carpeted with spheres of halite and angular gypsum, while Lac Abbé has towering deposits of travertine. The heat is only hospitable between November and mid-April, when easterly winds bring minimal rain and average temperatures of 25°C. Come June, July and August, the mercury rises to 45°C in the shade.

HISTORY IN A NUTSHELL

The discovery of basalt millstones near Lac Abbé has led some historians to believe agriculture may have been practised in Djibouti as long as 4000 years ago. Two millennia later Djibouti became part of the Ethiopian Aksumite kingdom, which introduced Christianity before collapsing in the 7th century AD. Islam was brought in shortly thereafter by Arabian merchants who crossed the Red Sea. During the 16th century, successive Islamic leaders waged holy wars against Christian Ethiopia; while they failed to convert the Ethiopian highlands, Islam obtained a firm hold on Djibouti. The country then fell under first Ottoman and then Egyptian rule, until the French strolled onto the scene in 1862: they eventually established a successful port at what would become Djibouti City. Independence from France was finally achieved on 27 June 1977 (Djibouti was the last African mainland nation to do so). Since the end of its bloody civil war (1991 to 1994), the country has remained stable.

PEOPLE

Djibouti's population is dominated by the Somali and Afar people, who make up 60 per cent and 35 per cent of the population respectively. The Somali, who occupy southern Djibouti, can be further divided into two clans: the Issa and the Issaqs (the term 'Issa' is often erroneously used to mean all Djiboutian Somalis). The Afar live in the north and are comprised of over 40 tribes, each historically linked to Ethiopia or Eritrea. Small French, Arab, Ethiopian and Italian populations make up the remainder of Djibouti's population. Over 80 per cent of the population live in urban areas, with two thirds of the nation's people living in Djibouti City alone. Almost 95 per cent of Djibouti's inhabitants are Sunni Muslim (although many nomads are not strictly orthodox).

TRADEMARKS

- ○ Port of Djibouti
- ○ Red Sea
- ○ Hostile deserts
- ○ Camels and salt caravans
- ○ Spherical Afar huts
- ○ Use of qat (a mildly intoxicating leaf)

MARKETPLACE

Due to a lack of natural resources and industry, Djibouti's economy is almost entirely dependent on its capital's port, which provides transit services for the region and acts as an international transhipment and refuelling centre. It continues to reap rewards from the Eritrean–Ethiopian conflict as the closure of the Ethiopia–Eritrea border means all Ethiopian foreign trade must go through the port. Services now account for an amazing 80 per cent of GDP. Nevertheless, unemployment still sits around 50 per cent and the nation relies heavily on foreign aid.

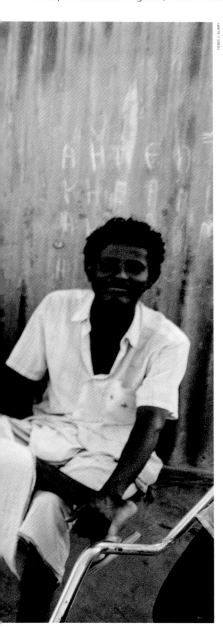

HANDICRAFT – INTRICATE HENNA DESIGNS MAKE EVERY GESTURE A WORK OF ART »

RANDOM FACTS

- Eight tonnes of qat are flown into Djibouti from Ethiopia each day.
- Almost 40 per cent of an average family's expenditure is devoted to procuring qat.
- It's estimated that chewing qat eliminates two months and sixteen days of productivity per worker per year in Djibouti.

NATURAL MOVEMENTS

Thanks to the fact that it sits directly above the meeting point of the diverging African, Somali and Arabian tectonic plates, Djibouti is currently, albeit very slowly (don't cancel your plans!), being ripped apart. The movements have stretched the earth's crust below Djibouti to only two or three kilometres thick (compared to a normal continental crust thickness of 35 to 70 kilometres) and the 'bridge of lava' separating the waters of Ghoubbet al Kharab from Lac Assal has started to collapse. In a few million years Djibouti will be no more, but until then, the volcanoes, sunken plains, salt lakes and fumaroles within this fascinating natural geological laboratory of a nation will be open for business.

IMPORT

- Qat
- Henri de Monfried
- Scuba equipment
- Food and beverages
- Petroleum products
- Most tourist souvenirs

EXPORT

- The waters of Lac Assal and Lac Abbé, courtesy of evaporation
- Monfried's letters of angst
- Henna tattoos
- Afar *fidama* (woven straw mats)
- Traditional Afar or Somali knives
- Coffee (courtesy of Ethiopia)

MYTHS & LEGENDS

Although the bay of Ghoubbet al Kharab is considered one of the best places in the world to dive with whale sharks, its waters are feared by many Afar tribespeople. According to legend, one of the stark islands in these waters was crowned by fire until a horrendous deluge extinguished it one memorable day. Since then, many believe the depths have been patrolled by demons who drag all those who venture onto the water's surface to the bay's dark bottom – hence the name 'Ghoubbet al Kharab', which translates to 'Devil's Cauldron'. To this day, few people fish visit these waters and even fewer set foot on the bay's bleak islands.

SURPRISES

- Despite the abundance and heavenly flavours of the local seafood, most Djiboutians don't care for it.
- Many Afar nomads still file their front teeth into ferocious-looking points.
- It's surprisingly pricey to travel in Djibouti, compared to other African nations.

⌃ THE HIDDEN JEWEL IN A VOLCANO'S PERFECT CONICAL CRATER

ESSENTIAL EXPERIENCES

- Descending to the crystallised shoreline of Lac Assal to watch Afar tribesmen gathering salt
- Lingering on Lac Abbé's ridiculously 'lunar' shoreline
- Searching for a rare Djibouti francolin in the shade of Mt Goda
- Following in the footsteps of nomads trekking the ancient salt route
- Floating in the midst of whale sharks and manta rays while diving in the Gulf of Tadjoura's Ghoubbet al Kharab
- Soaking up the Arab feel of Tadjoura, a whitewashed coastal town fringed with palms

ERITREA

Moulhoulé

Khor Angor

RED SEA

ETHIOPIA

Godoria

Balho

Dorra

As Dorra

Obock

Goda Mountains

Dittilou

Tadjoura

Gulf of Aden

Galafi

Lac Assal

Asa Ragid

⬦ DJIBOUTI CITY

Yoboki

Arta

Hol Hol

Lac Abbé

Ali Sabieh

Ali Addé

Dikhil

SOMALIA (SOMALILAND)

As Eyla

ETHIOPIA

MAP REF // R6

BEST TIME TO VISIT **NOVEMBER TO MID-APRIL**

⌃ A LAC ASSAL SALT MINER

'PLANET OF THE… GOATS'? LAC ABBÉ'S LUNAR LANDSCAPE WAS THE SETTING FOR THE FILM *PLANET OF THE APES* »

A DESERTED MOMENT AT THE CENTRAL MARKET »

PUTTING THE DONKEY BEFORE THE CART? WORK TIME IN DJIBOUTI CITY »

ERITREA

ALTHOUGH ERITREANS ARE CURRENTLY FACING THE WORST POLITICAL AND ECONOMIC CONDITIONS THEY'VE SEEN SINCE THEIR INDEPENDENCE, THEY STILL WELCOME VISITORS WITH OPEN ARMS, PEACEFUL SMILES AND WICKEDLY LOVELY CUPS OF COFFEE.

CAPITAL CITY ASMARA   POPULATION 4.8 MILLION   AREA 121,320 SQ KM   OFFICIAL LANGUAGES TIGRINYA, ARABIC, TIGRE, KUNAMA, AFAR

≫ ROUGH AND READY ALFRESCO IN ASSAB

LANDSCAPE

The eastern sliver of Eritrea, known as Dankalia, marks the northern limit of Africa's famed Rift Valley. The rifting has drastically thinned the earth's crust in this region, causing subsidence – meaning much of the area sits below sea level. Temperatures in Dankalia are extreme, and although it's strangely stunning, little of it resembles planet earth. The central highlands, which run almost north–south, can claim more moderate temperatures, fertile soils and elevations reaching 3018 metres. Lying between the highlands and the Sudanese border are the western lowlands. Although they're well watered by the Gash and Barka Rivers, the lowlands are less fertile than the highlands and therefore much less intensively cultivated.

ON PAPER

○ Michela Wrong's *I Didn't Do It For You* is a compelling and at times comedic account of Eritrea's contemporary history which delves deep into the national psyche and the failure of democracy in the country.
○ Dutch photographer Anne Alders' book *Eritrean Beauty* takes a look at each of Eritrea's nine ethnic groups; the text is by anthropologist Dr J Abbink.

○ *Asmara: Africa's Secret Modernist City*, by Edward Denison, Guang Yu Ren and Naigzy Gebremedhin, is a gorgeous coffee-table book that explores the history of Asmara's remarkable architecture.

MARKETPLACE

The beginning of the 21st century saw Eritrea's economy become one of the world's most restrictive, and now it's in a morass. The state has taken control of all private companies, and power cuts, food shortages, skyrocketing prices and rationing of staples are the order of the day. Most people have to wait in queues at state-run stores to get their monthly ration or buy them on the black market, but Eritreans have refined the art of belt-tightening and suffer in silence.

HISTORY IN A NUTSHELL

Eritrea was part of Ethiopia's Aksumite kingdom around the time of Christ, and hosted one of the greatest ports of the ancient world. The Aksumites introduced Christianity, but their dominance of the Red Sea ended in the 7th century and Islam soon rose to prominence, growing steadily and making great inroads along the coast. The Ottomans arrived in the 16th century and dominated the coast until the mid-

19th century, when Egypt gained control. Egypt's victory was short-lived, however, as the coast quickly fell into first Ethiopian and then Italian hands. Although Ethiopia routed the Italians in 1896, the Italians were able to split off Eritrea as a separate terrority. It became one of Africa's most industrialised colonies – only to collapse after World War II. In 1950 the UN controversially reunited Eritrea and Ethiopia, much to Eritrea's detriment. Happily, after 30 years of fighting for independence, in 1993 Eritrea was granted full sovereignty by Ethiopia's new post–civil war government. That same government went to war with Eritrea seven years later, however, and continued post-war tensions keep the Ethiopia–Eritrea border closed.

SURPRISES

○ Fashionable teenagers in Eritrea have dark blue gums – these 'tattoos' are supposed to make the teeth look whiter. To achieve this, the gums are pricked until they bleed and before being rubbed with charcoal.
○ By 1990 women made up 30 per cent of the Eritrean People's Liberation Front, and 13 per cent of the frontline combatants: some drove tanks, while others commanded battalions.

THE CATCH OF THE DAY IN THE DAHLAK ISLANDS? JAWS »

- The froth atop an Eritrean macchiato is an average of one and a half centimetres thick.
- From 1922 to 1941 a system of discrimination existed in Eritrea that was remarkably similar to the apartheid system of South Africa.
- Sixty-five thousand Eritreans lost their lives fighting for independence between 1961 and 1991.

PEOPLE

Despite Eritrea's petite size, it hosts nine ethnic groups, each with their own language and customs. The Tigrinya, who are largely Orthodox Christian, make up 50 per cent of the population and inhabit the densely populated central highlands. Almost 30 per cent of Eritreans are Tigré – who are mostly Muslim and call the western lowlands home. Inhabiting the coast and the hinterland south of Asmara and Massawa are the Saho, also generally Muslim, who comprise five per cent of the population. The Afar, Muslim nomadic pastoralists, make up another five per cent of the population and inhabit Dankalia. The remainder of Eritrea's populace is made up of Hedareb (2.5 per cent), Bilen (two per cent), Kunama (two per cent), Nara (1.5 per cent) and Rashaida (0.5 per cent).

TRADEMARKS
- Cinquecento taxis
- Marvellous macchiatos
- Asmara's Art Deco architecture
- Polite people
- Conflict with Ethiopia

URBAN SCENE

Asmara is an aberration. The litter-strewn, sprawling ghettos of many developing-world cities and the bleak high-rise office buildings of post-colonial Africa are absent. Instead, Rationalist, Art Deco, Cubist, Expressionist, Futurist and Neoclassical architecture from the Italian era frames lovely tree-lined boulevards. What's more, streetside cafés within these brilliant buildings use vintage Italian coffee machines to whip up marvellously mind-numbing macchiatos, cappuccinos and espressos for prices that would make Starbucks weak at the knees. The city's relaxed pace of life is infectious, and if it weren't for the friendly Eritreans, you'd be forgiven for thinking you were in southern Italy many decades ago. However, look further and you'll notice the queues at food stores and the plaintive whispers about the government and the woeful economy… Asmara is truly a city of pleasure and pain.

IMPORT
- Eritreans forced out of Ethiopia
- Italian cheese and salami
- Military equipment
- UN peacekeepers
- Fiats
- The evening *passeggiata*
- Italian words

EXPORT
- Ethiopians
- Shellfish, snapper and groper
- Salt
- Expelled NGOs
- Free press (it now lacks any)
- Sesame seeds
- Sheep

⌃ THE ERITREAN COMMUTE

ESSENTIAL EXPERIENCES

- **Sipping your second macchiato of the morning in one of Asmara's classic Art Deco cafés**
- **Perusing Massawa's narrow streets, looking past the decay of the remarkable Islamic architecture and absorbing the Arab atmosphere**
- **Getting cosy with the Dahlak Archipelago's colourful corals while diving in the Red Sea**
- **Taking leave from earth to visit the depths of planet Dankalia, a wasteland of stark splendour**
- **Making a modern-day pilgrimage to the mountain monastery of Debre Libanos**

SUDAN
SAUDI ARABIA
Nakfa
Afabet
Dahlak Islands
RED SEA
Agordat
Keren
Massawa
YEMEN
ASMARA
Adulis
Teseney
Barentu
Qohaito
Metera
Dankalia
ETHIOPIA
Assab
DJIBOUTI
MAP REF // Q5

BEST TIME TO VISIT **OCTOBER TO MAY**

⌃ A WOMAN PERCHED ON HER CAMEL, NEAR ADI KEYIH

FRANCES LINZEE GORDON // LONELY PLANET IMAGES

TIM DIRVEN // PANOS

ROUND-BALL FEVER IN A SCHOOL PLAYGROUND IN KEREN «

LIFE IN THE FAST LANE AT A BOWLING ALLEY «

THE TREASURE TROVE OF ART DECO ARCHITECTURE IN ASMARA IS ONE OF THE MORE PLEASANT COLONIAL LEGACIES «

SOMALIA & SOMALILAND

LAWLESS SOMALIA IS CURRENTLY PLAGUED BY CIVIL WAR, BUT AMID CHAOS, THERE IS A SUCCESS STORY: SOMALILAND, WHICH, LIKE A PHOENIX, HAS RISEN FROM THE ASHES.

CAPITAL CITY MOGADISHU (SOMALIA), HARGEISA (SOMALILAND)   **POPULATION** 5.4 MILLION (SOMALIA), 3.5 MILLION (SOMALILAND)   **AREA** 500,060 SQ KM (SOMALIA), 137,600 SQ KM (SOMALILAND)   **OFFICIAL LANGUAGE** SOMALI

LANDSCAPE

The terrain in Somalia and Somaliland is mostly desert or semidesert. There are three main topographical features: a mountainous highland region in the north, dominated by the Gollis Mountains; a relatively barren, hot and humid coastal region in the south; and a sweeping area of rich rainy-season pasture, prone to overgrazing and desertification. Serious drought continues to plague the country's south. With thousands of miles of coastline, Somalia has some of the longest beaches in the world.

HISTORY IN A NUTSHELL

Somalis have been subject to a strong Arabic influence since the 7th century, but in 1888 the country was divided among the European powers. The French got the area around Djibouti, Britain got much of the north, and Italy got Puntland and the south. It wasn't until 1960 that Somaliland, Puntland and southern Somalia were united – and after years of on-off civil war Somaliland broke away and unilaterally declared independence in 1991. A UN mission led by the US in 1992 wasn't able to restore stability in southern Somalia: factional fighting and anarchy followed. In 1998 Puntland also declared itself an autonomous state. Despite the setting up of a transitional government in 2000 and the election of a transitional president in 2004, the situation has been deteriorating. In 2006 Islamist militia defeated a US-sponsored alliance of warlords, which fuelled fears that southern Somalia would become 'Talibanised'.

The only reasonably stable (and safe) entity in Somalia currently is the self-proclaimed Republic of Somaliland – though its independence isn't formally recognised by any other government.

PEOPLE

All Somalis hail from the same tribe, which is divided into four main clans and loads of subclans. The clan in particular and genealogy in general are hugely important to Somalis, and interclan rivalry has fuelled decades of conflict. Well over a million Somalis, refugees from the civil war, are scattered across Europe, North America and the Middle East. All Somalis are Muslim.

TRADEMARKS

- Civil war
- The self-proclaimed Republic of Somaliland
- Warlords
- Narcotic qat leaves
- Secluded beaches

MARKETPLACE

Somalia remains desperately poor, as the ongoing clan rivalries and civil disturbances hamper development. Agriculture is the most important sector: livestock farming accounts for about 40 per cent of GDP and about 65 per cent of export earnings. Contraband, smuggling and overseas remittances from the Somali diaspora also play a key role. Somaliland's only asset is its port at Berbera, which is used by Ethiopia, its powerful landlocked neighbour.

RANDOM FACTS

- The daily cost of a gang of armed guards in Mogadishu is about US$500 each (negotiable).
- The daily cost of an armed bodyguard in Somaliland is US$15 (without meals).
- Artillery pieces, ammunition for high-calibre guns and landmines are all for barter at Bakara Market.
- Somaliland claims to have 10.4 million goats, 5.6 million sheep and 5.5 million camels.

NATURAL BEAUTY

Unfortunately, the civil war that's been raging for more than 15 years has overshadowed Somalia's great natural wonders. There are thousands of miles of pristine beaches along the Gulf of Aden and the Indian Ocean. The islands off Zeila, close to the Djibouti border, are also completely unspoilt and ablaze with technicolour tropical fish. The wild expanses of the Sheekh Mountains have a rugged beauty and afford stunning views over the coast, as far as Berbera.

IMPORT

- Kalashnikovs
- Livestock
- Mobile phones
- A parliament (in Somaliland)
- Tonnes of qat

EXPORT

- Kalashnikovs
- Al-Qaeda cells
- Refugees
- The US Armed Forces

ESSENTIAL EXPERIENCES

- **Ambling down the streets of Mogadishu in Somalia, the former 'Pearl of the Indian Ocean', some day when peace and order are restored**
- **Haggling over jewellery priced by the gram at the lively gold market in Hargeisa (Somaliland)**
- **Nursing a soft drink, feasting on fresh fish and relaxing on white-sand beaches in Berbera (Somaliland)**
- **Feeling like a National Geographic explorer while speculating on Somalia's mysterious past at the Las Geel archaeological site**

MAP REF // S7

BEST TIME TO VISIT OCTOBER TO MARCH

A WEIRD, WILD PART OF SOMALIA – CHECKPOINTS AND DEER (A NATIONAL SYMBOL) EVERYWHERE »

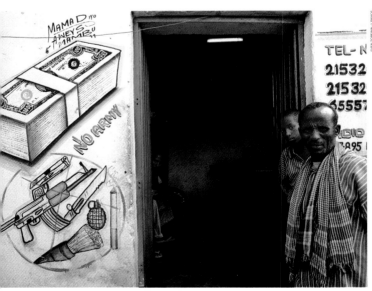

THE BUREAU DE CHANGE RULES: NO SMOKING, NO QAT AND LEAVE YOUR WEAPONS AT THE DOOR »

THE DESERTED 'GREEN LINE' IN MOGADISHU – A NO-MAN'S LAND DIVIDING NORTH FROM SOUTH

TEXT MATT PHILLIPS

KENYA

MORE THAN JUST THE MAASAI AND THE MARA'S SAFARI SAVANNAS, KENYA IS A COMPELLING NATION OF DIVERSE CULTURES, UNEARTHLY RIFT VALLEY LANDSCAPES AND SULTRY SWAHILI SHORES.

CAPITAL CITY NAIROBI   POPULATION 34.7 MILLION   AREA 582,650 SQ KM   OFFICIAL LANGUAGES SWAHILI, ENGLISH

LANDSCAPE

Kenya straddles more than just the equator. Its range of landscapes is truly staggering: from the north's hostile deserts and Mt Kenya's glaciated peaks to the dramatic depths of the Rift Valley and the sultry shores of the Indian Ocean and Lake Victoria. The diverse topography and consequent climatic conditions have endowed Kenya with an impressive array of flora and fauna – there are five Unesco Biosphere Reserves in Kenya alone (as many as in all of Southern Africa).

HISTORY IN A NUTSHELL

Kenya has seen its share of footsteps, including what may have been our ancestors' first attempts to walk upright some 6.1 million years ago. During the last 1000 years, Kenya's present-day tribes migrated in from other regions across Africa. The coast was just as busy, seeing a succession of outsiders from Arabia, Persia, Portugal and Britain step ashore and exert influence between the 8th and 19th centuries. The Maasai, weakened by civil war, finally succumbed to British settlement inland in the late 19th century – it wasn't until almost 80 years later, in 1963, that Kenya shed Britain's colonial yoke. Since that time Kenya's

government, though a pillar of stability, has been constantly eroded by corruption. There was a glimpse of hope after Kibaki's presidential win in 2002, but corruption scandals have started to crop up again.

TRADEMARKS

○ Safaris
○ Leaping and oh-so-colourful Maasai warriors
○ Lounging lions
○ Acacia trees punctuating savanna plains
○ Nairobbery

PEOPLE

Kenya's population is dominated by six major ethnic groups: Kikuyu (22 per cent), Luhya (14 per cent), Luo (13 per cent), Kalenjin (12 per cent), Kamba (11 per cent), Kisii (six per cent) and Meru (six per cent). Another 65 or so tribes comprise 15 per cent of the population, while Asians, Europeans and Arabs make up the remaining one per cent. Unsurprisingly, a plethora of tribal dialects are spoken as well as the official languages of Swahili and English. Almost 80 per cent of Kenyans are Christians, with the remaining population split evenly between Islam and traditional animist beliefs.

MARKETPLACE

Agriculture employs 75 per cent of the population and the nation is heavily reliant on the industry's export of tea, coffee and horticultural products. Plunging global commodity prices have reduced export earnings, however, and have unfortunately caused Kenyans' average annual income to drop below US$300. These economic woes mean that for Kenya, development is dependent on foreign aid – which is a hefty US$450 million per year. Kenya's government budget is US$3.88 billion: 1200 per cent of Niger's, 5.5 per cent of South Africa's and 0.4 per cent of the UK's.

RANDOM FACTS

○ The oldest primary school student in Kenya is 84 years old.
○ Over 30 varieties of cheese are produced at Eldoret's cheese factory.
○ The literal translation of the Swahili word for 'bald man', *mzee kipara,* is actually 'mosquito airport'.
○ A single horticultural farm in Naivasha supplied Europe with around a million roses for Valentine's Day in 2005.

MIRACLES 2000 IMPACT
UHURU PARK
BISHOP JOE SYMMON
SUNDAY, FEB. 20 2.00 p.m.
THE BLIND SEE
THE DEAF HEAR
THE LAME WALK
CAPTIVES ARE SET FREE
TELL THE DEVIL: THE RULES HAVE CHANGED!
DIAL-A-PRAYER 71-98-99
CHAPEL — VALLEY ROAD
8.00 AM, 10.00 AM, 4.00 PM.
ACHIEVERS CHAPEL — VALLEY ROAD
SUNDAY WORSHIP 8.00 AM, 10.00 AM, 4.00

≫ SAMBURU MEN AND WOMEN FEEL THE RHYTHM IN LORUBAE

≫ GIRAFFES CROSS THE SAVANNA UNDER A COAL-BLACK SKY

≫ CHILDREN FROM THE TOWN OF BURA DRESSED IN STYLE

A BLUE-TINGED VIEW ACROSS THE ROOFTOPS OF HARAMBEE AVENUE, LAMU ≫

A CHEETAH GIVES HER CUBS DEPORTMENT LESSONS, MASAI MARA NATIONAL RESERVE ≫

FROM THE TRAVELLER

It's January 5, midday. The sun has reached its highest point in the sky. On Diani Beach you see the Maasai, natives of Kenya, walking on bright, fine sands to their home village. As a rule, the Maasai don't like being photographed. You've only got a second to take a good picture. Well, here you are, experiencing an 'endless feeling', as my friend so well put it.

SIIRI LADVA // ESTONIA

SURPRISES

o Kenya has an adult literacy rate of 85.5 per cent.
o Kenya's glaciers are only a stone's throw from the equator.
o Nairobi has massive skyscrapers and a cosmopolitan population.

NATURAL BEAUTY

The Rift Valley, with its spectacular serrated escarpments, volcanic landscapes, ochre soils, grassy plains and soda lakes, is undoubtedly one of the most stunning sights on the continent. And although it is 696 metres shorter than Mt Kilimanjaro, Mt Kenya is easily East Africa's most dramatic mountain, thanks to its voluptuous valleys, craggy cliffs and steep summits. The single most striking image in Kenya, however, must be Mt Kulal's shattered purple lava fields set against the backdrop of the 'Jade Sea' (Lake Turkana).

URBAN SCENE

Lamu town is a remnant of the Swahili culture that formerly dominated the entire Indian Ocean coast. The winding streets, carved wooden doors and traditional houses of the town are simply captivating. Few experiences compare with taking a slow stroll down its narrow lanes immersed in the sights, sounds and smells of everyday Lamu life: the mysterious rustle of bui-bui-clad women, the echoing of unseen donkeys' hooves, the crackle of palm trees being jostled in the wind, the slow and serene bobbing of dhows, the aroma of seafood and the changing textures of a hundred coral and plaster walls.

WILD THINGS

Conjure up any African safari image, and Kenya's wildlife can provide in spades. The Big Five (lions, leopards, rhinos, elephants and buffaloes) loom large in the country, as do hundreds of other fascinating birds and beasts. One look at the shores of Lake Nakuru, painted pink with flamboyant flamingos, and it becomes clear just how prolific Kenya's birdlife is too. It's likely that visitors will leave the country having garnered a few new favourite animals; gerenuks – an elegant long-necked antelope – are a charming candidate.

IMPORT

↗ Maasai and Samburu tribes
↗ British colonial farmers
↗ Japanese minibuses
↗ A large Indian community
↗ Rail transportation

EXPORT

↖ Safari (it's Swahili for 'journey')
↖ Tea and coffee
↖ Fulfilled safari dreams
↖ *Lamu kikoi* (sarong-like wraps)
↖ Exotic flowers
↖ World-champion runners
↖ Maasai bangles

MODERN-DAY LEGEND

Recently the Kenyan government legislated to guarantee free primary education for all its citizens, a move that was universally applauded. One great-grandfather, Kimani Nganga Maruge, clapped louder than most. What the local schoolteacher thought when she saw this cane-wielding, knobbly-kneed 84-year-old sitting in the front row (he was hard of hearing after all) is anyone's guess. Decked out in the school uniform, shorts and all, with striped knee-socks pulled high, Mr Maruge was there to attain his long-overdue education and he wouldn't let anyone convince him otherwise. His stated purpose was to learn to read so that he could study the Bible and confirm his suspicions that his preacher wasn't actually following it! Mr Maruge has since been made prefect and has achieved some of the top marks in his class.

ECOTOURISM

While other countries have been losing the battle to preserve wildlife by separating animals and humans, some Kenyan communities are increasing animal populations (and their own standard of living) by embracing peaceful cohabitation. These communities consider wildlife a natural resource and protect its wellbeing both by combating poaching and by modifying their herding activities to minimise human–animal conflict and environmental damage. They also run magical ecolodges, whose income provides funds for their education, health and humanitarian projects. If these brave projects continue to prove that humans and wildlife are able not only to live in the same environment, but actually thrive in a mutually beneficial relationship, an amazing precedent will be set for the rest of Africa.

ESSENTIAL EXPERIENCES

o **Witnessing the glorious spectacle of rush-hour, wildebeest-style, during their annual migration at Masai Mara National Reserve**

o **Thanking the heavens for the sight of Lake Turkana and thanking your lucky stars your tyres survived to get you there**

o **Chilling, drinking and dhow-tripping around the fantastic Lamu archipelago**

o **Holding a frozen Kenyan flag in your frozen hands atop the frozen summit of Point Lenana on Mt Kenya, a mere 16 kilometres from the equator**

o **Sharing a smile and some shade with northern Kenya's most captivating tribes in Loyangalani**

o **Realising zebras do change their stripes in Samburu National Reserve, home to the rare Grevy's species**

o **Strolling the narrow streets of Mombasa Old Town**

MARK DAFFEY // LONELY PLANET IMAGES

≈ COLOURFUL BACKDROP FOR A WAIT AT A LAMU BUS STATION

MAP REF // Q8

BEST TIME TO VISIT **JANUARY TO FEBRUARY**

A MAASAI WARRIOR ON THE LAIKIPIA PLAIN, WITH MT KENYA DOMINATING THE HORIZON »

THE PEOPLE OF KIBERA FOCUSING ON THE IMPORTANT THINGS IN LIFE »

BEST FRIENDS FOREVER: POKOT BOY AND CAMEL »

UGANDA

IDI AMIN IS ALL MOST PEOPLE KNOW ABOUT THE PLACE, BUT THAT'S THEIR LOSS – UGANDA IS AFRICA CONDENSED, WITH THE BEST OF EVERYTHING THE CONTINENT HAS TO OFFER PACKED INTO ONE SMALL BUT STUNNING COUNTRY.

CAPITAL CITY KAMPALA   **POPULATION** 28.2 MILLION   **AREA** 236,040 SQ KM   **OFFICIAL LANGUAGE** ENGLISH

LANDSCAPE

Green! That covers most of Uganda and its landscape of rolling hills and verdant fields. To the southwest, the hills become mountains and rise to the jagged Virunga volcanoes on the Rwandan and Democratic Republic of Congo (DRC) borders. Water is another dominant feature in the landscape; the mighty Nile begins its journey in Jinja and cuts across the country. Much of the north is a world apart, however: arid desert and scrubland getting steadily more desolate as they merge with the mountains of southern Sudan.

TRADEMARKS

- Its nickname, 'the pearl of Africa'
- Source of the White Nile
- Idi Amin
- Murchison Falls
- The Mountains of the Moon (Rwenzori Mountains)

HISTORY IN A NUTSHELL

Uganda had a sophisticated political structure before the arrival of the Brits, thanks to the Buganda kingdom. Unfortunately, after independence Uganda found itself consumed by intertribal conflict. In January 1971, then-prime minister Milton Obote was overthrown in the coup that first brought Idi Amin to the world's attention. Amin's rule was characterised by thuggery and intimidation, and as many as 300,000 Ugandans lost their lives under his watch. He also destroyed the economy by expelling the Asian population in 1972, and by the end of his regime was proclaiming himself 'King of Scotland'. His decision to invade Tanzania brought about his own demise: the counter-attack saw him ousted from power in 1979.

The new dawn was short-lived, though, as a series of governments came and went. Finally, in 1986, Yoweri Museveni emerged victorious to usher in a new era. The National Resistance Movement abolished the political parties which had fractured the country along tribal lines, and set about rebuilding the economy. Still, a series of guerrilla conflicts continued to simmer, most notably those with the brutal Lord's Resistance Army (LRA) in the north. Uganda also found itself embroiled in the conflict in the DRC, Africa's first great war.

PEOPLE

Uganda has a pick'n'mix of tribal groups. Lake Kyoga is a natural boundary between the southern Bantu-speaking groups and the northern Nilotic groups. Bantu tribes include the Basoga, Bagisu and the politically influential Buganda; the Acholi, near the Sudanese border, are the most prominent Nilotic tribe.

MARKETPLACE

Before Amin, Uganda had a reasonable economy, thanks in part to the vibrant Asian-owned industrial sector. Almost two decades of violence, strife and mismanagement meant that the economy was in tatters, though, by the time Museveni came to power. He boldly invited the Asian exiles to reclaim their businesses and the economy subsequently emerged as one of the shining lights in Africa during much of the 1990s. Agriculture remains the driving force: important cash crops include cotton, tea and tobacco.

RANDOM FACTS

- Winston Churchill was one of the first 'tourists' to visit Uganda way back in 1907 and it was he who famously called it the 'pearl of Africa'.
- Idi Amin converted to Islam in the 1970s and spent his last years in luxurious exile in Saudi Arabia.
- There are only about 650 mountain gorillas left in the wild, half of them in Uganda – that's just one for every 10 million humans.

≫ A STICK IS THE ESSENTIAL ACCESSORY IN MURCHISON FALLS NATIONAL PARK

≫ WALKING IN THE CLOUDS: THE GIANT SENECIO FOREST FLOURISHES AT 3800 METRES

≫ WALL ART, KAMPALA

KICKING BACK IN THE CABBAGE PATCH ON MARKET DAY, BUNYONYI LAKE «

MAIN STREET, KAMPALA – THE NORMALLY CHAOTIC TRAFFIC THINS OUT «

SIPI FALLS, AT ONE OF THE TRIBUTARIES OF THE NILE «

NATURAL BEAUTY

Take a road trip out of the capital and you'll soon realise why Winston called Uganda the pearl of Africa. The country is so fertile, you almost feel that if you dropped something from your pocket a dozen of it would spring up from the earth. The landscape also has great contrasts, from the towering green volcanoes in the southwest, to the ochre rock bluffs of the northeast. Simply breathtaking.

URBAN SCENE

Kampala is chaotic but somehow charming. The city is spread over seven hills like Rome, but the comparisons end there. Nakasero is the dynamic heart of the city, boasting a sprinkling of skyscrapers and plenty of action. For a glimpse of 'the real Africa', though, head south to the densely packed taxi and bus parks, where it's a miracle that anything can move! By night the action moves out to the suburbs: for the brave of heart, Gaba Road rumbles on until the morning.

IMPORT

↗ Vehicles
↗ Asian business savvy
↗ Rhinos, to replace those wiped out in the bad old days
↗ Adrenaline-seekers and adventurers
↗ Refugees from Sudan and the DRC

EXPORT

↖ Coffee
↖ Electricity to Kenya
↖ Tea
↖ Cobalt
↖ Guerrilla know-how (think Kagame in Rwanda, Kabila in Congo)

WILD THINGS

Uganda's wildlife was decimated during the long years of civil strife. Rhinos were wiped out and other mammals suffered a huge drop in numbers – many went into fighters' cooking pots. The war was not all bad news, however: it did give the previously overpopulated national parks time to recover. Despite the devastation, Uganda remains the primate capital of the world, with mountain gorillas and chimpanzees the star attractions. The country is also drawing bird-watchers in increasing numbers, as it plays host to more than 1000 species – including the most sought after of all, the shoebill stork.

SURPRISES

○ The number of people that can squeeze into a *matatu* (minibus)
○ That Jinja is fast catching up with Victoria Falls as Africa's adventure centre
○ Kampala's soaring skyline

ECOTOURISM

As visitor numbers rise, ecotourism is developing in Uganda, and many of the new camps and lodges are being designed with environmental concerns to the fore. There are also many community tourism initiatives in the country, seeking to help local communities benefit from the tourism in their midst.

IN ART

The Last King of Scotland by Giles Foden chronicles the experience of Idi Amin's personal doctor, as he slowly finds himself becoming the dictator's confidant. In 2005 a Hollywood film crew came to town to shoot the big-screen version of the book, which eventually won Forest Whitaker a Best Actor Oscar for his role as 'Big Daddy'. *The Abyssinian Chronicles,* by Moses Isegawa, tells the story of a young Ugandan coming of age during the turbulent years of Idi Amin and the civil war.

FUTURE DIRECTION

Long a darling of international donors, President Museveni's U-turn to seek a third term in office and his subsequent victory has cast a cloud in some quarters over his excellent record. Unflattering comparisons were made by some with the Robert Mugabes of this world. Politics aside, the economy remains fragile. However, tourism is likely to be a wild card when the word spreads that Uganda has the wildlife without the masses, and offers some of the most accessible adventures in the continent of Africa.

↟ FIVE KILOMETRES ABOVE IT ALL ON ALEXANDRA PEAK, MOUNT STANLEY

↟ 'TAME YOUR THIRST!' AT THE PEOPLE'S BAR ON BUGALA ISLAND

ESSENTIAL EXPERIENCES

○ **Riding the wild, wild waters at the source of the Nile, which has some of the best white-water rafting in the world**

○ **Penetrating the Impenetrable Forest at Bwindi National Park to get up close and personal with the mountain gorillas**

○ **Trekking the mystical Mountains of the Moon, one of the most challenging yet rewarding hikes on the continent**

○ **Enjoying life in the slow lane at Lake Bunyoni, in its otherworldly landscape of terraced hillsides and secluded bays**

○ **Joining the Kampala nightshift to experience some of the best bars and clubs in the region**

MAP REF // P8

BEST TIME TO VISIT JUNE TO SEPTEMBER

ICONIC AFRICA – A UGANDAN GIRL CARRYING WATER ⪢

GGABA FISHERMEN SAY THE FISH ARE SHRINKING ALONG WITH LAKE VICTORIA ⪢

RWANDA

A BEAUTIFUL YET BRUTALISED COUNTRY, RWANDA IS KNOWN TO THE WORLD FOR ALL THE WRONG REASONS, BUT SHATTERS VISITORS' PRECONCEPTIONS WITH ITS OUTRAGEOUS NATURAL BEAUTY, WARM AND WELCOMING LOCALS AND LEGENDARY MOUNTAIN GORILLAS.

CAPITAL CITY KIGALI   POPULATION 8.7 MILLION   AREA 26,340 SQ KM   OFFICIAL LANGUAGES KINYARWANDA, FRENCH, ENGLISH

⌃ OPEN WIDE! A MOTHER AND CHILD FROM THE 'SUSA' GROUP OF GORILLAS STUDIED BY DIAN FOSSEY

LANDSCAPE

It's not known as *le pays des milles collines* (land of a thousand hills) for nothing. Rwanda's hills stretch into the infinite horizon in every direction, making bus travel akin to a dose of the bends. To the west is the stunning shoreline of Lake Kivu, with its hidden bays, plunging cliffs and secret beaches. In the east, the hills finally trail off towards Tanzania and the land turns to the grassy plains and acacias of Akagera National Park.

HISTORY IN A NUTSHELL

For most people, Rwanda is synonymous with the tribal warfare between the Hutu and Tutsi, which culminated in the genocide of 1994. The original inhabitants, the Twa Pygmies, were muscled out by Hutu farmers from the south and Tutsi herders from the north from the 16th century onwards. The Belgian colonialists favoured the Tutsi during most of their rule (which began after World War I), but switched allegiance in the run-up to independence in 1962, setting the stage for decades of conflict and brutality to follow.

Relations between the two tribes remained tense throughout the 1970s and '80s, and periodic massacres were common. The tinder box finally ignited in the early 1990s when the Rwandan Patriotic Front (RPF) invaded from Uganda, seeking to overthrow the government.

As peace talks dragged on, a minority of extremists in the Hutu-dominated government decided to carry out a sort of 'final solution' to the Tutsi 'problem'. Both the Rwandan and Burundian presidents were killed in April 1994 in a plane crash – it's believed they were most likely shot down by Hutu extremists. In the following 100 days of bloodlust, more than 800,000 people lost their lives while the world stood by and watched.

An international tribunal was established in Arusha, Tanzania to try those responsible for the genocide, and many have now been convicted. In 1996 the new RPF government also undertook several lengthy incursions into the Democratic Republic of Congo (DRC) in an effort to flush out extremists sheltering there – but by doing so it helped spark the long civil wars in the DRC which subsequently claimed nearly four million lives.

More than a decade on from the genocide, Rwanda is finally at peace, and though there's still a way to go to clear the backlog of trials, many of those who were involved are either behind bars or have been reintegrated into their communities.

PEOPLE

Tiny as it is, Rwanda is one of the most densely populated countries in Africa, with more than 300 people per square kilometre. More than 80 per cent of Rwandans are Hutu; Tutsis make up more than 15 per cent. Less than one per cent of the population is Twa Pygmy.

TRADEMARKS

- ○ Gorillas in the mist
- ○ The Virunga volcanoes
- ○ *Le pays des milles collines*
- ○ Arguably the furthest source of the Nile
- ○ Primus beer

MARKETPLACE

The 1994 genocide in Rwanda not only took its toll on the population, it dealt a dire blow to the small economy. Tourism was one of the biggest earners before the genocide, thanks to the magical mountain gorillas, but for obvious reasons it ceased for a period afterward. Fortunately, it's once again playing its part in balancing the books. Agriculture remains the major employer, however, with about 90 per cent of the population living off the land. Coffee and tea are big business, along with pyrethrum, a natural insecticide.

YOU WANT TOMATOES? WE'VE GOT TOMATOES (KIGALI MARKET) »

THE LAND OF A THOUSAND HILLS ALSO DOES A PRETTY GOOD WATERFALL (NYUNGWE FOREST NATIONAL PARK) »

○ Rwandan president Paul Kagame helped propel President Museveni of Uganda to power. Before he launched the liberation movement in Rwanda, Kagame had been first a guerrilla commander and then head of the Ugandan army while living in exile there.
○ Mountain gorillas are the largest primates in the world – adult males regularly weigh in at more than 200 kilograms.

NATURAL BEAUTY
Small but perfectly formed, Rwanda can compete with the big boys of Africa in beauty. Almost every square inch of the country is farmed and terraces have been etched, impossibly, into the most precipitous hillsides, where farmers scratch out a living on slopes as steep as ski runs.

URBAN SCENE
Kigali, set on its series of rolling hills, is on the comeback trail. Though it was badly damaged during the genocide – to say nothing of the thousands of residents butchered in the streets – the city is back on its feet once more. Much of the hustle and bustle of daily life takes place in the city centre, but by night it's another story: the action moves to the hip suburbs of Kiyovu and Kacyiru. Elegant restaurants, happening bars and big nightclubs make this city more fun by night than by day.

WILD THINGS
It's all about the mountain gorillas. One of the world's rarest and most captivating mammals, they are also some of our closest relatives in the wild. A gorilla encounter on the forested slopes of the Virungas is one of the most magical experiences on earth – with no bars, no windows separating us, we are privileged guests in their domain. The late Dian Fossey studied the Susa group, consisting of over 35 individuals living on the slopes of Kalisimbi.

IMPORT
↗ Petrol
↗ NGOs
↗ Returning exiles
↗ Refugees from the DRC and Burundi
↗ Brochettes and frites from Belgium

EXPORT
↖ Coffee
↖ Pyrethrum
↖ Primus beer
↖ Conflict (to the DRC)
↖ Optimism about reconciliation

FUTURE DIRECTION
The country has travelled a remarkably long way on the road to reconciliation, and is probably in better shape than anyone could have imagined back in 1994 after the genocide. President Kagame has been keen to promote a new Rwandan identity, free from the tribal divisions of the past: no Hutu, no Tutsi, only Rwandans. It may sound rather idealistic, but realistically it's the only way forward for this traumatised country.

⌃ OUT FOR A STROLL IN RWANDA

⌃ A COLOMBUS FINDS A COMFORTABLE NOOK

⌃ KIGALI IS ON THE COMEBACK TRAIL

ESSENTIAL EXPERIENCES

○ **Scaling the slopes of the Virunga volcanoes to encounter gorillas in the mist**
○ **Coming face-to-face with the horrors of the past at the Kigali Memorial Centre, a haunting genocide museum in the capital**
○ **Checking out Rwanda's very own Costa del Kivu at Gisenyi, with its unspoilt beaches and clear waters**
○ **Penetrating the lush canopy of the Nyungwe Forest, home to chimpanzees and huge troops of colobus monkeys**
○ **Settling into a garden bar in Kigali, ordering a large bottle of Primus beer and taking in a sunset over Rwanda's other 999 hills**

DEMOCRATIC REPUBLIC OF THE CONGO (ZAIRE)
UGANDA
Parc National des Volcans
● Ruhengeri
● Byumba
● Gisenyi
Lake Kivu
✪ KIGALI
TANZANIA
● Kibuye
● Gitarama
● Kibungo
Parc National Nyungwe Forest
● Cyangugu
Butare ●
BURUNDI

MAP REF // O9

BEST TIME TO VISIT JUNE TO SEPTEMBER

IN THE COMPANY OF THE DEAD AT THE KANYAMANZA GENOCIDE MEMORIAL ≫

EERIE PRIMEVAL-LOOKING FOREST IN THE VIRUNGA MOUNTAINS ≫

PLAYING VOLLEYBALL – AND CATCH-UP – AT A SCHOOL FOR STUDENTS WHO MISSED CLASSES DURING THE GENOCIDE ≫

BURUNDI

BACK ON THE MAP AFTER A LONG CIVIL WAR, BURUNDI'S SMALL SIZE HIDES SOME SURPRISES, INCLUDING A FREEWHEELIN' CAPITAL, BROCHURE-WORTHY BEACHES AND HAUNTING LANDSCAPES.

CAPITAL CITY BUJUMBURA **POPULATION** 8.1 MILLION **AREA** 27,830 SQ KM **OFFICIAL LANGUAGES** KIRUNDI, FRENCH

LANDSCAPE

Rwanda may be the 'land of a thousand hills', but Burundi isn't far behind. The north is a stunning landscape of dramatic peaks and deep valleys, best experienced on the bus between Bujumbura and Kigali. To the southwest, it levels out along the shores of lovely Lake Tanganyika, home to fishing villages and blissful beaches.

HISTORY IN A NUTSHELL

The original Burundians were the Twa Pygmies, but they were soon squeezed out by bigger groups. First came the Hutu farmers around AD 1000, and then later the Tutsi, pastoral cattle herders from the north. Relations between the two were reasonable until the Belgian colonial authorities began to classify the population by ethnicity. After independence, power was concentrated in the hands of the Tutsi minority under a succession of military governments, and thousands died in periodic purges.

In 1993 full-scale civil war broke out between the Tutsi-dominated government and Hutu rebel groups and lingered until 2005, claiming about 300,000 lives. Today, Burundi is enjoying peace for the first time in a generation.

TRADEMARKS

- Lake Tanganyika's best beaches
- The southernmost source of the Nile
- Les Tambourinaires dancers
- *La Pierre de Livingstone et Stanley*, where the infamous 'Dr Livingstone, I presume?' encounter may have taken place

PEOPLE

About 84 per cent of Burundi's population is Hutu. About 14 per cent are Tutsi and just one per cent are Twa Pygmy.

MARKETPLACE

Burundi's tiny economy has been ravaged by almost 15 years of civil war and five decades of ethnic division. It's overwhelmingly agricultural, with 90 per cent of the population working the fields. Coffee and tea are two of the biggest commodities.

NATURAL BEAUTY

Choose from majestic mountains in the north and glorious beaches in the south on the shores of Lake Tanganyika. Many of the mountains are carved with gravity-defying terraces all the way down to the deep valleys below, on which farmers somehow eke out a living.

RANDOM FACTS

- The neighbouring DRC is more than 80 times the size of little old Burundi.
- President Pierre Nkurunziza was a physical education teacher and rebel leader before he became head of state.
- Burundi still has more than 200,000 displaced persons from the civil war, including refugees in Tanzania and the Democratic Republic of Congo (DRC).

URBAN SCENE

'Bujumbura'… the name just rumbas off the tongue, doesn't it? Burundi's urban scene begins and ends in 'Buj', as locals call their capital. Though it was comatose during the long civil war, this once-charming city is waking up once more, and even the 34-year-long curfew has finally been lifted. With restaurants that wouldn't feel out of place in Brussels, underground nightclubs that rumble on till dawn and the mighty Lake Tanganyika as a backdrop, Buj could soon be back on the map as one of Africa's hidden gems.

SURPRISES

- Bujumbura International Airport looks like something that was lifted straight out of Tatooine, Luke Skywalker's home in the original *Star Wars* movie.
- Burundi recently banned the use of real Christmas trees as a method of combatting its dramatic deforestation problem.

FUTURE DIRECTION

The future is bright in Burundi for the first time in living memory. Peace has come to this beautiful yet blighted land, and the population has embraced its democratic freedoms with abandon. The new government is a delicate balance of Hutu and Tutsi, and is attempting to govern for all Burundians, rather than solely for the interests of one ethnic group or another. Look out for a trickle of travellers to arrive in the country over the next few years, as the word gets out.

ESSENTIAL EXPERIENCES

- **Wining and dining in surprising style before dancing the night away in Bujumbura, a city that is bouncing back**
- **The Bahamas? No, it's Burundi – checking out the white sand beaches of Lake Tanganyika, some of the best in landlocked Africa**
- **Seeking the source of the Nile with a pilgrimage to Burundi's very own pyramid, which marks what's claimed to be the southernmost source of the world's longest river**
- **Experiencing the novelty of being one of the only tourists in the country**

MAP REF // O9

BEST TIME TO VISIT JUNE TO SEPTEMBER

A TRIBAL DANCER LETS THE RHYTHM MOVE HIM IN NINGA »

THESE INNOCENT-LOOKING MUSHROOMS ARE ACTUALLY HARSH FORCED RELOCATION CAMPS »

IT'S NOT SOME KIND OF UNUSUAL AND DRAMATIC HEADDRESS – IT'S A LOAD OF CARROTS »

TEXT MARY FITZPATRICK

TANZANIA

WILDEBEEST STAMPEDING ACROSS THE PLAINS MIX WITH THE SIGHTS AND SCENTS OF THE ZANZIBAR ARCHIPELAGO FOR AN UNBEATABLE COMBINATION IN THIS CLASSIC AFRICAN NATION.

CAPITAL CITY DAR ES SALAAM   LEGISLATIVE CAPITAL DODOMA   POPULATION 37.5 MILLION   AREA 945,090 SQ KM   OFFICIAL LANGUAGES SWAHILI, ENGLISH

LANDSCAPE
On its jagged course down the continent, the Great Rift Valley cuts a giant swath across Tanzania, leaving in its wake volcanoes and collapsed volcanoes, dramatic escarpment scenery around Lake Manyara, and deep blue lakes on Tanzania's western fringes. The rest of the country has its share of stunning landscapes as well, with the sublime coastal region rising to verdant hill ranges in the northeast and southwest. In addition to the continent's highest mountain (Kilimanjaro), Tanzania has its lowest point (Lake Tanganyika's floor).

HISTORY IN A NUTSHELL
Kicking up the dust alongside humanity's earliest ancestors have been a succession of other arrivals, including nomadic hunter-gatherers, and immigrants from Ethiopia, Sudan and the Niger Delta. While they were jostling for turf in the interior, traders from Arabia and Persia came ashore on monsoon winds, mixing with the coastal population and creating Swahili culture. From the late 15th century, a stream of European adventurers and missionaries joined the picture. After rather fitful German and British colonial ventures, an independent Tanganyika emerged in 1962 (later to join with Zanzibar as Tanzania) under the leadership of Julius Nyerere. Since independence, Tanzania has distinguished itself for its tolerance and stability among often volatile neighbours, and today is one of the continent's stars.

TRADEMARKS
o Wildlife
o Safaris
o Dhows
o Mt Kilimanjaro
o The Serengeti migration
o Red-garbed Maasai warriors
o Zanzibar's carved doorways
o *Karibu* (Welcome)

PEOPLE
Mainland Tanzania is home to over 100 tribes, including the colourful Maasai, the seminomadic Hadzabe, the Makonde, Chagga and Sukuma. Most are very small, with almost 100 tribes combined accounting for only one third of the total population. On the Zanzibar Archipelago, most non-Africans consider themselves Shirazi, with ties to Persia. Close to 50 per cent of Tanzanians are Christians, and almost 40 per cent are Muslim, with the rest following traditional religions.

MARKETPLACE
Following Nyerere's failed socialist experiment the country's economic statistics have been moderately optimistic, with modest growth rates and controlled inflation. Yet annual per capita income hovers at barely US$400, and daily life remains a struggle for many Tanzanians. The extended family forms an essential support network to fill in some of the gaps, and those with jobs are expected to share what they have. Agriculture and, increasingly, tourism are economic mainstays.

RANDOM FACTS
o Tanzania is the only country boasting indigenous inhabitants from all major African ethnolinguistic families (Bantu, Nilo-Hamitic, Cushitic and Khoisan).
o Less than seven per cent of eligible students are enrolled in secondary school – one of the world's lowest rates.
o In rural areas, a woman drops her own name to become known as *Mama* followed by her eldest son's name.

ALL SET FOR UNDERWATER ADVENTURE IN BEAUTIFUL MIKINDANI BAY »

ⵚ OL DOINYO LENGAI HAS A FORBIDDING PRESENCE – IT'S NO WONDER THE MAASAI CONSIDER THIS ACTIVE VOLCANO A HOLY PLACE

ERIC L WHEATER / LONELY PLANET IMAGES

ⵚ LONG BEFORE PLASTIC WATER BOTTLES, THERE WAS THE CONVENIENT AND PORTABLE GOURD

ⵚ 'IT REALLY WAS *THIS* BIG!'

BUG-EYED MONSTER – WELL, A CHAMELEON, ANYWAY »

PLAYGROUND BOOGIE, ZANZIBAR »

NGORONGORO CRATER IS BUFFALO HEAVEN »

NATURAL BEAUTY

Tanzania assaults the senses: gnarled baobabs silhouetted against the sunset in Tarangire National Park; hippos snorting in Katavi's lakes; the scents of cloves and vanilla on Zanzibar; sea breezes and palms rustling along the coast; pine-shaded paths in the Usambaras. The mundane (hillsides dotted with small farm plots) mixes with the spectacular (Mt Meru and Mt Kilimanjaro) for scene after unforgettable scene.

URBAN SCENE

Zanzibar's Stone Town is one of Africa's most evocative destinations. Its winding alleyways echo with the sounds of children playing, while elderly men in their *kanzu* and *kofia* sit on stone benches playing *bao*. In the evenings, the waterside Forodhani Gardens come to life with vendors serving up grilled seafood, locals chatting on the grass and boys jumping into the water for a swim.

WILD THINGS

Over one million wildebeest are joined by thousands of elephants, zebras, giraffes, lions, massive pods of hippos, solitary rhinos and so many flamingos that the air takes on a pink hue. For many, Tanzania is defined by its unrivalled collection of wildlife, which is at its most accessible in the northern safari circuit. Offshore is an abundance of colourful fish, corals and sea turtles; head west for up-close encounters with chimpanzees.

CULTURE

On a continent renowned for its traditions of hospitality and extended family, Tanzania holds a distinguished place, with a remarkably egalitarian and harmonious social outlook. Children acknowledge their elders with a respectful *'shikamoo'*, while strangers are addressed as *dada* (sister), *mama* (for an older woman), *kaka* (brother) or *ndugu* (relative or comrade). Greetings are essential, and no-one ever starts a conversation without first inquiring about the latest news.

LOCAL CRAFTS

At Dar es Salaam's bustling Mwenje market, skilled Makonde carvers bring hard blocks of wood to life. 'Tree of life' carvings show interlaced human and animal figures around a common ancestor, all supporting and connected with each other, while abstract *shetani* carvings embody images from the spirit world. Brightening things up are *tinga-tinga* paintings, with their colourful, magical animal motifs.

SURPRISES

- Kilimanjaro's melting ice-cap, which will soon disappear if ice loss continues at its present rate.
- Orchids and wildflowers in Tanzania's new Kitulo Park, one of Africa's few parks centred on flowers.
- Wonderfully intimate and luxurious safari lodges.

MYTHS & LEGENDS

Former president Julius Nyerere – known as *Mwalimu* (teacher) – is a larger-than-life figure in Tanzania, and his photo still graces walls throughout the country. From his beginnings as the son of a local chief, he became leader of then-Tanganyika's independence movement and the country's first president. His *ujamaa* (familyhood) ideals still permeate society, and he was almost single-handedly responsible for putting Tanzania on the world stage, and for promoting Swahili as a national language. Other claims to distinction are his pan-Africanism and support for regional independence movements.

CUISINE

No experience of Tanzania is complete without dipping your hand into a bowl of *ugali* (a thick mass of cooked maize or cassava flour), rolling it into a ball and using it to scoop out some of the accompanying sauce. It's the national dish, and most Tanzanians were eating it before they could talk. More appealing to foreign palates is the delicious coconutty seafood.

MUSIC

Wander Zanzibar Town of an evening and listen for the haunting wail of *taarab* music, with its African, Arabic and Indian strains, its two-edged lyrics, zither-like *kanun*, *nay* (flute) and drums. The audience is as interesting to watch as the musicians: listeners giving money to the singer, women dressed to the nines sitting separately from the men, and a lively repartee.

≈ PESTER POWER WITH CLAWS: A LION CUB

≈ SOLVING THE PROBLEMS OF THE WORLD

ESSENTIAL EXPERIENCES

- **Bumping down the steep, rutted track into Ngorongoro Crater, watching blue-green vistas open up before you and seeing lions and more on the wildlife-filled crater floor**
- **Hearing hoof beats echoing across the Serengeti plains, and savouring the rhythms of life in the wild**
- **Straining up Mt Kilimanjaro's scree slope in the dark, and then watching dawn break over the plains below from the summit**
- **Wandering along cobbled streets in Stone Town, past carved wooden doors and women in black bui-buis**
- **Sweating up while climbing densely vegetated slopes in search of chimpanzees at Mahale Mountains park**
- **Tiptoeing through Kilwa Kisiwani's ruins and getting acquainted with centuries of Swahili history along the coast**
- **Relaxing under the palms on one of Zanzibar's powdery white beaches, while gazing out at fantastically turquoise seas**
- **Slipping along the Rufiji River past basking hippos in the Selous Game Reserve**

FROM THE TRAVELLER

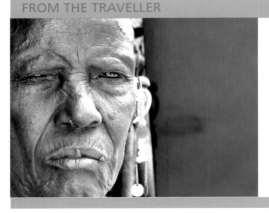

The photo was taken during a trip across the Serengeti plains. The Maasai really don't like to be photographed so I asked before shooting. The woman answered yes but it was clear she didn't like my camera. I took only this picture. Too often, in eastern Africa, I saw tourists paying to enter horrible false *manyattas* (extended family homes) just to steal photos. The eyes of the woman showed me the Maasai resentment towards the insensitivities of tourists which unfortunately my camera symbolised. We should spend more time trying to communicate rather than taking pictures to change this resentment.

BARBARA LOMONACO // ITALY

MAP REF // P10

BEST TIME TO VISIT JUNE TO OCTOBER, DECEMBER TO JANUARY

KICKING THE FOOTBALL AROUND MIKINDANI'S CRUMBLING STREETS »

PER-ANDERS PETTERSSON // GETTY

KEEPING UP WITH THE PREMIER LEAGUE »   MAKING A SPLASH IN ZANZIBAR'S VEGETABLE MARKET »

TEXT MATT PHILLIPS

COMOROS & MAYOTTE

BORN IN FIRE, RAVAGED BY MALAGASY PIRATES, RULED BY THE FRENCH AND SUBSEQUENTLY THE SITE OF COPIOUS COUPS, THIS VOLCANIC ARCHIPELAGO CONTINUES ITS CLIMB OUT OF THE INDIAN OCEAN.

CAPITAL CITY MORONI (COMOROS), MAMOUTZOU (MAYOTTE)   POPULATION 690,950 (COMOROS), 201,230 (MAYOTTE)
AREA 2170 SQ KM (COMOROS), 370 SQ KM (MAYOTTE)   OFFICIAL LANGUAGES ARABIC, FRENCH (COMOROS), FRENCH (MAYOTTE)

≈ WEDDINGS, PARTIES, ANYTHING – A COMORAN WEDDING BAND

LANDSCAPE

This four-island archipelago is dominated by mountainous volcanic landscapes. Grande Comore's Mt Karthala (2361 metres) continues to be one of the world's largest active volcanoes – an eruption in 2005 ended a period of dormancy that had lasted a mere 14 years. Being the youngest islands, Grande Comore and Mohéli have immature soils that aren't very suitable for agriculture, enabling large sections of rainforests to escape the till. The same can't be said for the older islands of Anjouan and Grande Terre, but these islands do have well-developed coral reefs that are rich in marine life. The archipelago is hot and sticky, with the monsoon bringing torrential rain between October and April. It's coolest between April and September, though temperatures rarely drop below 19°C.

HISTORY IN A NUTSHELL

Seagoers from Indonesia and Polynesia were the earliest inhabitants of these islands, and traces of their culture linger, despite the subsequent waves of African and Arab immigrants. The Shirazi Arab clans were the most influential among the new arrivals, setting up Islamic sultanates after arriving in the 15th and 16th centuries. The French took hold in the mid-19th century, however, through a cunning mixture of strategies that included divide and conquer ploys, chequebook politics and a serendipitous affair between a sultana and a French trader that was turned to good use. Comoros history from this era reads like a cross between a Walt Disney animated movie, a Merchant Ivory production and a Shakespearean tragedy. Nevertheless, France kept an iron grip on the islands until 1975, when Comoros was finally established as an independent republic – Mayotte remained with France. Since then, Mayotte has enjoyed stability while Comoros has endured failed experiments with socialism and more coups than anyone cares to remember. In 2006 Comoros finally witnessed its first peaceful change of power since independence. Its unique new constitution sees the presidency rotated every four years between the three major islands of Grande Comore, Anjouan and Mohéli (or to give them their local names, Njazidja, Nzwani and Mwali respectively).

PEOPLE

Over 90 per cent of the population in Comoros and Mayotte have mixed Bantu, Arab, Malay and Malagasy roots. Most of the remaining populace is comprised of minority ethnic groups such as the Antalote, Cafre, Makoa, Oimatsaha and Sakalava. Approximately two per cent of Mayotte's population is French. Comorans speak Arabic, French and Shikomoro, which is a blend of Swahili and Arabic; most Mahorais, as the people of Mayotte are called, speak the Swahili dialect of Mahorian. For the most part Comorans are outgoing, extroverted and emotional people, ready to discuss their problems, life stories and political opinions at the drop of a hat. Oddly, the opposite mood seems to prevail on Mayotte – Mahorais have a reputation of being standoffish.

Islam is entrenched on both islands, with almost 98 per cent of Comorans and Mahorais Sunni Muslims. Just over half the remaining citizens of each nation are Roman Catholic.

TRADEMARKS

- Political coups (we've lost count at 20)
- Magnificent blue-green ocean waters
- Fragrant fields of ylang-ylang, jasmine, cassis and orange flowers
- Volcanic eruptions
- Fiery sunsets
- Long white beaches
- Beautiful rainforests
- Succulent seafood

GALAWA BEACH – SLICED STRAIGHT FROM PARADISE »

THE 500-YEAR-OLD FRIDAY MOSQUE GLOWS IN MORONI'S GOLDEN SUNLIGHT »

MARKETPLACE

Low education levels, high unemployment and few natural resources have seen the Comorian economy sputter along at subsistence levels. And despite the fact that 80 per cent of the population works in the agricultural sector, Comoros is obliged to import the bulk of its foods, even its staple rice. Mayotte's economy would be in the same state as that of Comoros if it weren't for the financial assistance it receives from France.

URBAN SCENE

The former seat of an ancient sultanate, Moroni is a friendly place and offers a perfect introduction to Comoros. In the narrow streets of Moroni's old Arab quarter there are women in their colourful wraps chatting on their doorsteps, and grave groups of white-robed men whiling away the hours between prayers with games of dominoes played on smooth stone benches. At dusk, silhouetted against what are perhaps the Indian Ocean's most stunning sunsets, hundreds of men and boys swim between the harbour's volcanic rock jetties.

RANDOM FACTS

○ Although the islands were discovered by the Portuguese around 1500, it wasn't European explorers who were the biggest headache for locals prior to French annexation – it was pirates from Madagascar. Many Comorans still harbour a lingering mistrust of the Malagasy.

○ The average time between Comoros coups is 1.55 years.

WILD THINGS

Thanks to its 400-million-year-old fossils showing protuberances resembling limbs, the coelacanth fish was long considered a hot contender to be one of the species that crawled from the sea to found life on dry land. You can imagine the surprise, then, when a fisherman hauled in a recently deceased coelacanth in 1938! Since another high-profile catch off Anjouan in 1952, scientists have been returning to Comoros. However, no-one has yet succeeded in establishing how many of the fish exist, and none have yet been taken alive.

IMPORT

⤢ Rice (and lots of it)
⤢ Bob Dénard (repeatedly)
⤢ The French military
⤢ A melange of cultures

⌃ COMORAN WOMEN AND THE RHYTHM OF LIFE

EXPORT

⤡ Ylang-ylang (perfume essence)
⤡ Vanilla
⤡ Cloves
⤡ Copra
⤡ Coconuts
⤡ Coffee
⤡ Cinnamon

KING OF THE COUPS

Wade through Comoros' recent political turmoil and you'll notice one name cropping up again and again: Bob Dénard (born Gilbert Bourgeaud). Perhaps the world's most influential mercenary during the past half-century, he's had a hand in four Comoros coups, as well as conflicts in Zimbabwe, Yemen, Iran, Nigeria, Benin, Gabon, Angola and the Belgian Congo (now the Democratic Republic of Congo).

Dénard deposed Comoros' first president, Ahmed Abdallah, only a month after independence in 1975 – allegedly at France's behest. Less than three years later, Dénard ousted the man he'd helped put in power, and returned the one he'd previously removed. He then remained as president Ahmed Abdallah's head of security until Abdallah was murdered in a 1989 coup. In 1995 he returned for yet another coup, but although he succeeded in removing president Said Mohamed Djohar, he was soon arrested by French forces. He received a suspended sentence in a Paris court… Friends in high places?

⌃ PEEK-A-BOO! A COLOURFUL TRADITIONAL CHIROMANI WRAP

ESSENTIAL EXPERIENCES

○ **Hovering over the corals before settling into the soft sands at Chiroroni**

○ **Tiptoeing through crumbling palaces at Hari ya Moudiji**

○ **Gawking at the green sea turtles at Chissioua Ouénéfou**

○ **Fishing, diving and boating in the waters of Mayotte**

○ **Summiting Mt Ntingui and gazing over the entire archipelago**

○ **Meandering through Moroni's maze-like medina and the Place de Badjanani**

○ **Savouring the scents of Bamboa's ylang-ylang distillery**

○ **Procuring the perfect hand-crafted piece of art at Mitsoudjé on Grand Comore**

MAP REF // R11- S11

BEST TIME TO VISIT **MAY TO OCTOBER**

AT A PRESTIGIOUS 'GREAT WEDDING', BRIDE, GROOM, GOLD GALORE AND GUESTS WAVING BANKNOTES ARE THE ORDER OF THE DAY »

SLICING AND DICING TO ORDER AT THE LOCAL MARKET »

THE SERIOUS BUSINESS OF LIFE ON COMOROS – A GAME OF BAO »

SEYCHELLES

THE BEAUTIFUL, SAND-RINGED ISLANDS OF THE SEYCHELLES ARE ABOUT A THOUSAND MILES FROM ANYWHERE – THE NEAREST CONTINENTAL LANDFALL IS KENYA, AROUND 1500 KILOMETRES EAST ACROSS THE INDIAN OCEAN.

CAPITAL CITY **VICTORIA**   POPULATION 81,540   AREA 455 SQ KM   OFFICIAL LANGUAGES **ENGLISH, CREOLE**

⌃ PRASLIN ISLAND, THE PERFECT PLAYGROUND

LANDSCAPE

The land area of the Seychelles is tiny; the sea area is extraordinary. More than 115 coral and granite islands are scattered across 400,000 square kilometres of ocean. The northern granite islands are all that remains of a massive granite shelf that tore away from the coast of Africa around 65 million years ago. The 73 coral islands were formed from ancient coral reefs, set in atolls around shallow lagoons. Their remoteness has bred a remarkable biodiversity on the islands: many species are found nowhere else. Cousin Island, for example, has more than 300,000 seabirds, although it's less than a kilometre wide.

HISTORY IN A NUTSHELL

The earliest residents of the Seychelles were pirates but the first recorded landing came in 1609, when a British merchant ship stopped off to search for water and provisions. The islands were formally claimed by the French in 1742 and counter-claimed by the British in 1814, and became an important depot for shipping spices and slaves. Tourism took off in the final years of British rule, under the direction of the charismatic first president of the Seychelles, James Mancham. The islands gained independence in 1976; a year later, the socialist leader Albert René seized power in a coup.

The socialist Seychelles People's Progressive Front has been in power ever since, though centrist parties are gaining seats at each new election.

PEOPLE

All but two per cent of the population of the Seychelles live on Mahé, Praslin and La Digue. Most of the outlying atolls have no permanent residents at all. The majority of Seychellois are descended from European plantation owners or African slaves, but there are small populations of Indians and Chinese, descended from indentured plantation workers. Around 90 per cent of Seychellois speak Creole (pidgin French) as their first language.

MARKETPLACE

According to the UN, the Seychelles have the strongest economy in sub-Saharan Africa, but both fishing and tourism (which account for around 20 per cent and 13 per cent of GDP respectively) are vulnerable industries. The tuna plant in Victoria processes a staggering 400 tonnes of tuna per day, so a collapse in Indian Ocean tuna stocks would be devastating. Apart from fish, most goods are imported, so many day-to-day essentials are disproportionately expensive even for locals.

TRADEMARKS

○ White-sand beaches
○ Granite boulders
○ Swaying palm trees
○ Giant tortoises
○ Coups d'état

NATURAL BEAUTY

The 115 islands of the Seychelles are jaw-droppingly beautiful. The granite islands in the north rise dramatically from the ocean, ringed by white beaches and curiously eroded granite boulders; the coral-fringed outer islands stand not much higher than the lagoons that surround them. In the centre of Praslin is one of the most striking landscapes on earth – the World Heritage–listed Vallée de Mai, a dense jungle full of otherworldly coco de mer palms.

RANDOM FACTS

○ People used to think that the Seychelles' most famous plant, the coco de mer tree, grew under the sea.
○ The Seychelles were once home to six species of giant tortoise; today only one survives.
○ In 1981 South African mercenaries arrived at Mahé airport disguised as a rugby team and tried to seize the Seychelles.

MY BEAUTIFUL BALLOON: A WHITE-SPOTTED PUFFERFISH »

URBAN SCENE

The Seychelles have only one city, Victoria on Mahé, but anywhere else, this would be a village. Only 24,900 people live in the Seychelles' quiet capital, most on the tree-lined avenues that straggle into the jungle behind the harbour. Several viewing areas on the Morne Seychellois massif offer stunning outlooks over the city, the surrounding jungle and the flight path into Mahé airport.

WILD THINGS

Unique species are the Seychelles' stock in trade. Topping the bill is the coco de mer, found only on Praslin and Mahé. Female trees produce enormous, grooved coconuts, said to resemble the female buttocks, while male trees produce a long, dangling inflorescence, resembling… well, you get the idea. Other intriguing residents include the Aldabran giant tortoise, found only on Aldabra Atoll, and the sinister-looking robber crab, a four-kilogram monster that lives entirely on land, foraging for coconuts and carrion.

≫ A SUBMERGED BOAT IN PRISTINE WATERS

≫ THE LUSCIOUS SEYCHELLES LILY

CUISINE

The main influences on Seychelles cuisine come from India and France, reflecting the old trade routes from Europe to Asia. Fish crops up everywhere, grilled and served with incendiary chilli relish or simmered in rich, coconutty sauces with Indian spices. Among the more unusual Seychellois dishes are millionaire's salad (made from the core of the palmiste tree) and fruitbat curry – it's said to taste a little bit like rabbit.

SURPRISES

○ Although they're nominally Christian, many Seychellois still maintain a belief in witchcraft. The islands' *bonhommes* (witch doctors) use fetish objects called *gris-gris* to either fend off or summon evil spirits.

○ The official car of the Seychelles is the mini-moke, a mechanically unpredictable Tonka Truck–style jeep powered by the engine from an English Mini.

MYTHS & LEGENDS

Probably the most famous modern legend from the Seychelles is the story of the 1981 coup. With backing from the South African government, the ex-Congo mercenary 'Mad' Mike Hoare landed at Mahé International Airport with a private army, disguised as rugby players and tourists. The gang was rumbled when an airport guard spotted an AK-47 in their luggage, and they fled back to South Africa in a hijacked Air India jet.

ESSENTIAL EXPERIENCES

○ **Getting cosy with a coco de mer in the primordial Vallée de Mai on Praslin island**

○ **Sprawling on the sand on exquisite Anse Lazio beach, the Seychelles' finest**

○ **Living the easy life on laid-back La Digue, the least developed of the Seychelles' granite islands**

○ **Swimming with sharks at Shark Bank, Îlot and Brissare Rocks, just three of the Seychelles' amazing dive sites**

○ **Feasting on seafood on Beau Vallon beach, looking across to the cloud-shrouded massif of Silhouette Island**

○ **Doing a Robinson Crusoe on an island resort in the remote outer atolls**

MAP REF // T10

BEST TIME TO VISIT **APRIL TO OCTOBER**

≫ ISLAND LIFE… THERE'S ALWAYS TIME FOR A CHAT

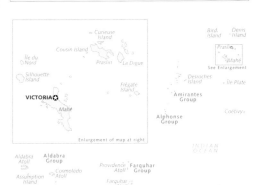

THE GIANT TORTOISE ON COUSINE ISLAND IS CLASSIFIED AS A VULNERABLE SPECIES «

MUSHROOM ATOLL APPEARS TO HOVER ON THE LAGOON «

THE DAY'S CATCH – WITH A COUPLE OF BOTTLES OF COKE – GLISTENS IN THE SUN «

TEXT ANDREW STONE

MADAGASCAR

LITTLE-VISITED AND OTHERWORLDLY, MADAGASCAR FEELS LESS LIKE AN ISLAND NATION OFF THE AFRICAN COAST AND MORE LIKE AN ALTERNATE REALITY.

CAPITAL CITY ANTANANARIVO (TANA)   POPULATION 18.6 MILLION   AREA 587,040 SQ KM   OFFICIAL LANGUAGES FRENCH, MALAGASY

LANDSCAPE

It may be dwarfed by its continental mothership but Madagascar is still the world's fourth-biggest island, and is home to some very weird and wonderful terrain: limestone mountain ranges sharpened to razor edges by the elements, high plateaus that plunge into semitropical rainforest, a fantastical spiny desert, and along the coast, mangrove swamps, coral reefs and sandy beaches. Those who fly over all these natural wonders will spot another, more sinister, feature: serious deforestation, which is gouging canyons into the earth and bleeding Madagascar's red soil into the sea.

HISTORY IN A NUTSHELL

Madagascar's geological history, defined by a slow continental drift out into the Indian Ocean over hundreds of millions of years, is the key to its extraordinary natural history. Its flora and fauna have been evolving on their own for thousands of millennia, and the result is fantastic, unique and downright odd. Man's arrival was much more recent (about 1500 to 2000 years ago), and most islanders are descended from Malay Polynesians who washed up here from Southeast Asia. The French held sway just long enough over the 20th century to introduce the language and decent bread, before the country gained independence in 1960.

TRADEMARKS

- Cuddly lemurs
- Bulbous baobabs
- Chilled-out chameleons
- Paradise for pirates
- Rutted roads

PEOPLE

Walk down the streets of the capital and you'll see a striking array of people from different ethnic groups, from those with very dark African skin and features, to those with lighter Malaysian looks and even Polynesian faces worthy of a Gauguin painting. Madagascar's 18 tribes form a complicated genealogical mosaic – some closely related, others claiming separate ethnic descent. The Malayo-Indonesian groups include the Merina and Betsileo; the Betsimisaraka, Tsimihety, Antaisaka and Sakalava groups are descended from a mix of Malayo-Indonesian, African and even Arab ancestors. All speak Malagasy (from the Austronesian family of languages) and many speak French, but very few speak English.

MARKETPLACE

Agriculture accounts for more than a quarter of Madagascar's GDP and employs four out of five of its people. Encouraged by the World Bank and the International Monetary Fund (IMF), Madagascar ditched socialism in the 1990s to pursue privatisation and economic liberalisation. The result has been steady economic growth, albeit from a very low base.

RANDOM FACTS

- Madagascar's President Ravalomanana is known as the 'yoghurt king' after the dairy products empire he built from nothing.
- The striking pachypodium shrub (or elephant's foot), looks just like a baby baobab but is in fact no relation.
- The name of Madagascar's unofficial national dessert, the Banane Flambé, is also Malagasy slang for a stud or romeo.
- Air Madagascar, the national airline once officially called Madair and now known affectionately as Airmad, has never suffered a crash.

THIS IS MADAGASCAR – THE GORGEOUS, WACKY SURAKA SILK MOTH ON A PACHYPODIUM SHRUB »

⌃ EMPTY STREETS AND DECREPIT COLONIAL BUILDINGS GIVE MAJUNGA ITS SOPORIFIC FEEL

CAROL POLICH // LONELY PLANET IMAGES

⌃ BEAUTIFUL SHELL, GRUMPY TORTOISE – THE ANGONOKA TORTOISE IS ONE OF THE WORLD'S TEN MOST ENDANGERED SPECIES

⌃ TINFOIL-SHINY FISH AND AN EMPTY BEACH AT ANAKAO

AVENUE OF GIANTS: SOME OF THE BAOBABS ON THIS FAMOUS ROAD ARE 1500 YEARS OLD »

WAITING FOR A FARE… NO HURRY! »

A FIELD OF UMBRELLAS BLOOM IN THE SQUARE ON MARKET DAY, TANA »

NATURAL BEAUTY

So otherworldly is this odd, benign, enchanting isle, that if you visit, you may well wonder afterwards if you dreamt the whole experience. Were the Ankàrana limestone massif's eerie caves, canyons and fields of razor-sharp *tsingy* (pinnacles) for real? Did that bone-shaking ride through red-earthed plains studded with baobabs or the thermal bath in the rainforest really happen? Were those hypnotic sifakas (white lemurs) bounding across the scrub a mirage? Did you really get mugged by cute ring-tailed lemurs hoping for a snack? Yes, but just to be sure, book a return trip.

WILD THINGS

Madagascar is home to the fabled, the weird and the unique: the fossa (a cougar-like predator), the giant coua (a flightless bird) and the otherworldly aye-aye (a very rare lemur with a skeletal, elongated middle finger), not to mention several dozen other lemur species. Sadly, however, Madagascar's most mythic creatures – like the pygmy hippo and the three-metre, ostrich-like aepyornis – have long been extinct.

IMPORT

↗ Battered Peugeot taxis
↗ Souped-up car sound systems
↗ American rap and R&B (to play eternally on souped-up car sound systems in battered Peugeot taxis)
↗ Lonely Planet authors on holiday

EXPORT

↖ Vanilla
↖ Textiles
↖ Coffee
↖ Ylang-ylang
↖ Rice
↖ Precious and semiprecious gemstones

CULTURE

Outside the cities, many Malagasy hold traditional beliefs centred on *razana* (the respect for ancestors and observance of customs honouring them). *Fady* is the complex system of taboos governing these customs and beliefs. The 'turning of the bones', or *Famadihana*, is an amazing (and expensive) funerary ritual and party held for the deceased by their living relatives. The deceased are exhumed, cleaned, dressed in fresh shrouds, spoken to and even danced with by their descendants, before being returned to the grave with a few well-chosen gifts.

SURPRISES

○ Madagascar's forests contain 1000 orchid species, some reliant for pollination on their very own species of moth.
○ The language with the closest relationship to Malagasy is spoken in Borneo.
○ Written Malagasy bears remarkably little resemblance to the spoken language. The rule of thumb is 'swallow as many syllables as you can and drop the last one'.

MUSIC

Good suspension? A needless luxury. Working electrics? A nice idea. Air-conditioning? For wimps. A good sound system? Absolutely bloody essential. This is the creed of the Malagasy taxi-brousse (bush taxi) driver, who treats passengers to upbeat, often frenetic and infectiously rhythmic mix tapes featuring a blend of popular Malagasy music, sounds from over the water in continental Africa and some mainstream US R&B and rap. The home-grown music can range from folk to pop, and uses a variety of instruments, including guitar, accordion, flute, whistle and traditional instruments.

ECOTOURISM

With much of the booming population still scraping a meagre living from the soil and economic development still modest, the pressure on Madagascar's ecosystems is relentless and heartbreaking. Land clearance for crops, slash-and-burn rice-growing and the relentless demand for charcoal are stripping the land's riches and its topsoil. What Madagascar badly needs is affluent, ecologically responsible visitors in numbers to boost the economy and assist some of the excellent conservation efforts going on in its reserves and national parks.

CUISINE

Rice, rice and more rice. It's the staple of the country, and most often served with stewed chicken, fish or zebu (the Malagasy cattle). Good seafood is plentiful near the coasts; fresh fruit is abundant everywhere. *Achards*, a fiery vegetable curry, is ubiquitous, as surprisingly is *soupe Chinoise*, an often decent meat broth with vegetables, noodles and coriander. France's culinary legacy is excellent bread and coffee.

ESSENTIAL EXPERIENCES

○ **Wondering at the amazing indris' cacophonous whoop as Madagascar's largest, tailless lemur long-jumps from tree to tree at the Périnet Reserve**

○ **Trekking to the Piscine Naturelle in Isalo National Park, Madagascar's fun-size Grand Canyon**

○ **Exploring the Pirate's Graveyard on Isle St Marie, former bolt hole of legendary buccaneer Captain Kidd**

○ **Haggling for delicately embroidered cloth, exotic spices and vanilla pods in Tana's bustling Zoma (the Friday market)**

○ **Shoehorning yourself in with the locals, their luggage, livestock, sacks of rice and quite possibly the kitchen sink for the ride of your life aboard a Malagasy taxi-brousse (bush taxi)**

○ **Hitting the lemur jackpot on a trek through Ranomafana National Park (can you spot all the park's 12 species?)**

○ **Gazing down at Fort Dauphin, Madagascar's southern redoubt, from the 500-metre summit of Pic St Louis**

≈ FIRST CLASS TO MANAKARA, EARLY MORNING

≈ A PANAMA HAT AND A PIERCING GAZE

MAP REF // S12

BEST TIME TO VISIT **APRIL TO OCTOBER**

≈ A WARM WELCOME TO A SOUTHERN-DESERT VILLAGE

A FREE RIDE FOR A CHEEKY PARSON'S CHAMELEON – GOOD THING HIS MOTHER HAS EYES IN THE BACK OF HER HEAD! ⤒

MOUNT TSARANORO RISES ABOVE THE VALLEY LIKE A CATHEDRAL FOR ROCK CLIMBERS ⤒

TOM COCKREM // LONELY PLANET IMAGES

FISHING IN HEAVEN, LOKOBE RESERVE ⤒

TEXT JAN DODD

RÉUNION

WITH ITS TROPICAL PALMS AND CREOLE CUISINE, ITS PAVEMENT CAFÉS AND BERET-CLAD BOWLS PLAYERS, THIS INDIAN OCEAN ISLAND HAS ONE FOOT IN FRANCE, THE OTHER IN AFRICA – AND ITS MAGNIFICENT, MOUNTAINOUS HEAD UP IN THE CLOUDS.

CAPITAL CITY ST-DENIS   POPULATION 787,580   AREA 2520 SQ KM   OFFICIAL LANGUAGE FRENCH

WAITING FOR A WAVE ON A SURFING SAFARI

LANDSCAPE

Forming the tip of a volcano rising from the ocean floor, Réunion's highest peak is Piton des Neiges (3069 metres). Around it fan the three spectacular cirques of Mafate, Cilaos and Salazie, while the still-active Piton de la Fournaise rumbles away to the south surrounded by lava-strewn landscapes. Elsewhere, abundant rainfall and a marked altitude range foster some of the most varied plant life in the world. Winter temperatures average 22°C on the coast and 11°C in the mountains. Cyclones stalk the region from December to March.

HISTORY IN A NUTSHELL

Although France claimed the island in 1649, it only began to take its colony seriously after 1715, when it established highly profitable coffee and sugar plantations there, worked by African and Malagasy slaves. The *colons* (settlers) grew fatter still on the trade between Asia and Europe in the 19th century, which brought Chinese, Malay and Indian indentured labourers to join the by-now freed slaves. But the opening of the Suez Canal in 1869, followed by a slump in sugar prices, brought the good times to a shuddering halt. Nevertheless, while many other colonies gained independence, Réunion has remained under French rule as an overseas department, and seems relatively content with its lot, thanks to generous state aid.

RANDOM FACTS
○ The high plains near Takamaka receive roughly 10 metres of rainfall a year.
○ A 30-kilometre-long, 3.5-metre-high tunnel is being drilled to funnel water from the island's interior to the drought-ridden west, but work stopped in 2002 because of floods.
○ 'Millionaire's salad' is made using the single bud of a palm tree. When the bud has been removed, the tree dies.

PEOPLE

Most of Réunion's population is squeezed into the narrow coastal plains, as far as possible from the corner that lies beneath the brooding volcano. Creoles (people of Afro-French ancestry) and Malabars (Hindu Indians) account for the vast majority of the population, with Creoles outnumbering Malabars by about two to one. The remainder are made up of Z'oreilles (French mainlanders) and small communities of Chinese and Z'arabes (Muslim Indians). Seventy per cent of Réunionnais belongs to the Catholic faith and most speak both French and Creole. One third of the people are under 20 years of age.

MARKETPLACE

Réunion's economy is heavily reliant on *la métropole* (mainland France). It imports some 60 per cent of its needs from the mainland and in return sends back three quarters of its exports – largely sugar and other agricultural and marine products. However, efforts to diversify into services and tourism, and to create closer links with mainland Africa, have met with some success. Despite the fact that the unemployment rate remains stubbornly high at around 30 per cent, the relatively bright lights of Réunion continue to attract immigrants from the nearby Comoros and Mayotte islands.

TRADEMARKS
○ Piton de la Fournaise
○ Creole culture
○ Grand Raid cross-country race
○ Vanilla
○ Maloya music
○ Cirque de Mafate
○ Cyclones

CELEBRATING DIPAVALI, THE FESTIVAL OF LIGHTS, IN ST-ANDRE »

ONE OF THE MOST ACTIVE VOLCANOES IN THE WORLD, PITON DE LA FOURNAISE, PUTS ON A SHOW »

NATURAL BEAUTY

Réunion's spectacular mountainscapes are a magnet for hikers, photographers and nature lovers. Before helicopters, the only way into the Cirque de Mafate was on foot. This meant hiking over precipitous passes before plunging into a mystical region of ancient forests and hidden valleys, where tiny hamlets cling beneath razor-sharp ridges. The island is home to 700 indigenous plant species, including 150 trees. Native forest survives in inaccessible ravines and in the Forêt de Bélouve, where gnarled mountain tamarind trees are at their eerie best when wreathed in cloud.

ADRENALIN RUSH

From heart-pumping hikes to high-soaring paraglide rides, Réunion is a dream for adventure-sports enthusiasts. You can hurtle from Le Maïdo down to the coast by mountain bike, go canyoning or white-water rafting in the Cirque de Salazie, or surf the renowned left-hander off St-Leu. Check your insurance cover and go for it!

CULTURE

Though it's predominantly France with a tropical twist, Réunion's cultural heritage also blends African, Indian and Chinese traditions. African slaves brought with them an easy-going attitude and compelling music; Indian imports include vibrant ceremonies and piquant curries; while the Chinese contribute an entrepreneurial spirit, inimitable New Year festivities and another distinctive cuisine. Binding this diverse community is a shared sense of being simply 'one of the people'.

MYTHS & LEGENDS

All over Réunion you'll see blood-red shrines dedicated to St Expédit, who is known for his snappy ability to resolve problems. According to some scholars, he owes his sainthood to the Italian post. When a box of religious relics marked *espedito* (expedited) was sent from Rome to Paris, the nuns who received it mistakenly assumed this was the saint's name. The cult arrived in Réunion in 1931 and spread like wildfire. Over the years, believers have incorporated voodoo practices into their worship.

CUISINE

A blend of French, African, Indian and Chinese traditions, Réunionnais cuisine offers plenty to titillate the tastebuds. The staple dish is *rougail saucisse*, sausages in a tomato-and-onion sauce, served with rice, lentils and a side-dish of fiery chilli sauce. Indian-influenced snacks include lip-smacking samosas, rotis and dhal puris, and from China come sweet-and-sour soups and spring rolls. Smarter restaurants serve French cuisine and fabulous seafood. To wash it down, there's imported French wine and the potent local brew *rhum arrangée* or a thirst-quenching vanilla-flavoured tea.

MUSIC

The true spirit of Réunion is to be heard in the slow, reflective beat of *maloya*. The words and rhythms of this slave music are heavy with history. Slavery, poverty and the search for a cultural identity are favourite subjects. Lyrics became so political in the 1970s that *maloya* was temporarily banned. Accompaniment is provided by the accordion and home-made *houleur* drums and the *caïambe*, a maraca-like instrument. Two of the hottest stars are Danyel Waró and the group Ziskakan.

≈ DON'T LOOK DOWN! TAKAMAKA GORGE

KEVIN O'HARA // AGE PHOTOSTOCK

GUICHAOUA // ALAMY

ESSENTIAL EXPERIENCES

○ Teetering on the cliff at Le Maïdo for vertiginous views into the island's almost impenetrable interior – beat the clouds with a crack-of-dawn start

○ Taking a crash course in Creole architecture in Hell-Bourg, before tucking into a plate of *chou-chou* (a local vegetable) and river trout

○ Hiking over precipitous rock ramparts to explore the wild and rugged Cirque de Mafate, Réunion's 'lost world'

○ Sharing in a Christian feast day, Hindu fire-walking ceremony, country market or impromptu music fest

○ Circling the smouldering crater of the Piton de la Fournaise to appreciate the full grandeur of this restless volcano

ST-DENIS
• La Grande Chaloupe
• Le Port
• St-André
• St Paul
• St-Gilles-les-Bains
INDIAN OCEAN
• St-Benoît
Saline-les-Bains
• Trois Bassins
• Cilaos
• Plaine-des-Palmistes
• Ste-Rose
• St-Leu
• Trévelave
Piton de la Fournaise
• Le Gouffre
• St-Louis
• Le Tampon
• Tremblet
• St-Pierre
• Grand Bois
• St-Joseph
• St-Philippe

MAP REF // U12

BEST TIME TO VISIT **APRIL TO OCTOBER**

≈ DRESSED UP FOR DIPAVALI

VILLAGE IN THE CLOUDS: HELL-BOURG »

A RAINBOW OF BOATS AT THE ST-GILLES-LES BAINS QUAY »

BEFORE HELICOPTERS, THE ONLY WAY INTO THE PRECIPITOUS CIRQUE DE MAFATE WAS ON FOOT »

TEXT JOE BINDLOSS

MAURITIUS

MODELLED ON PARADISE, ACCORDING TO MARK TWAIN, THIS ISLAND NATION OF BEACHES AND SUGAR CANE IS CLOSER TO INDIA THAN AFRICA IN ITS CULTURE AND PHILOSOPHY, WITH A NAME THAT CONJURES UP ALL THE EXOTICISM OF THE INDIAN OCEAN.

CAPITAL CITY **PORT LOUIS**   POPULATION **1.2 MILLION**   AREA **2040 SQ KM**   OFFICIAL LANGUAGES **ENGLISH, CREOLE**

⌃ PARADISE ISLAND: LE MORNE BRABANT, A BASALT OUTCROP, GLOWS IN THE AFTERNOON LIGHT

LANDSCAPE

The island of Mauritius was formed (together with Réunion, 200 kilometres southwest) by ancient volcanic eruptions, which created a surreal landscape of volcanic lakes, waterfalls and curiously eroded peaks, ringed by perfect beaches. In the south, the coastline is scarred by black lava flows, a marked contrast to the whispering white sand found elsewhere on the island. The interior was once covered in tropical rainforest, but most of the jungles were cleared to provide space for sugar cane in the 19th century. The island has a classic Indian Ocean climate: temperatures rarely drop below 20°C, and it's lashed by rain and cyclones from December to March.

HISTORY IN A NUTSHELL

The first human beings to set foot on Mauritius were merchant seamen, who made light work of the island's dodos and giant tortoises. Arab and Portuguese traders also dropped in, but never stayed long. The first permanent settlers were the Dutch, who landed in 1598 and established the first sugar cane plantations – these plantations were, as usual, tended by slaves from Africa. The French picked up the reins in 1710, massively expanding the sugar industry, and the British followed in 1810, abolishing slavery but importing thousands of Indian and Chinese indentured workers. Mauritius was finally granted independence in 1968. Sugar, textiles and tourism then became the major engines driving the Mauritian economy.

RANDOM FACTS

- The dodo, which is indigenous to Mauritius, was made famous by Lewis Carroll's *Alice's Adventures in Wonderland*.
- Everything we know about dodos is based on the three or four skeletons that are now kept in European museums.
- No fewer than one in four Mauritians works in the sugar industry which produces an impressive 550,000 tonnes (or 18 billion lumps) of sugar every year.

PEOPLE

Two thirds of the Mauritian population are descended from indentured Indian plantation workers, one third are creoles descended from freed African slaves, and the remainder are Chinese (three per cent) or French (two per cent). Indo-Mauritians dominate the political and cultural spheres, but Franco-Mauritians are the major landowners. While English is the official language, only around one per cent of Mauritians speak it fluently. Creole is the most widely spoken language, followed by Bhojpuri (a dialect of Hindi) and French.

MARKETPLACE

During the 1970s and 1980s, Mauritius was one of the tiger economies (or lion economies?) of Africa. Sugar exports and textile manufacturing fuelled massive economic growth (five to six per cent over most of this time), and developers ploughed billions into developing the island for tourism. With sugar and textile sales falling, tourism is the only industry still showing favourable growth. However, the prognosis isn't entirely bleak; Mauritius still has the second largest per capita GDP in Africa, just behind oil-rich Equatorial Guinea.

TRADEMARKS

- White-sand beaches
- Swaying casuarinas
- Honeymoons
- Brown sugar
- Sunday picnics
- Smoked marlin

A FANTASTICALLY CARVED MAURITIAN TEMPLE »

LOCALS MAKE A COLOURFUL CONTRAST TO THE GIANT *VICTORIA REGIA* WATER LILY »

NATURAL BEAUTY

Wriggling your toes in the sand at the end of a tropical day is the definitive Mauritius experience. The island's beaches are legendary, backed by wispy casuarinas, and dusted with cool, white sand. Inland are rolling sugar cane fields, interrupted by man-made pyramids of volcanic stone and tortured peaks drenched in green foliage. Offshore are coral reefs teeming with divers, snorkellers and iridescent fish. You can see what Mark Twain meant!

WILD THINGS

The most famous species in Mauritius became extinct a hundred years before it received its official Latin name. Obviously, we're talking about the unfortunate dodo (*Didus ineptus*). When the first Dutch sailors landed on Mauritius in 1598, dodos were common as pigeons; within 70 years, the dodo was as dead as a… dodo. The demise of the dodo is popularly blamed on hungry sailors, but recent studies suggest that most dodos were wiped out in their nests by imported dogs and rats.

CUISINE

Mauritian cuisine blends influences from France, India, China and Africa, turning workaday dishes like fish soup into exotic taste sensations. The Indian Ocean produces a breathtaking variety of seafood, from octopus and lobster to tuna, swordfish and marlin. Smoked marlin is a national delicacy – traditionally, smoking was the only way to preserve this gargantuan fish in the steamy tropical climate.

MYTHS & LEGENDS

Probably Mauritius' most controversial hero was the 18th-century French privateer Robert Surcouf. Surcouf plundered 47 British merchant ships from his base in Port Louis, earning him the nickname *Roi des Corsaires* (King of Privateers). He later returned to France, dying in genteel retirement in St Malo, despite a five million franc bounty on his head. Legends persist of buried treasure, allegedly dumped into Port Louis harbour or buried on the coast near Baie du Tombeau.

SURPRISES

○ After decades of dependence on sugar, textiles and tourism, Mauritius is attempting to reinvent itself as a 'cyber island', tapping into the huge market for outsourcing in Britain and France.

○ Mauritius is one of the first nations in the world to turn sugar into electricity. Sugar cane–powered steam turbines produce a fifth of the island's electricity during the annual harvest season.

TOP FESTIVAL

Hindu festivals are celebrated with aplomb in Mauritius, particularly the flamboyant Maha Shivaratri festival in February or March. According to local Hindus, the Grand Bassin holy lake is spiritually connected to the holy River Ganges in India, and hundreds of thousands of pilgrims march to the lake from across the island to pay their respects to the Hindu god Shiva. The festivities rage for three days. The surface of the lake vanishes under a sea of floating offerings and flower garlands.

⌃ HINDU WOMEN PERFORM A SUN RITUAL

ESSENTIAL EXPERIENCES

○ **Splashing, snorkelling and sunbathing on the gorgeous beaches around Île aux Cerfs**

○ **Getting lost among the fabulous flora in the Sir Seewoosagur Ramgoolam Botanical Gardens in Pamplemousses**

○ **Living the life aquatic at Mauritius' dive sites; Rempart Serpent, La Passe St François and Colorado all deserve special attention**

○ **Getting lost in the crowds at the Maha Shivaratri festival in Grand Bassin, the holy lake**

○ **Trekking to forested peaks in Black River Gorges National Park**

○ **Making the retreat complete on the sleepy island of Rodrigues, 600 kilometres out into the Indian Ocean**

Île Plate ⊙   ⊙ Île Ronde

Coin de Mire

Grand Gaube

Grand Baie   ⊙ Île d'Ambre

Pamplemousses

INDIAN OCEAN

PORT LOUIS ✪

Beau Bassin   ⊙ Moka   Belle Mare
Rose Hill
Flic en Flac   Militaire Quartier
   Quatre Bornes   Île aux Cerfs
Tamarin   Vacoas   Blanche Montagne
   Curepipe
  Tamarin Falls
Île aux   Black River
Bénitiers   Gorges   Mahébourg
   National Park
Bel Ombre
   Souillac

MAP REF // U12

BEST TIME TO VISIT APRIL TO NOVEMBER

⌃ 'GOING TO THE CHAPEL…' IN A HONEYMOONERS' HEAVEN

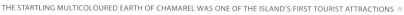

THE STARTLING MULTICOLOURED EARTH OF CHAMAREL WAS ONE OF THE ISLAND'S FIRST TOURIST ATTRACTIONS ≫

SHARPER THAN A *HAIL MARY*: BODY-PIERCING AS A PENANCE ≫

'A BEACH PLUS FRIENDLY LOCALS PLUS MUSIC – WHAT MORE COULD YOU WANT ON A TROPICAL IDYLL? ≫

SOUTHERN AFRICA

PERHAPS IT'S FITTING THAT SOUTHERN AFRICA SITS AT THE END OF THIS COLOURFUL FORAY INTO AFRICA. IT'S A MICROCOSM OF THE CONTINENT ITSELF, CONCENTRATING MANY OF THE OTHER AFRICAN REGIONS' GREATEST ASSETS IN ONE NEAT AND OH-SO-DELECTABLE PACKAGE.

East Africa's famous Big Five (lion, leopard, elephant, rhino and buffalo) are here in force, as are hundreds of other alluring species, both lurking in national parks and roaming in the wild. Although Southern Africa can't claim to have invented the safari, it can certainly say it has refined it. Visitors can dodge hippos and crocodiles while exploring the Zambezi by canoe in Zambia or Zimbabwe, or simply rent a compact car and explore the tamed roads within the wilds of South Africa's massive Kruger National Park. Stunning underwater worlds are on display within the azure waters of Mozambique's Indian Ocean archipelagos, offering an irresistible temptation to take the plunge.

At the other end of the landscape spectrum, Southern Africa boasts sublime sands that would make even the Sahara green with envy – the Namib is the oldest desert in the world and its dunes at Sossusvlei are the highest on the planet. And although it's typically associated with East Africa, the Rift Valley's dramatic landscapes cut through three Southern African nations: Zambia, Malawi and Mozambique.

Throughout Africa, massive rivers shape the landscape and bring life to the land and people. Southern Africa is no exception, with the Zambezi River (Africa's fourth largest) flowing from its source in Zambia through Angola, along the border of Namibia, Botswana, Zambia and Zimbabwe, and finally crossing Mozambique before emptying into the Indian Ocean. Along the way, it plunges over Victoria Falls (shared by Zimbabwe and Zambia), one of the world's seven natural wonders.

Creative minds have turned some of Southern Africa's best physical attributes into adrenaline outlets. Victoria Falls is the adventure capital of Africa, with white-water rafting, jet boating, microlight flights, bungee jumping, abseiling and the wonderful swing across the Batoka Gorge. The Namib Desert is a distant second for thrill seekers; it antes up with sand boarding, quad-biking and spectacular skydiving.

As in the rest of Africa, borders here don't precisely reflect the boundaries between different peoples, nor could they ever hope to: Southern Africa's mixture of cultures and languages is too complex. However, unlike elsewhere on the continent, parts of Southern Africa (South Africa is the most notable example) have substantial white populations, which has led to two seemingly parallel societies, one African and one European.

Southern Africa is truly a cross-section of everything African, which means it also has its fair share of problems. The region contains nine of the ten highest HIV/AIDS infection rates in the world – in Swaziland almost 40 per cent of the population is infected, and Botswana is also very hard hit. And while the political strife in Angola may finally be over, the situation in Zimbabwe has turned from bad to worse.

Still, take the sour with the sweet, and let Southern Africa move you.

TEXT: MATT PHILLIPS

Cabinda
(Angola)

DEMOCRATIC
REPUBLIC OF
CONGO (ZAÏRE)

INDIAN
OCEAN

Uige

TANZANIA

LUANDA ✪

Malanje   Saurimo

SEYCHELLES

Mpika

COMOROS

Lake
Malawi

Lobito   Kuito
Benguela   Huambo

Kitwe   Mzuzu

Ndola   MALAWI

Mayotte
(France)

Pemba

Mongu   Kabwe

LILONGWE ✪

Nampula   Nacala

Namibe
(Moçâmedes)   Lubango
Tomboa

ANGOLA

LUSAKA ✪

Tete   Blantyre

ZAMBIA

MOZAMBIQUE

Oshakati   Rundu

Livingstone
(Victoria Falls)

HARARE ✪

Quelimane

MADAGASCAR

SOUTH
ATLANTIC
OCEAN

Tsumeb

ZIMBABWE

Okavango
Delta

Bulawayo   Mutare

Chimoio

NAMIBIA

Francistown   Masvingo   Beira

Réunion
(France)

Swakopmund   WINDHOEK ✪

Selebi-Phikwe

Walvis Bay
Rehoboth

BOTSWANA

Namib
Desert

GABORONE ✪

PRETORIA ✪

Inhambane

Keetmanshoop

Kalahari
Desert

Johannesburg

Xai-Xai

Lüderitz

MBABANE ✪   MAPUTO ✪

Karasburg

Kimberley   BLOEMFONTEIN ✪

SWAZILAND

Port Nolloth

MASERU ✪

LESOTHO

Durban

SOUTH
AFRICA

Mthatha

Drakensberg

Beaufort West

East London

SOUTHERN
OCEAN

CAPE TOWN ✪   Mossel Bay

Cape of
Good Hope

Port Elizabeth

TEXT MARY FITZPATRICK

MOZAMBIQUE

IMAGES OF WAR AND FLOODS ARE FAST FADING INTO THE BACKGROUND, AS REPORTS OF IDYLLIC BEACHES, ISLANDS AND A FASCINATING CULTURAL MELANGE TAKE OVER THE HEADLINES ABOUT MOZAMBIQUE.

CAPITAL CITY **MAPUTO**   POPULATION **19.7 MILLION**   AREA **801,590 SQ KM**   OFFICIAL LANGUAGE **PORTUGUESE**

≫ THE SUNSET'S RAYS BATHE THE WALLS OF A MOSQUE IN GOLDEN LIGHT, ILHA DE MOÇAMBIQUE

LANDSCAPE

Mozambique's 2500-kilometre coastline is one long succession of unspoiled, spectacular beaches fringed by archipelagos. Much of its interior is featureless bush, though there are several lush and exceptionally biodiverse highland areas, including the forested Chimanimani Mountains along the Zimbabwe border. Nampula boasts a profusion of towering granite outcrops or inselbergs, while Lake Niassa dominates the northwest. The mighty Zambezi cuts a giant swath through the country on its way to the sea, while the Rovuma winds along the Mozambique–Tanzania border. Average temperatures range from 24°C in the cooler season along the coast to well over 30°C in the arid inland areas around Tete.

HISTORY IN A NUTSHELL

From Bantu-speaking farmers and fisherfolk to Arabic traders, Goan merchants and adventuring Europeans, Mozambique has long been a crossroad of cultures. One of its earliest centres was the gold-trading port of Sofala, linking inland goldfields with the powerful Kilwa sultanate. The Portuguese arrived in the late 15th century, but they never managed to establish the control they sought over the region, and distinguished themselves by a particularly repressive style of governing. Gunshots in the unlikely northern village of Chai set off the war that led to independence in 1975. But the mix was a bad one: a rapid colonial pull-out (complete with the sinking of ships and the pouring of concrete down wells), the new government's overly idealistic Marxist ideology, and insufficient economic and educational bases paved the way for years of warfare between the Frelimo government and foreign-sponsored Renamo rebels. Since the 1992 peace agreement, however, the country has blazed ahead with reconstruction. It is now one of the continent's most inspiring success stories.

PEOPLE

Major ethnic groups include the Makua and Makonde in the north and the Ronga and Shangaan in the south. About 35 per cent of Mozambicans are Christians, about 30 per cent are Muslims, and the rest are followers of traditional local religions.

TRADEMARKS

- *Marrabenta* music
- Makonde woodcarvings
- Prawns and crayfish
- José Craveirinha's poetry
- Malangatana's paintings
- Cahora Bassa Dam
- Idyllic islands and beaches

MARKETPLACE

Once an economic basket case, Mozambique is now one of the continent's shining stars, thanks to local determination plus massive influxes of foreign aid. It's near the top in terms of economic growth in Africa, although daily life remains a struggle and it's hard to make ends meet. Average annual per capita income is about US$300 (versus about US$26,000 in the UK), and most Mozambicans strive to earn a living in the lively informal sector as traders, street vendors and subsistence farmers.

RANDOM FACTS

- Mozambique's waters are among Africa's best for diving with manta rays and dugongs.
- To seal an engagement, the matrilineal Lomwe-Makua people around Gurùè require an exchange of services for the man to prove he can work.
- As a legacy of the war, many of the most remote northern district capitals have airstrips, and some can even accommodate jets.

A YOUNG WOMAN SPORTS THE LOCAL ANSWER TO SUNSCREEN »

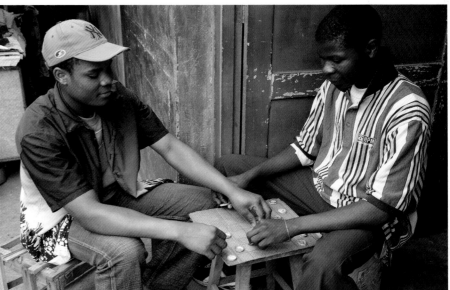

CHECK IT OUT: BOYS PLAY DRAUGHTS IN THE MARKETPLACE AT MAPUTO »

This photo was taken in the small village of Metangula on the shore of Lake Niassa (Lake Milawi). I knelt down on the beach to change the battery in my camera and automatically drew a crowd of curious children. When I looked up, task completed, I snapped this shot of a young fellow intent upon being the centre of my attention.

TOM NEWMAN // CANADA

NATURAL BEAUTY

Viewed from the air, the Bazaruto Archipelago is a stunning sight – seas in brilliant turquoise and jade hues laced with shimmering white sand banks. Rivalling it are the Quirimbas islands to the north, where pristine patches of sand alternate with dense mangrove forests and stands of waving palms. Along the coast are seemingly endless stretches of beach, often backed by cliffs or low dunes, while inland is Lake Niassa, with crystal-clear waters and low mountains rising up from narrow slivers of shoreline.

URBAN SCENE

Ilha de Moçambique – part ghost town and part lively fishing village – is an ideal place to get a taste of the monsoon cultures that once dominated this part of the coast. In Stone Town, the island's northern half, wide praças (squares) are rimmed by once-grand churches and stately colonial-era buildings keep watch over quiet, cobbled streets. In the adjoining Makuti Town, with its thatched-roof huts, narrow alleyways echo with the sounds of playing children and squawking chickens, while fishermen repair their long, brightly coloured nets on the sand. In its 17th- and 18th-century heyday, the island was the capital of Portuguese East Africa and home to a fascinating cultural mix of Christian, Muslim and Hindu communities. Over the centuries, immigrants from East Africa, Goa, Macau and elsewhere mixed with the local Makua culture, which is now once again dominant.

WILD THINGS

Swimming in Mozambique's turquoise waters are dugongs, whale sharks, dolphins, sea turtles, seasonal humpback whales and a plethora of different kinds of colourful fish. On the terrestrial side, the rivers are filled with hippos and crocs. There are enough lions and elephants roaming around, especially in the

north, to be the stuff of local lore, although the animals' skittishness, challenging access and dense vegetation can make spotting them tricky.

IN DANCE

Mozambicans are superb dancers – from the nightclubs of Maputo, with their Afro-Latino fusion beats, to the more genteel, Arabic-inspired tufo dancing in the north. In mapiko, a mask-wearing dancer embodies an ancestral spirit who brings harm to the women and children, from which only the men can protect them. Chopi timbila players accompany a troupe of dancers and singers; their ability to master different beats simultaneously with each hand is renowned.

CUISINE

Local cuisine such as xima (pap) and matapa (cassava leaves with peanut sauce) is enlivened by an abundance of prawns and crayfish, and peixe grelhada – grilled catch of the day. Coconut milk is a common feature, and everything is liberally spiced with piri-piri (hot pepper).

ESSENTIAL EXPERIENCES

- ○ Wandering in the predawn stillness through Ilha de Moçambique's streets, taking in the time-warp atmosphere

- ○ Slipping into the Bazaruto Archipelago's turquoise waters amid shoals of colourful fish

- ○ Walking on almost deserted white-sand beaches or sailing a dhow through narrow mangrove channels in the Quirimbas Archipelago

- ○ Cruising along Maputo's Avenida Marginal in a laranjinha taxi on a weekend afternoon, before digging into a plate of grilled prawns at Costa do Sol

- ○ Heading into Gorongosa National Park, hearing the amazing nocturnal symphony of birds and insects, and maybe even glimpsing an elephant or lion

- ○ Spending time at the wonderful Nkwichi Lodge on Lake Niassa (Lake Malawi), exploring secluded coves, snorkelling and wildlife spotting

⌃ LITTLE YELLOW TAXI: A *LARANJINHA* WAITS FOR PASSENGERS

TANZANIA • Palma
ZAMBIA   Mocímboa • Quirimbas
Niassa   da Praia • Archipelago
(Malawi) Mecula   National
          • Lichinga • Pemba   Park
Cassacatiza   • Nacala
        • Nampula • Ilha de
Songo • Mogincual • Moçambique
            Pebane • Moma
Nyamapanda • Quelimane
ZIMBABWE
    • Chimoio   INDIAN OCEAN
      • Beira (Mozambique Channel)
Inhassoro • Bazaruto
            Archipelago
            National Park
          • Inhambane
SOUTH
AFRICA   • Xai-Xai
✈ MAPUTO
SWAZILAND

MAP REF // Q11

BEST TIME TO VISIT MAY TO JULY, SEPTEMBER TO NOVEMBER

TRY BEFORE YOU BUY: AN OPEN-AIR FURNITURE STORE PROVIDES AN EXCUSE TO LOUNGE ABOUT «

MOZAMBICAN WOMEN IN VIBRANT CLOTHING «

BUSY AT WORK IN THE SHADOW OF A RUSTING HULK AT BEIRA, MOZAMBIQUE'S SECOND-LARGEST CITY «

TEXT JUSTINE VAISUTIS

MALAWI

BLESSED WITH ONE DADDY OF A LAKE, VIVID BIRDLIFE AND ONE OF AFRICA'S FRIENDLIEST POPULATIONS, MALAWI REMAINS ONE OF THE CONTINENT'S BEST-KEPT SECRETS.

CAPITAL CITY **LILONGWE**   POPULATION **13 MILLION**   AREA **118,840 SQ KM**   OFFICIAL LANGUAGE **CHICHEWA**

⌃ WITH A SMILE ALMOST AS WIDE AS THE PIROGUE BEHIND HIM, A YOUNG BOY KNEELS IN THE SAND ON THE SHORES OF LAKE MALAWI

LANDSCAPE

Malawi is celebrated for its lake, also known as Lake Niassa. At close to 580 kilometres long and 75 kilometres wide, it occupies a fifth of the country's total area and is the third-largest lake in Africa. Over 500 species of fish flutter within its confines. On terra firma, escarpments ascend into rolling plateaus, which cover much of the landscape, particularly in the north. Malawi's southern reaches are flatter and drier. In other areas there are thick woodlands and swamps. Although the climate is subtropical, Malawi's rainfall is reliably unreliable; a predicament that commonly results in drought.

HISTORY IN A NUTSHELL

With fingers of territory stretching to East, Central and Southern Africa, Malawi was a thoroughfare for the Bantu migration from Africa's heart to its south. Between AD 1000 and 1600 several groups left their stamp, including the Maravi, from whom Malawi derives its name. In the 17th century, Portuguese explorers crossed the lake from Mozambique, but it was Dr David Livingstone, who accidentally (re-)discovered Lake Malawi in 1859, who had the most significant European influence on the country. Presbyterian missionaries and colonisation ensued

and the country was declared the colony of Nyasaland in 1907. In 1964 Malawi became independent and in 1966 it became a republic headed by Hastings Banda, who remained president for almost 30 years.

PEOPLE

The main ethnic group is the Chewa people, who account for 58 per cent of the population and dominate central and south Malawi. Yao people also populate the south and Tumbuka the north. English and Chichewa are both spoken widely, although there are at least eight other tongues spoken. Over three quarters of Malawians practise Christianity, and around 13 per cent are Muslim.

MARKETPLACE

Most of Malawi's exports are agricultural. Sadly, droughts and falling returns on the main export crop, tobacco, mean foreign aid is still 30 to 40 per cent of the budget. The government's push for alternative crops has fallen largely on deaf ears. Although agriculture employs the bulk of Malawi's labour, it provides less than half of the GDP (US$600 per capita annually). Government spending is US$913.9 million, compared to US$1.9 billion in Mozambique and US$70.6 billion in South Africa.

TRADEMARKS

- Lake Malawi
- Birdlife
- Malawian Chief's chair
- Snorkelling
- HIV/AIDS

NATURAL BEAUTY

So big that its shoreline is imperceptible in parts, Lake Malawi is the country's undisputed geographic jewel. Skirting its circumference are banks of green hills in the north and stretches of creamy sand in the south. The landscape itself is a who's who of sub-Saharan stereotypes and then some. Mopane and grasslands sidle up to scrubby marshlands. Tea plantations blanket pockets of the south and the cool, elevated planes of the Nyika Plateau look like they've been carved out of the Scottish highlands.

RANDOM FACTS

- The runways are paved at only six of Malawi's 42 airports.
- Prior to 1994, women were forbidden to wear trousers and men were forbidden to have long hair.
- White-skinned folk are known as *mzungus* in Malawi.

LONE PHONE: A MAN USES THE ONLY PHONE IN HIS VILLAGE

'Mzungu, shoot me, shoot me!' these kids were yelling at me from the car that was taking them to school in Mzuzu. They loved their photograph to be 'shot'. Every time I see this picture I'm reminded of the typical Malawian sunny spirit and hospitality; the country's nickname 'The warm heart of Africa' could not be more well chosen.

CÉCILE OBERTOP // NETHERLANDS

WILD THINGS
What Malawi lacks in celebrity African wildlife, it makes up for in its florid feathered stock. Boasting over 600 bird species, the country has top billing on twitchers' itineraries. Among the most enigmatic are Pel's fishing owl, Lilian's lovebirds, iridescent malachite kingfishers, African sacred ibis, red cormorants and Bohm's bee-eaters.

IN WOOD
Navigating a Malawian market without purchasing a woodcarving is tougher than navigating the lake in a teacup. There's plenty in the way of ornaments and chess sets but the endemic chief's chair is the Malawian speciality. This two-piece, three-legged Leggo-like arrangement has a modest seat and a high, intricately carved back. Although it's designed to be used, ergonomics are not its key feature. It's best appreciated as a beautiful home decoration.

ANDREW MACCOLL // LONELY PLANET IMAGES

⌃ WOMEN SELLING BEANS AT THE OLD TOWN MARKET, LILONGWE

MYTHS & LEGENDS
Tagged the 'King of Reggae', Evison Matafale was one of Malawi's most promising musicians. His songs inspired millions, and his outspoken social and political attitudes earned him a loyal following. Unfortunately, not everyone shared these views and he frequently found himself in police custody. In 2001 he was arrested for allegedly writing a seditious letter, and he died in custody three days later. His demise ensured him martyr status, however, and he remains something of a folk hero.

CUISINE
Two items dominate Malawian cuisine: *nsima* (maize meal) and fish. It's pretty hard to get excited about *nsima*, but the fish is another matter entirely. The most common species to end up as dinner is *chambo*, a type of cichlid. It usually arrives at your table barbecued to a smoky crisp, unceremoniously splayed with head and spine still attached. It ain't pretty – but it tastes incredible.

MUSIC
Shaped by its rhythmic roots and an international influence, the most popular mainstream music is Malawi soft reggae. Championed best by local artists such as Lucius Banda (who has also served as a member of parliament) and Billy Kaunda, the genre often delivers a political or social comment wrapped in mellow bass.

- ○ **Dodging hippos, elephants and azure kingfishers in Liwonde National Park**
- ○ **Watching Tanzanian tin roofs shimmer from a retreat on Lake Malawi's northern banks**
- ○ **Busting your biceps conquering the lake aboard a kayak**
- ○ **Navigating the green folds of Nyika National Park atop your trusty steed on a horse safari**
- ○ **Snorkelling, diving, walking and meeting the locals on the enigmatic Likoma and Chizumulu Islands**
- ○ **Hiking the hazy heights of Mt Mulanje**
- ○ **Sleeping under the stars on the *Ilala* ferry; Malawi's dame of river vessels**

TANZANIA
Chitipa • Kaporo
Lake
Malawi
Nyika • (Lake Niassa)
National Park
ZAMBIA
Mzuzu •
• Nkhata Bay

MOZAMBIQUE

LILONGWE ✪
• Monkey Bay
Liwonde
Lake Malombe National Park
MOZAMBIQUE Liwonde • • Nayuchi
Zomba • Lake Chilwa
Mwanza • Blantyre • • Mt Mulanje
• Mulanje
Bangula •
• Nsanje

MAP REF // P11

⌃ HIPPOS HEAD FOR THE WATER, LIWONDE NATIONAL PARK

PENNY TWEEDIE // GETTY

DON'T SHAKE ME UP: OFFLOADING CRATES OF FIZZY DRINK FROM THE ILALA FERRY, LAKE MALAWI ≫

ANTIPODEAN ANTICS AT CAPE MACLEAR, LAKE MALAWI ≫

CHILDREN AT THE MAPIRA REFUGEE CAMP GET A GROOVE ON ≫

TEXT MATT FIRESTONE

ZAMBIA

ALTHOUGH ITS NEIGHBOURS ZIMBABWE, ANGOLA AND THE DEMOCRATIC REPUBLIC OF CONGO ARE STRUGGLING, ZAMBIA HAS REASONS TO CELEBRATE: ITS 73 POPULATION GROUPS ARE COEXISTING PEACEFULLY, ITS WILDLIFE IS THRIVING AND ITS ECONOMY IS ON THE RISE.

CAPITAL CITY **LUSAKA**   POPULATION **11.5 MILLION**   AREA **752,610 SQ KM**   OFFICIAL LANGUAGE **ENGLISH**

≪ AN ELEPHANT MAKES TRACKS BESIDE THE ZAMBEZI RIVER

LANDSCAPE

Landlocked Zambia is shaped like a contorted figure-eight, and consists of rolling plains, winding rivers and tropical lakes. Although the country has 19 national parks and game management areas (GMAs), decades of poaching, mismanagement and bush clearing have taken their toll on the country's wildlife. Since the 1990s, however, Zambia has actively rehabilitated its parks with the help of international donors, and wildlife populations are slowly returning to their previous levels.

HISTORY IN A NUTSHELL

The celebrated British explorer David Livingstone travelled up the Zambezi in the 1850s, searching for a route into the interior of Southern Africa. In response to his rallying cry of 'Christianity, Commerce and Civilisation', Zambia (then known as Northern Rhodesia) was taken into the control of the British South Africa Company (BSAC) in 1911 to prevent further Portuguese expansion in the area. A few years later, vast copper ore deposits were discovered in the north-central part of the territory, which led to the granting of colony status in 1924. Following World War II, white settlers began arriving en masse from Southern Rhodesia (Zimbabwe) and Nyasaland

(Malawi), sparking a wave of Zambian nationalism. In 1963 British rule in Southern Rhodesia ended, and Zambia declared itself independent under the rule of President Kenneth Kaunda. Although Kaunda virtually bankrupted the country during his 27-year rule, it has since been marked by increasing stability and optimism.

TRADEMARKS

- Victoria Falls
- Zambezi River
- David Livingstone
- Copper
- Political corruption

PEOPLE

Tourism is on the rise in Zambia and although travelling through the country is for the adventurous, chances are visitors will be greeted by a few smiling locals along the way. Zambians are renowned for their friendly and laid-back demeanour, so even if things were collapsing around them you'd probably still be greeted with a smile. Zambians pride themselves on their diverse ancestry and have 73 traditional dialects. The country nevertheless has one of the lowest population densities in the world – only

14 people per square kilometre. More than half of all Zambians live either in Lusaka or in urban areas throughout the Copperbelt.

MARKETPLACE

Following independence, President Kaunda drained the country with a bloated civil service and a nationalisation scheme rife with corruption and mismanagement. Falling copper prices and rising fuel prices accelerated the slide, and by the end of the 1970s Zambia was one of the world's poorest countries. Although the installation of multiparty democracy in the 1990s led to increased stability, Zambia has suffered its share of riots, famines and attempted coups. In recent years, however, increasing world copper prices have ushered in a period of relative prosperity.

RANDOM FACTS

- In mid-2006, copper hit a record high of US$7000 per ton in response to increased demand from developing countries such as China and India.
- Although Livingstone named Victoria Falls after the queen of England, they were (and still are) known as Mosi-oa-Tunya in the Kololo language – 'The Smoke That Thunders'.

A FARMER WITH HIS CATTLE AT KAUNGA MASHI, SHANGOMBO DISTRICT »

SUNSET AT VICTORIA FALLS; THE ZAMBEZI RIVER PLUNGES OVER A GIANT RIFT IN THE BEDROCK INTO A NARROW CHASM »

Our driver in South Luangwa National Park took us closer to the animals than we had ever been before. We came upon this young female elephant and what must have been her young one nearby. She gave a warning charge, as our driver quickly reversed and turned around. Though we weren't in any real danger, it felt like a real African safari adventure!

KERRY KLETTER // USA

WILD THINGS

South Luangwa National Park is the birthplace of the 'walking safari', conceived by conservationist Norman Carr. It's easy to miss small things from a vehicle, but everything's visible on foot. Spoor (tracks), scat (dropping), nests, scrapes and scent marks provide information about wildlife and may even help locate it. However, lion encounters are a real possibility, so it's advisable to stay in single file behind the scout.

SURPRISES

○ Contrary to popular belief, heat-stressed hippos do not actually sweat blood – they actually lack sweat glands. Instead, they have mucous glands that excrete a gluey, bright-red fluid which hardens on their skin to form a natural sunblock.
○ The Nile crocodiles, which are by far the largest reptile in Africa, can reach a length of six metres and weigh over a tonne.

MYTHS & LEGENDS

In response to the growing mystery surrounding David Livingstone's whereabouts, the *New York Herald* arranged to send journalist Henry Morton Stanley to Africa in 1869. After setting out with nearly 200

porters, Stanley finally found Livingstone on 10 November 1871 in Ujiji near Lake Tanganyika. Although Livingstone may well have been the only European in the entire region, Stanley famously greeted him with 'Dr Livingstone, I presume?'

IMPORT

↗ Machinery
↗ Transportation equipment
↗ Petroleum
↗ Clothing
↗ Donor money
↗ Food aid

EXPORT

↖ Copper
↖ Tobacco
↖ Flowers
↖ Cotton
↖ IOUs

FUTURE DIRECTIONS

With the turmoil in Zimbabwe, tourists are visiting the Zambian side of Victoria Falls more, initiating a construction boom. Local business owners are riding the tourism wave straight to the bank, and the Zambezi waterfront is rapidly being developed as one of the most exclusive destinations in Southern Africa.

ESSENTIAL EXPERIENCES

○ **Catching a glimpse of a lunar rainbow over Victoria Falls, one of the seven natural wonders of the world**

○ **Spotting rare species including African wild dogs, Thornicroft's giraffes and Cookson's wildebeests in South Luangwa National Park, Zambia's premier wildlife venue**

○ **Taking a safari in Kafue National Park, a reserve that's among the largest on earth, and famous for its diverse landscapes**

○ **Being swept and flung headlong down the Zambezi River in a raft, a kayak or on a river-board**

○ **Canoeing in the vicinity of crocs, hippos, buffaloes and elephants in the Lower Zambezi National Park**

○ **Exploring the swamplands of Kasanka National Park, which boasts over 400 unique species of birds**

⌃ THORNICROFT'S GIRAFFES, SOUTH LUANGWA NATIONAL PARK ZAMBIA

MAP REF // N11

BEST TIME TO VISIT **MAY TO SEPTEMBER**

⌃ STRIPES ALIVE! TWO ZEBRAS, SOUTH LUANGWA NATIONAL PARK

A YOUNG MAN SITS AT THE FOCAL POINT OF THE BOLD DECORATIONS ON THIS HOUSE WALL

EVERY EXPRESSION UNDER THE SUN: MASKS IN A MARKET

A BASKET CASTS WELCOME SHADE OVER THIS YOUNG ZAMBIAN WOMAN

ANGOLA

THE LAST 500 YEARS FOR ANGOLA HAVEN'T BEEN PRETTY, BUT THINGS ARE IMPROVING. WITH LUCK – AND A LITTLE LESS CORRUPTION – ANGOLA WILL SOON BE SHOWCASING ITS COOL COASTLINE, RAW INTERIOR AND CHAOTIC CULTURE TO THE REST OF THE WORLD.

CAPITAL CITY LUANDA   POPULATION 12.1 MILLION   AREA 1.2 MILLION SQ KM   OFFICIAL LANGUAGE PORTUGUESE

⌃ A SWING SET FOR TWO

LANDSCAPE

Angola has more than 1600 kilometres of beautiful Atlantic coastline, mountains in the central provinces and rich rainforest in the north (closer to Congo). The countryside is green and fertile, with many rivers and even more minerals.

HISTORY IN A NUTSHELL

To sum up: 500 years of colonialism (where slaves were the country's biggest export), three minutes of independence (in 1975), then 27 years of bloody civil war. Angola was a playground for the Cold War (the Soviet Union, Cuba, South Africa and the US all had their fingers in the pie), and its civil war has meant an entire generation has grown up knowing only the devastation of war. Visiting Angola is the only way you can really begin to know the impact this has had.

PEOPLE

Angolans don't offer a lot of themselves to strangers. It's something of a survival technique – every one of them has endured a lifetime of fighting and a government uninterested in what they have to say. Still, they're certainly not shy. One of Africa's more beautiful people, Angolans have found that the best therapy for their woes is escapism. Their method?

Parties and love. Combine the two and you get wild parties and sexily clad bodies cramming the dance floors till dawn.

MARKETPLACE

Although many people believe Angola mortgaged much of its future oil earnings during the last years of its war, there's no doubt that the massive hike in oil prices has been a boon for the country. Angola now produces more than a million barrels a day – making it Africa's second-biggest producer after Nigeria, and a key supplier to the USA. The country is also rich in diamonds, but as most African nations will attest, wealth in diamonds and/or oil is a route to disaster more often than development. Half of the population still survives on subsistence agriculture, and half of the country's food must be imported.

TRADEMARKS
○ Land mines
○ Diamonds
○ Oil
○ War (there's still one going in the north)
○ Corruption
○ Babies (Angola has the second-highest birth rate in the world)

WILD THINGS

A combination of land mines, bored soldiers taking pot shots at elephants and hungry soldiers shooting anything else with four legs has meant Angola's wildlife was massively depleted over the last quarter-century or so. But the situation is improving. Recently the national animal, the palanca negra (giant sable), was spotted, and efforts to reintroduce animals into national parks are ongoing. Angola's coastline is the second-richest fishing zone in the world, though that's also a problem, as masses of huge foreign fishing boats pay to enter and pillage the crucial breeding areas.

RANDOM FACTS
○ There was a time, not long ago, when Angola had as many land mines as children (five million, or so they said).
○ Angola remains one of the few countries in Africa where English will not get you anywhere. (Try Portuguese.)
○ Forty-nine of Angola's 50 richest people are in government.
○ In 2003 the World Bank announced that US$1 billion had gone missing from Angola's accounts in each of the previous five years.

TWO FRIENDS SURVEY THE CITY AND SEAFRONT FROM THE WALLS OF THE OLD FORT, LUANDA

URBAN SCENE

Luanda is very nearly beautiful. Catch the rays off the harbour, or through a wine glass at the beach, and the whitewashed churches, Art Deco façades and foxy girls in midriff tops are dazzling. At another time of day, however, the potholes, foul smells and chaos are more likely to frazzle. War across Angola – and relative safety in Luanda – means the capital harbours people from all corners of the country. The result is a messed-up, frenetic, sometimes fun and sometimes hellish capital city.

MYTHS & LEGENDS

At the end of the '90s, while Angola's war raged, a local businessman decided to invest in a national park and to start reintroducing zebras. A week after an airdrop of four zebras (at a total cost of US$10,000 per zebra), they were dead, and their meat was being sold in the market for a few dollars.

⌃ ILLEGAL DIGGERS PICK OVER THE CATOBA

⌃ AT LEAST ONE KUITO RESIDENT SEEMS UNTARNISHED BY THE WAR

TOP FESTIVAL

Angola's Carnival doesn't have the glamour of Rio's, but it gives a mesmerising insight into what three decades of war does to youth. Held in February and taking place along Luanda's palm tree–lined Marginal (on the harbour), it's *the* time for gays, geeks, gremlins and ghouls. The pick of the event is probably the musclemen who carry troupes of beautiful girls. The freakiest statistic is the number of dead cats strung to people's costumes. It's not always pretty, but then neither is Angola.

SURPRISES

o Angola has some of the best surf beaches in Africa (though getting to them, and past the land mines, is trickier than the rips).
o Angola has one of the lowest HIV rates in southern Africa.
o The further you get from Luanda, the friendlier the locals get.
o Angola surprised the world footballing community in 2006 by knocking out Africa's biggest nation, Nigeria, from the FIFA World Cup. It was the nation's biggest sporting moment ever. Ironically, the team was then pitched against former coloniser Portugal in the first game of the tournament – as so often happens in Africa, justice went on walkabout, and despite a brave effort Angola lost 1–0.

FUTURE DIRECTIONS

Elections were promised for 2005. They are now long overdue, and are unlikely to occur for a while yet. The government that came to power by winning the 27-year war is less than keen to risk throwing it away at an election. An outbreak of Marburg virus in 2005 and a cholera epidemic in 2006 haven't exactly been the peace dividends Angolans were looking for. But they continue to hope that things will improve.

ESSENTIAL EXPERIENCES

o **Arriving, surviving, exploring**

o **Watching some of the most beautiful bodies dance on the beach**

o **Fishing in the rich waters around Lubango**

o **Taking it easy while drinking caipirinhas on the beach in Luanda**

o **Heading into the heart of Angola, where tourists haven't been seen for more than a quarter-century**

MAP REF // L11

BEST TIME TO VISIT **APRIL TO OCTOBER**

⌃ SCHOOLCHILDREN HAVE THE DANGERS OF MINES SPELLED OUT TO THEM

THE STARK REALITY OF ANGOLA'S ENDLESS CIVIL WAR: A LAND-MINE VICTIM WITH A PROSTHETIC LEG IN A CLINIC AT LUENA «

A CARNIVAL PARTICIPANT IN LUANDA «

TOPOLOGICAL DRAMA: A PLATEAU GIVES WAY TO A SPECTACULAR ERODED GULLY «

NAMIBIA

WEDGED BETWEEN THE KALAHARI AND THE SOUTH ATLANTIC, NAMIBIA IS A LAND OF DESERTS, SEASCAPES, WILDLIFE RESERVES AND SHEER UNADULTERATED BOUNDLESSNESS – NO WONDER IT ENJOYS VAST POTENTIAL AND PROMISE.

CAPITAL CITY WINDHOEK   POPULATION 2 MILLION   AREA 825,418 SQ KM   OFFICIAL LANGUAGE ENGLISH

LANDSCAPE
In addition to having a striking diversity of cultures and migrants, Namibia is a photographer's dream – it boasts wild seascapes, rugged mountains, lonely deserts, stunning wildlife, colonial cities and nearly unlimited elbow room. A predominantly arid country, Namibia can be divided into four main topographical regions: the Namib Desert and coastal plains in the west, the eastward-sloping Central Plateau, the Kalahari along the borders with South Africa and Botswana and the densely wooded bushveld of the Kavango and Caprivi regions. Despite its harsh climate, Namibia has some of the world's grandest national parks, ranging from the game-rich Etosha National Park to the dune fields and desert plains of the Namib-Naukluft Park.

HISTORY IN A NUTSHELL
Because of its barren and inhospitable coastline, Namibia was largely ignored by Europe until Germany annexed the country during the scramble to claim Africa in the late 19th century. However, the German colony's forces surrendered to a South African expeditionary army fighting on behalf of the Allies during World War I. Following that war, South Africa was given a mandate to govern the territory (then known as South West Africa) and they sought complete annexation, despite international opposition. In 1949 the South African government tightened its grip on the territory by granting parliamentary representation to the white population. This prompted the formation of the South West Africa People's Organization (Swapo), which launched a campaign of guerrilla warfare against the illegal occupiers. After several decades of insurgency, a deal was struck between Cuba, Angola, South Africa and Swapo, in which Cuban troops would be removed from Angola and South African troops from Namibia. In February of 1990 Namibia adopted a new constitution and independence was granted the following month under the presidency of Swapo leader Sam Nujoma.

PEOPLE
Namibia has one of world's lowest population densities – approximately two people per square kilometre. The major tribal groups include the Owambo, Kavango, Herero, Damara, Caprivian, Nama, Afrikaner, Baster, German, San and Tswana. The remainder is mostly comprised of Asians, Portuguese and refugees from other African countries. About 75 per cent of Namibians inhabit rural areas, though recent years have been characterised by increased migration to the cities. It's also estimated that nearly a quarter of the adult population is living with HIV/AIDS.

MARKETPLACE
Namibia has a solid modern infrastructure. Rich in resources, its economy is largely driven by the extraction and processing of minerals. It's the world's fifth-largest producer of uranium and the fourth-largest exporter of minerals (particularly lead, zinc, tin, silver and tungsten) on the continent. In the southwest, De Beers operates an enormous diamond-mining concession in an area known as the *Sperrgebiet* (a German word meaning 'forbidden zone').

TRADEMARKS
o Namib Desert
o Kalahari
o Etosha Pan
o Desert elephants
o Oktoberfest

GEMSBOK CAST ELEGANT SHADOWS ON THE SANDS OF THE NAMIB DESERT IN THE LATE AFTERNOON »

≪ THE STARK SILHOUETTES OF DEAD ACACIA TREES RISE ABOVE A SALT PAN

TOM SHEPPARD // GETTY

≪ THE GRANITE MASSIF AT SPITZKOPPE IS HOME TO THIS SPECTACULAR NATURAL ROCK ARCH

≪ ANCIENT ART: A MEMBER OF THE SAN USES FRICTION TO COAX A FIRE INTO LIF

A HIMBA WOMAN WITH BRAIDS DAUBED WITH RED CLAY »

HIMBA CHILDREN PEER FROM THE DOORWAY OF THEIR DOMED MUD HUT »

FROM THE TRAVELLER

The Himba people are unique to Kaokoland in Namibia (and southwestern Angola). On our return from Epupa Falls towards Opuwo, we came upon these Himba ladies who literally came out of the bush. We asked permission to take a photo in exchange for a small bag of flour and sugar – things that are precious to the Himba. I took just the one photo and we went on our way.

KLAUS THORSEN // UK

○ Surface temperatures in the Namib can reach as high as 70°C (158°F).
○ Beetles, lizards and spiders in the Namib get their moisture by condensing fog on their bodies.
○ Contrary to popular belief, male lions are in fact active and competent hunters, though they tend to allow lionesses to initiate a hunt.

NATURAL BEAUTY

The Namib is one of the oldest and driest deserts in the world – the result of the Benguela Current sweeping north from Antarctica and capturing and condensing humid air before it reaches the land. Its western strip is a sea of mainly apricot-coloured sand dunes interspersed with dry pans, of which Sossusvlei is the best known. In fact, the photogenic dunes near Sossusvlei, towering 300 metres above the underlying strata, are among the tallest in the world. The inhospitable landscapes of the Namib are markedly different from the Kalahari. Unlike 'true' deserts, the Kalahari is a semiarid landscape, covered with trees and crisscrossed by ephemeral rivers and fossil watercourses. One of Africa's most prominent geographical features, it stretches across parts of Congo, Angola, Zambia, Namibia, Botswana, Zimbabwe and South Africa.

URBAN SCENE

Windhoek (population 260,000) isn't your typical African capital – the city centre is characterised by a blend of German colonial architecture and taffy-coloured modern buildings. Its population reflects the country's ethnic mix, and the streets buzz with the optimism of a young country working hard to define itself. Namibia's remaining German enclaves, Swakopmund and Lüderitz, are sandwiched between

the Namib and the South Atlantic, and recall Bavarian *Dörfer* (villages), with their churches, bakeries, cafés and Art Nouveau architectural stylings.

ON PAPER

○ *Sheltering Desert* by Henno Martin recounts the author's adventures with fellow German geologist Hermann Korn; the pair spent two years in the Namib Desert avoiding Allied forces during World War II.
○ *Lost World of the Kalahari* by Laurens van der Post is an anthropological classic that depicts the traditional lifestyles of the San.

WILD THINGS

Namibia's diverse ecosystems support vast populations of elephants, giraffes, elands, oryx, kudu and wild cats, as well as one of the last remaining free-ranging black rhinoceros populations in the world. The country's coastline is also home to large colonies of jackass penguins and Cape fur seals, which inhabit the icy cold waters of the South Atlantic.

IMPORT
↗ Mining equipment
↗ Petrol
↗ Foodstuffs
↗ Chemicals
↗ Angolan refugees
↗ German tourists

EXPORT
↖ Diamonds
↖ Precious metals
↖ Uranium
↖ Processed fish
↖ Salt
↖ Sand

MYTHS & LEGENDS

The San have a legend that the wildly twisting Fish River Canyon was gouged out by a frantically scrambling snake, Koutein Kooru, as he was pursued into the desert by hunters.

SURPRISES

○ Windhoek Lager is brewed according to the 1516 German *Reinheitsgebot* (purity law), which states that beer can only contain barley, hops and water.
○ Among Namibia's many botanical curiosities is the welwitschia, which resembles a giant wilted lettuce and can survive on nothing more than condensed fog droplets.
○ Although English was chosen by the government as the official language, Afrikaans is spoken by the majority of the population – the legacy of South African occupation.

TOP FESTIVAL

True to its partially Teutonic background, Windhoek plays host to the continent's largest Oktoberfest, complete with *Lederhosen*, German polka and stein upon stein of sweet, delicious beer.

ESSENTIAL EXPERIENCES

○ **Watching the sun rise from the tops of flaming red dunes at Sossusvlei**
○ **Going on a self-drive safari in Etosha National Park, one of the continent's premier wildlife venues**
○ **Getting your adrenaline fix at the desert oasis of Swakopmund, the extreme-sports capital of Namibia**
○ **Tracking rhinos and elephants on foot in northwest Namibia's Damaraland**
○ **Testing your endurance on the five-day hike through Fish River Canyon or on an ascent of Spitzkoppe, the 'Matterhorn of Africa'**
○ **Spotting rusting shipwrecks and enormous seal colonies from above on a scenic fixed-wing flight over the Namib Desert**
○ **Feasting on *Wurst und Kartoffelklösse* (sausage and potato dumplings) in the surreal colonial relic of Lüderitz**
○ **Getting off the beaten path (and the tarred road) on the Skeleton Coast, a desolate strip of windswept and fog-covered coastline**

PAUL WEINBERG // PANOS

⌃ THESE TWO SAN CHILDREN ARE AS SNUG AS BUGS DESPITE THE MORNING'S CHILL

MAP REF // K12

BEST TIME TO VISIT **MAY TO SEPTEMBER**

TWO LOST SOULS AMID THE TOWERING DUNES OF THE NAMIB DESERT »

MITCH REARDON // LONELY PLANET IMAGES

LOOK WHAT THE TIDE BROUGHT IN: A SHIPWRECK SOUTH OF WALVIS BAY »

AN ELDERLY SAN WOMAN PUFFS AWAY »

TEXT MATT FIRESTONE

BOTSWANA

BESIDES BOASTING THE BEAUTIFUL OKAVANGO DELTA, BOTSWANA ENJOYS HIGH STANDARDS OF ECONOMIC STABILITY, EDUCATION AND HEALTH CARE, WHICH, WITH THE EXCEPTION OF SOUTH AFRICA, ARE UNEQUALLED ELSEWHERE IN SUB-SAHARAN AFRICA.

CAPITAL CITY GABORONE   POPULATION 1.6 MILLION   AREA 600,370 SQ KM   OFFICIAL LANGUAGE ENGLISH

≫ LIONS MATING IN THE MOREMI WILDLIFE RESERVE

LANDSCAPE
Landlocked Botswana extends 1100 kilometres from north to south and 960 kilometres from east to west, making it about the same size as Kenya or France and somewhat smaller than Texas. Most of the country lies at an average elevation of 1000 metres, and consists of a vast and nearly level sand-filled basin characterised by scrub-covered savanna. The Kalahari, a semiarid expanse of sandy valleys, covers nearly 85 per cent of the country, including the entire central and southwestern regions. In the northwest, the Okavango River flows in from Namibia and soaks into the sands to form the Okavango Delta. In the northeast are the great salty clay deserts of the Makgadikgadi and Nxai Pans, which are home to some enormous baobab trees.

HISTORY IN A NUTSHELL
During the early 19th century, the Boers began their Great Trek across the Vaal River, confident that they had heaven-sanctioned rights to any land they might choose. At the Sand River Convention of 1852, Britain recognised the Transvaal's independence, and the Boers informed the Batswana (people of Botswana) that they were now subjects of the South African Republic. However, following the British annexation of the Transvaal and the first Boer War, Britain designated lands north of the Molopo River as the British Protectorate of Bechuanaland. The protectorate proved economically invaluable to the British Empire, and was also strategically valuable as a corridor for Rhodes' Cape–Cairo railway. By 1955, however, it became apparent that Britain was preparing to release its grip on Bechuanaland. In 1962 Tswana leader Seretse Khama helped form the Bechuanaland Democratic Party (BDP), which formulated a schedule for independence. On 30 September 1966 the Republic of Botswana gained independence and Khama was elected as the country's first president.

PEOPLE
Sixty per cent of the population of Botswana claims Tswana heritage, though the country is also home to significant numbers of Herero, Mbukushu, Yei, San, Kalanga and Kgalagadi people. Botswana is rapidly urbanising, although the bulk of the population is still concentrated in the southeast, and large areas of the country are wilderness. Despite a progressive health-care system, it is estimated that as much as 40 per cent of Botswana's population is living with HIV/AIDS.

TRADEMARKS
o The Kalahari
o Okavango Delta
o Chobe River
o Diamonds
o HIV/AIDS

MARKETPLACE
Botswana is one of Africa's economic success stories. After the nation achieved democratic rule in 1966, three of the world's richest diamond-bearing formations were discovered within its borders. As a result, Botswana has transformed itself from one of the poorest nations in the world into a rapidly developing country. Today, diamonds account for over one third of Botswana's total GDP.

RANDOM FACTS
o The diamond mine at Jwaneng produces around 10 million carats annually, and processes nearly 500,000 metric tonnes of rock monthly.
o Once a vehicle enters one of the closed diamond mines it's never permitted to leave, as a precaution against smuggling.
o The Okavango Delta contains 95 per cent of all the surface water in Botswana.

ONE OF THE SAN OUT HUNTING NEAR D'KAR »

I was at the most peace with myself in an entire year of travel during this boat ride along the Okavango Delta. The locals were poling us in dugout *mokoro* canoes, pushing us through the reed grass towards our campsite for the next couple of nights. The sun was shining and there were elephants on either side of the water staring at us.

DARA LEONARD // USA

NATURAL BEAUTY

Despite Botswana's modern veneer, there's no hiding the fact that much of the country is strictly for the intrepid (not to mention relatively wealthy) traveller. With its vast open savannas teeming with free-ranging wildlife, Botswana is the Africa of everyone's dreams. Most of the country is covered with scrub brush and savanna, although small areas of deciduous forest thrive near the Zimbabwe border. Because the Okavango Delta and the Chobe River provide a year-round water supply, nearly all of the southern African mammal species are present in the Moremi Wildlife Reserve and in Chobe National Park. In the Makgadikgadi and Nxai Pan National Parks, however, thousands-strong herds of wildebeest, zebra and other hoofed mammals migrate annually in search of permanent water and stable food supplies.

IMPORT
↗ Foodstuffs
↗ Machinery
↗ Electrical goods
↗ Petrol
↗ Zimbabwean immigrants
↗ Khaki-clad tourists

EXPORT
↖ Diamonds
↖ More diamonds
↖ Precious metals
↖ Soda ash
↖ Cattle
↖ Textiles

URBAN SCENE

Although the lack of integration and unchecked sprawl deprive Gaborone of a true heart, 'Gabs', as it's affectionately called by locals, is the most cosmopolitan city in Botswana. The capital is packed with office towers, shopping malls and fast-food restaurants, but Gabs remains true to its humble roots. Produce markets still cling to the city fringe and local eateries continue to serve up steaming hot plates of *mabele* (sorghum). Gaborone might not be a thing of beauty, but to most Batswana, it is the modern face of the nation.

SURPRISES
○ Despite the apparent progressiveness of Botswana's government, recent years have been characterised by the high-profile forced relocation of San populations from the Central Kalahari Game Reserve (CKGR).
○ Travellers looking for a splurge can take a five-day luxury elephant-back safari through the Okavango Delta for US$11,000 – that's US$2200 per night or US$1.50 per minute.

TOP FESTIVAL

Established in 1987, the Maitisong Festival is the largest performing arts festival in Botswana and is held every year for seven days during the last week of March or the first week of April. The festival features an outdoor programme of music, theatre, film and dance, as well as an illustrious indoor programme that stars some of the top performing artists from around Africa.

○ **Gliding through the watery mazes of the Okavango Delta in a *mokoro*, a traditional dugout canoe**

○ **Driving (or boating) past thousands of elephants along the riverfront in Chobe National Park**

○ **Testing the limits of your survival instincts on a four-wheel drive expedition through the Central Kalahari Game Reserve**

○ **Setting out on a safari in one of Africa's most pristine (and exclusive) wildernesses at the Moremi Game Reserve**

○ **Following herds of migrating zebras and wildebeests in the baobab-dotted Makgadikgadi and Nxai Pan National Parks**

○ **Marvelling at the ancient San rock art scattered amid the mystical Tsodilo Hills**

MAP REF // N13

⌃ A SAN WOMAN UNEARTHING EDIBLE ROOTS

THE HOST WITH THE MOST: RED-BILLED OXPECKERS ON THE LOOKOUT FOR TICKS IN A GIRAFFE'S PELAGE (MANE) ⤢

MEERKATS ON THE ALERT ⤢

DECORATED HOUSES PAINT A PRETTY PICTURE IN MAKGADIKGADI ⤢

TEXT HARRIET MARTIN

ZIMBABWE

BEHIND THE GRIM MEDIA REPORTS LIES ONE OF SOUTHERN AFRICA'S MOST BEAUTIFUL – AND TODAY, UNTOURISTED – COUNTRIES, FULL OF CHARM, POLITICAL INTRIGUE AND MAGNIFICENT WILDERNESS.

CAPITAL CITY HARARE   POPULATION 12.2 MILLION   AREA 390,580 SQ KM   OFFICIAL LANGUAGE ENGLISH

LANDSCAPE

Zimbabwe has a stunning landscape – from the Limpopo River in the south to the Zambezi in the north, evergreen highlands line its eastern border. And although the country is in a tropical zone, the mostly high altitudes produce a beautiful and moderate climate (which even the worst government can't destroy) – perfect for animal-spotting safaris and gin and tonics.

HISTORY IN A NUTSHELL

The ancient rock art dotted around Zimbabwe is the work of the early Khoisan people, hunter-gatherers who inhabited Zimbabwe from the 5th century. In 1888 Cecil John Rhodes, an ambitious entrepreneur, formed the British South Africa Company and colonised the country, modestly naming it Rhodesia. In the 1950s and 1960s two African parties emerged, the Zimbabwe African People's Union (ZAPU) and the Zimbabwe African National Union (ZANU), but it wasn't long before they were banned and their leaders imprisoned. In 1966 a long bush war between freedom fighters and Rhodesian forces began, and was waged until the late 1970s. Hostilities only ended with independence in 1980, when Rhodesia became

Zimbabwe and Robert Mugabe, the ZANU candidate, its first prime minister (in 1989 he became the executive president). Today, after two stolen parliamentary elections, Zimbabwe is living under a dictatorship.

TRADEMARKS

○ President Bob
○ The weather – sun glorious sun
○ Inflation, inflation, inflation
○ Gin and tonics
○ No fuel

MARKETPLACE

In 1980 US$1 was worth Z$1.50. By 1990, after 10 successful years of independence, the Zimbabwe dollar was still strong and one of the healthiest in Africa (US$1 was worth Z$2.60). At the time of writing, the black-market rate was US$1 to Z$350,000. The biggest bank note so far has just been released – a Z$100,000 note (around 30 cents). Unemployment is at 70 per cent. The government's budget is a fraction of what it was, as the tax base has collapsed. And due to tensions with foreign governments, there's virtually no aid. Sixty-five per cent of the population earns

over Z$5 million a month but despite this, it's still below the poverty line.

PEOPLE

The two main ethnic groups are the Shona (76 per cent), who occupy the north and east, and the Ndebele (18 per cent), who live in the west. The majority are Christian, although traditional spiritual beliefs and customs are still practised, especially in rural areas, where merciless economic times are leading to an increase in faith and fraud.

RANDOM FACTS

○ President Robert Mugabe is the only African ruler who came to power at independence and is still clinging on.
○ The average monthly pension of a university lecturer who retired before 1998 does not buy a loaf of bread.
○ One in three Zimbabwean children are orphans, yet despite the economic crisis, 90 per cent of them are cared for by extended family.
○ Zimbabwe lost at least 25 per cent of its wildlife population in the years between 2000 and 2002 to poaching.

NOTHING BEATS AN ELEPHANT'S-EYE VIEW OF THE ZIMBABWEAN LANDSCAPE »

NATURAL BEAUTY

Zimbabwe has its share of surprises – for the visitor, most of them good – but it's unlikely anything will compare with Victoria Falls. Despite its fame, it's essentially unchanged since Livingstone first saw it 170 years ago, and is every bit a 'wonder of the world'. However, Great Zimbabwe National Monument is an intriguing archaeological site where a powerful ancient city once stood. Its stone structures are the largest in Africa south of the Egyptian pyramids.

WILD THINGS

We can talk birds, or we can talk herds, but let's be straight: Zimbabwe is one of the best countries in the world for viewing lions. Okay, there are not as many as in, say, the Serengeti, but it has the only national park in Africa that allows unguided walking safaris. And there's nothing more nerve-racking than hunting lions… without the gun.

MUSIC

Zimbabwean musicians are turning from the West and finding their inspiration within – and they're making a lot of noise at home and abroad. Notable are Oliver Mtukudzi, Dudu Manhenga, Chiwoniso Maraire and Plaxedes Wenyika. From gospel to pop, urban grooves, jazz and township, the common thread is the way Zimbabweans use music to advise each other – about the environment, HIV/AIDS, respecting where you come from and, above all, about hope.

TOP FESTIVAL

Harare International Festival of Arts is *the* event, held annually in the last week of April. Embassies and corporate sponsors cram the timetable with both international acts and Zimbabwean artists, spanning classical music, jazz, soul, funk, theatre and dance.

BEER MONEY

The cost of a beer today in a pub in Zimbabwe is Z$250,000. If you paid for it with one-cent coins – common just a few years ago – you'd have to wait for the bartender to count to 25 million! What's more, the coinage would weigh about 45,000 kilograms. Your best bet would be to sell the coins on the international metal market. Using a very conservative estimate, you'd reap US$184,500. Even if you resisted the temptation to change your money at the black-market rate of US$1 to Z$350,000, and changed at the bank rate of US$1 to Z$99,201, you'd still end up with Z$18,302,584,500! If beer prices haven't increased, your coinage will buy you 73,210 beers.

FUTURE DIRECTIONS

Inflation has topped 1000 per cent and some warn it may go to 3000 per cent; the president has promised to no longer follow 'orthodox economic policies' and to print money when he wants to. Fortunately, he's currently ensuring a smooth departure from office – though 2008 is a little later than was expected. Until he's gone, the international community is unlikely to show Zimbabwe any warmth.

⌃ A FEMALE CORN HARVESTER CARRYING A BABY

⌃ SUNLIGHT CASTS A GOLDEN GLOW IN MATOBO NATIONAL PARK

⌃ A DANCER HIDES BEHIND A TRADITIONAL MASK

ESSENTIAL EXPERIENCES

○ Taking an ultralight flight, white-water rafting or bungee jumping at Victoria Falls, then relaxing in five-star comfort with a cocktail and sunset

○ Canoeing past – not through! – hippos and crocs on the Zambezi at Mana Pools National Park

○ Fishing, taking a safari on horseback, winning millions (read: $5) at the casino or climbing Zimbabwe's second-highest peak – all possible near Nyanga

○ Walking with lions and sleeping under the stars in Hwange National Park

MAP REF // O12

BEST TIME TO VISIT MAY TO OCTOBER

TWO CHILDREN POSE FOR THE CAMERA »

TOWN CHIEF, RUSAPE »

CHILDREN FROM MAJORHO SCHOOL PLAY VOLLEYBALL »

TEXT JOE BINDLOSS

SOUTH AFRICA

CLOSER TO ANTARCTICA THAN TO THE SAHARA, SOUTH AFRICA IS WHERE AFRICA AND EUROPE COLLIDE, A RAINBOW NATION FORGING A NEW FUTURE AFTER DECADES OF OPPRESSION.

CAPITAL CITIES PRETORIA (ADMINISTRATIVE), CAPE TOWN (LEGISLATIVE), BLOEMFONTEIN (JUDICIAL)   POPULATION 44.2 MILLION   AREA 1.2 MILLION SQ KM
OFFICIAL LANGUAGES AFRIKAANS, ENGLISH, NDEBELE, NORTHERN SOTHO, SOUTHERN SOTHO, SWATI, TSONGA, TSWANA, VENDA, XHOSA, ZULU

LANDSCAPE

South Africa is a vast and varied country. The south is mountainous and temperate, the north arid and tropical. In the centre are the rolling grasslands of the Highveld, enveloping Johannesburg and Pretoria; the northeast is dominated by huge national parks. South Africa is unique for having two independent nations within its borders – Lesotho, with its dramatic highland scenery, and tiny Swaziland, tucked against the Mozambique border.

HISTORY IN A NUTSHELL

The earliest South Africans were the San, a hunter-gatherer tribe that settled the southern tip of Africa 40,000 years ago. In the south the San adopted agriculture while the north saw an influx of Bantu-speaking peoples from the Niger Delta. Little changed until the 17th century, when land-hungry Dutch settlers arrived. The British Empire annexed South Africa in 1814, but tensions flared with Afrikaans-speaking Boer farmers over the abolition of slavery and the importation of Indian workers (including one Mohandas Gandhi). After the Anglo-Boer war, Afrikaner nationalists gained the upper hand. South Africa became a republic in 1961 and the new government introduced a policy of apartheid – the forced separation of the races – ushering in South Africa's darkest days. The African National Congress led the fight for freedom, finally achieved by Nelson Mandela in 1991. Mandela's policy of reconciliation has largely been continued by his successor, Thabo Mbeki.

TRADEMARKS

- Springboks
- Nelson Mandela
- Peace and reconciliation
- Wildlife safaris
- Giant steaks
- Table Mountain
- Apartheid – gone but not forgotten

PEOPLE

In many ways there are two South Africas – one African and one European. Power and wealth are still concentrated among white South Africans, who make up just 10 per cent of the population. Around 79 per cent of the population are black Africans and a further nine per cent are of mixed race – 'coloured' in local parlance. The country is 80 per cent Christian, with small communities of animists, Muslims and Hindus – although those of all religions adhere to a host of tribal beliefs as well. South Africa has 11 official languages, more than any country apart from India.

MARKETPLACE

South Africa is the financial powerhouse of Africa. A quarter of the GDP for the entire continent is produced within its borders. Mining, electricity production, finance, car manufacturing and tourism are major industries; indeed, South Africa was one of the first nations to welcome tourists from China. However, unemployment stands at a staggering 25 per cent, and is highest among the black township population.

RANDOM FACTS

- South Africa alone produces two thirds of all Africa's electricity.
- Nelson Mandela wrote his famous Long Walk to Freedom secretly in Robben Island prison, hiding the pages behind a loose section of wall in the exercise yard.
- Half of South Africa's wealth is concentrated among 10 per cent of the population.

THE LEADER OF THE PACK: ONE CURIOUS OSTRICH OGLES THE CAMERA WHILE FELLOW BIRDS HANG BACK »

⋀ SOUTH AFRICA IS SYNONYMOUS WITH WORLD-CLASS SURFING

⋀ THE VIEW ACROSS BLYDE RIVER CANYON IN THE KLEIN DRAKENSBERG MOUNTAINS

⋀ LIFEGUARDS AT DURBAN BEACH

THE QUIVER TREE IS SO CALLED BECAUSE THE SAN MADE QUIVERS FOR THEIR ARROWS FROM ITS BRANCHES »

A CELEBRATION OF THE VERTICAL LINE IN PORT ELIZABETH »

PERFECT POSTURE : A ZULU WOMAN CARRIES A POT ON HER HEAD »

NATURAL BEAUTY

The diversity of the landscapes across South Africa is breathtaking, taking in the Kalahari Desert, subtropical areas, scrubland plateau and mountains. The looming mass of Table Mountain is a South African icon, of course, but the peaks of the Drakensberg are even more dramatic, falling suddenly away towards the coastal plain – this is prime trekking country. Just north is Kruger National Park, the most popular destination for wildlife-spotting safaris. Further south are the wave-lashed coves of the Wild Coast, perhaps the most unspoilt part of South Africa.

URBAN SCENE

Johannesburg may be bigger, but Cape Town is definitely South Africa's favourite city, relaxed and genteel. Table Mountain rises gloriously overhead and the waves of the South Atlantic crash magnificently on a string of gorgeous surfing beaches. Downtown has the feel of an old colonial capital, while the seafront is closer to Miami or Surfers Paradise. Cape Town also has a huge Indian population, concentrated in colourful Bo-Kaap. Thousands of black South Africans, however, still eke out a meagre living in the townships of Crossroads and Khayelitsha. Within easy driving distance of the city are the Winelands region, the famous Garden Route and a couple of national parks.

IMPORT

↗ British sport
↗ Dutch words
↗ European prejudices
↗ The frontier spirit
↗ Cadbury chocolate
↗ Viticulture
↗ Minibus taxis

EXPORT

↖ Nelson Mandela
↖ Cage diving
↖ Year-round fruit
↖ Cape wines
↖ Enlightened attitudes to overcoming and recovering from oppression

CUISINE

European settlers to South Africa imported the habits of home, including a love of good food and wine. Modern South African food is an enticing mix of European, African and Indian flavours, with lots of unusual meats and legendary wines from the Cape of Good Hope. Afrikaans cuisine is a different story, however – designed as it was to help Afrikaners withstand the rigours of travel in the veld. Probably the most famous Afrikaans dish is biltong, dried strips of beef or antelope meat flavoured with salt, pepper and coriander.

SURPRISES

○ Penguins! The Cape of Good Hope has a native population of jackass penguins, which are unexpected interlopers all the way from Antarctica.
○ Brotherly love – though grievances remain, generally South Africans on both sides of the racial divide seem to be committed to putting the past behind them.

WILD THINGS

Lions, elephants, hippos, zebras, giraffes… every conceivable African animal can be found in South Africa's national parks. Kruger National Park in the north is an African legend, home to all the 'big five' and a host of antelope and monkey species as well.

Uniquely South African species include the tiny aardwolf, which is related to the hyena, and the famous aardvark, best known for the second entry in most English-language dictionaries. Fynbos, the low-lying vegetation of the Southern Cape, is found nowhere else.

MYTHS & LEGENDS

South Africa is home to a living legend – Nelson Mandela. In his 80s, the former South African president and activist remains one of the most charismatic and inspirational leaders in Africa. Despite spending 27 years in prison, Mandela never bowed to the oppression of apartheid, refusing offers of early release without the promise of free elections. Mandela was also almost single-handedly responsible for the present policy of peace and reconciliation, turning the transition from apartheid to democracy into a process of nation-building instead of a quest for revenge.

FUTURE DIRECTIONS

South Africa has come on in leaps and bounds since the fall of apartheid, but there have still been a number of hiccups on the road to democracy, most notably when President Thabo Mbeki refused to acknowledge the AIDS crisis that afflicts one third of the population. Another issue is the redistribution of land and jobs from white citizens to black citizens. While it seems a logical step towards equality, you only have to look at Zimbabwe to see how easily such well-intentioned policies can go awry.

ESSENTIAL EXPERIENCES

○ **Climbing an African icon – Cape Town's magnificent Table Mountain**
○ **Sampling the local pinotage on a tour of the Cape Winelands**
○ **Diving with great white sharks at Hermanus – reality bites!**
○ **Plugging into the energy of township life in sprawling Soweto**
○ **Stretching a leg through the mighty Drakensberg range**
○ **Seeking out the big five in Kruger National Park**
○ **Witnessing dolphins surf while trekking the Otter Trail**

ERIC L WHEATER // LONELY PLANET IMAGES

⌃ BOYS AND THEIR TOY WINDMILLS IN MPUMALANGA

ARIADNE VAN ZANDBERGEN // LONELY PLANET IMAGES

⌃ A DANCER'S ANKLE DECORATIONS

FROM THE TRAVELLER

This image depicts the Drakensberg mountain range at sunrise. After spending the night on the amphitheatre in the Drakensberg, I woke up to a cold but clear morning. After walking to the edge of the plateau and the point where Tugela Falls makes its 947-metre drop I saw the lower mountains of the Drakensberg range covered in clouds. Here, the peaks are seen just coming through the clouds.

SACHAR DE VRIES // NETHERLANDS

MAP REF // N14

BEST TIME TO VISIT JUNE TO SEPTEMBER FOR HIKING, NOVEMBER TO MARCH FOR SUNSHINE

COME STAY WITH ME: A WELCOMING SMILE FROM THE OWNER OF VICKY'S B&B, KAYELITSHA, CAPE TOWN »

AFRICAN SYNTHESIS: THE BEADED MOTIFS OF THIS NDEBELE WOMAN'S TRADITIONAL DRESS MELD INTO THE MURAL BEHIND HER »

THE LEGGY BEAUTIES OF SOUTH AFRICA »

TEXT MATT FIRESTONE

SWAZILAND

SWAZILAND IS RENOWNED FOR ITS LAID-BACK ATMOSPHERE AND WELCOMING PEOPLE – THEN AGAIN, IT PAYS TO HAVE A SENSE OF HUMOUR WHEN YOU'RE RULED BY AFRICA'S LAST ABSOLUTE MONARCH, KING MSWATI III, WHO'S INFAMOUS FOR HIS EXCESSIVELY LAVISH LIFESTYLE.

CAPITAL CITY MBABANE   POPULATION 1.1 MILLION   AREA 17,363 SQ KM   OFFICIAL LANGUAGE ENGLISH

⌃ SWAZI MAIDENS PREPARE TO DANCE BEFORE THE KING AT THE ANNUAL UMHLANGA REED DANCE HELD AT THE LUDZIDZINI ROYAL VILLAGE

LANDSCAPE

Landlocked Swaziland is sandwiched between the mountainous Mozambican border and the mid- and highveld of South Africa. The northwest extremity of the country is largely characterised by rainforest, while the agricultural industry is sustained by the country's numerous rivers, including the Lusutfu. In terms of conservation, King Mswati III has ushered in a progressive approach to wildlife preservation that has endowed Swaziland with a striking bunch of national parks.

HISTORY IN A NUTSHELL

In the mid-18th century, the first Swazi king, Ngwane III, led his people south from Mozambique to the Pongola River in present-day Swaziland. Under pressure from the Zulu, the next king, Sobhuza I, withdrew to the Ezulwini Valley, which remains the centre of Swazi royalty and rituals. In 1877 the British flexed their military muscle and annexed the kingdom, though independence was granted on paper during the Swaziland Convention of 1881. In 1968 British rule was overturned peacefully, and the independent country of Swaziland inherited a constitution that was largely the work of the British. In 1973, however, King Sobhuza II suspended it, on the grounds that it did not reflect Swazi culture, and four years later parliament reconvened under a new constitution that vested all power in the king. Since 1986 Swaziland has been governed by King Mswati III, whose rule has been marked by regular funding requests for luxury cars, private jets, exotic travel and palaces for his wives (13 at present count).

TRADEMARKS

○ Mkhaya Game Reserve
○ Ezulwini Valley
○ Royal weddings
○ Swazi arts and crafts
○ HIV/AIDS

MARKETPLACE

The Swaziland economy is inextricably tied to South Africa, from which it receives about 90 per cent of its imports and to which it sends about two thirds of its exports. However, the country remains dependent on remittances from workers employed in South Africa, as well as duties from the Southern Africa Customs Union. Although the manufacturing sector has grown in recent years, it's estimated that nearly 80 per cent of the population survives through subsistence agriculture and pastoralism.

PEOPLE

The population of Swaziland is largely comprised of ethnic Swazi, though there is a significant minority of white people. It's estimated that over 40 per cent of the population is living with HIV/AIDS, which is the highest infection rate in the world.

RANDOM FACTS

○ The king's personal car is a DaimlerChrysler Maybach 62, and features a television, DVD player, 21-speaker surround-sound system, minifridge, cordless telephone and sterling silver champagne flutes. It costs around US$500,000.
○ In 2002 Swaziland's parliament voted against a government request to purchase a US$50 million luxury jet for Mswati III.
○ The World Health Organisation (WHO) estimates that HIV testing and counselling services typically cost under US$30 per person.

WILD THINGS

Swaziland is one of the few countries in Africa where it's still possible to spot black rhinoceroses. Despite their formidable appearance, black rhinos are extremely nervous animals. When disturbed, they are quick to flee the scene, though they will confront an

SISTERLY SOLIDARITY IN A SWAZILAND VILLAGE »

STEMMING THE TIDE OF AIDS: COLOURED TASSELS WORN AROUND THE HEAD IDENTIFY VIRGINS IN SWAZILAND »

aggressor head-on, particularly if their young are present. As a result, they are difficult to observe for extended periods of time in the wild. Black rhinos can easily be identified by their triangular (rather than square) lip and their lack of a neck hump.

IMPORT
↗ Machinery
↗ Transport equipment
↗ Foodstuffs
↗ Petroleum products
↗ Luxury cars
↗ Wedding cakes

EXPORT
↖ Soft-drink concentrates
↖ Sugar
↖ Wood pulp
↖ Cotton yarn
↖ Refrigerators
↖ Canned fruit

MYTHS & LEGENDS
The Incwala or 'First Fruits' ceremony is both a harvest festival and a ritual cleansing of the king and country. Incwala is also intended to sanctify the king's ability

to father children (the previous king, Sobhuza II, fathered more than 600). Many of the rituals associated with the Incwala ceremony symbolise the wanderings of the ancient queen mother, who survived on sugar cane, maize and wild pumpkin. She also sheltered herself and her son with the branches of the lusekwane shrub, which is now considered sacred.

SURPRISES
○ In order to combat the HIV/AIDS epidemic, King Mswati III decreed in 2001 that men were prohibited from having sex with teenage girls for five years.
○ Just two months after imposing the ban, Mswati III fined himself a cow for breaking the ban by taking a 17-year-old girl as his ninth wife.
○ The ban against sex with teenagers was prematurely lifted in 2005, just weeks before Mswati III chose another 17-year-old girl as his thirteenth wife.

TOP FESTIVAL
The Umhlanga Reed Dance, which typically takes place annually in August, features an assembly of about 20,000 bare-breasted young maidens who dance before the king, and present him with a mature reed. Traditionally, the dance was meant to encourage young women to remain abstinent.

≫ A RURAL SWAZI MAN PREPARES A SIMPLE MEAL

≫ SWAZI KING MSWATI III AND HIS ENTOURAGE

≫ A CONTEMPORARY REWORKING OF TRADITIONAL CARVING SKILLS

ESSENTIAL EXPERIENCES

○ **Tracking the last remaining black and white rhinos in Swaziland at the Mkhaya Game Reserve, the country's premier wildlife venue**

○ **Watching Incwala Ceremony and the Umhlanga Reed Dance, both of which take place at the Royal Kraal in the Ezulwini Valley**

○ **Visiting the largest protected area in Swaziland, Hlane Royal National Park, which is located near the former royal hunting grounds**

○ **Hiking or birding your way through the Malolotja Nature Reserve, a rugged wilderness that boasts a 200-kilometre network of trails**

○ **Spotting rare black eagles at the Milwane Wildlife Sanctuary, a small private reserve that protects a variety of game**

Piggs Peak
Malolotja Nature Reserve
Mhlume
Mlawula Nature Reserve
✪ MBABANE
Lobamba
Hlane Royal National Park
Manzini
Siteki
MOZAMBIQUE
Mankayane
Mkhaya Nature Reserve
Big Bend
Hlathikulu
Nhlangano
SOUTH AFRICA
Lavumisa

MAP REF // P14

BEST TIME TO VISIT **MAY TO SEPTEMBER**

MOTHER AND BABIES HANG OUT BY THE WATER ≫

TRIO OF SWAZI WOMEN IN BOLD TRADITIONAL DRESS ≫

A YOUNG CATTLE HERDER: CATTLE ARE IMPORTANT SYMBOLS OF WEALTH AND STATUS IN SWAZI CULTURE ≫

KARL LEHMANN // LONELY PLANET IMAGES

JODY DENHAM // ART DIRECTORS

LESOTHO

THE MOUNTAINOUS ENCLAVE OF LESOTHO IS ENTIRELY SURROUNDED BY SOUTH AFRICA, THOUGH ITS NATIONAL IDENTITY IS UNIQUE.

CAPITAL CITY MASERU   POPULATION 2 MILLION   AREA 30,355 SQ KM   OFFICIAL LANGUAGE ENGLISH

LANDSCAPE

Rightfully known as the Kingdom in the Sky, Lesotho has the highest lowest point of any country in the world (1400 metres), and is the only country that's entirely above 1000 metres. In fact, over 80 per cent of the country lies at an elevation of more than 1800 metres, and it's largely characterised by the jagged peaks and fertile valleys of the Drakensberg. Although the country's snowcapped mountains and lush green valleys have often been likened to those of Switzerland, there's no mistaking its cultural heritage. Lesotho's hillsides are richly adorned with San rock art, and its small towns and villages fiercely protect their Basotho identity.

HISTORY IN A NUTSHELL

The Basotho emerged as a people in the 1820s, when Moshoeshoe the Great gathered the tribes scattered by Zulu raids and established the stronghold of Thaba-Bosiu near present-day Maseru. In 1868, after a series of wars against the Boers, Moshoeshoe placed the region under the protection of the British government. Following his death, however, the British signed control of the region over to the Cape Colony in 1871, only to have it shuttled back into British control in 1880. This was eventually revealed to be a lucky break for the Basotho – had they remained part of the Cape Colony, they would have been subjected to apartheid under the newly formed Union of South Africa. In the 1950s, the Basotholand National Council requested internal self-government, and it was granted in 1966. Lesotho became independent under Prime Minister Leabua Jonathan. However, when Leabua was defeated at the 1970 poll, he declared a state of emergency, suspended the constitution, expelled the king and banned the opposition. Since then, Lesotho's political climate has been characterised largely by coups d'états and meddling from various foreign powers, particularly the South African government.

PEOPLE

The population of Lesotho is almost entirely comprised of Basotho, who trace their origins back to the disparate Sotho clans united by Moshoeshoe the Great in the early 19th century. Having been spared the torturous policies of apartheid, Lesotho is a relaxed and welcoming country to travel in and the Basotho people are renowned for their warmth and hospitality. Today a large number of Basotho work as migrant labourers in the gold mines of South Africa. Unfortunately, along with their foreign income the returning migrants import HIV/AIDS, resulting in a rampant epidemic – it's estimated that 30 per cent of the population lives with the virus.

MARKETPLACE

The fledgling Lesotho economy is dependent on remittances from miners employed in South Africa as well as duties from the Southern Africa Customs Union. In recent years, though, the completion of a large hydropower facility has enabled the country to generate income through the sale of water to South Africa, and there's a growing manufacturing sector based on farm products and apparel assembly. Nevertheless, the economy is still largely based on subsistence agriculture and pastoralism, especially in the area around Quthing.

TRADEMARKS

○ Moshoeshoe the Great
○ Thaba-Bosiu
○ Malealea
○ Basotho ponies
○ Drakensberg

A BOY'S BEST FRIEND: WORKING DOGS ARE PART AND PARCEL OF LESOTHO'S PASTORAL ECONOMY »

RANDOM FACTS

○ Sani Pass, which connects KwaZulu-Natal in South Africa to northern Lesotho, is regarded as one of the most dangerous roads in southern Africa. The remains of vehicles that did not succeed in navigating its steep gradients and poor surfaces are littered on both sides of the pass.

○ Because of its mountainous terrain, Lesotho is one of the only places in southern Africa that experiences four distinct seasons.

NATURAL BEAUTY

The Drakensberg (meaning 'Dragon Mountains') are the geological remnants of the original African plateau. The escarpment has a sandstone base and a thick cap of basalt, and is characterised by its unusual combination of steep-sided blocks and pinnacles (which are reminiscent of a dragon's back). Heavy snow falls regularly in winter, and rains and mists are fairly common year-round.

WILD THINGS

Basotho ponies are world-renowned for their agility, hardy frames, docility and stamina. The foundation breed is believed to be the Cape horse, which was a Java horse of strong Persian and Arab descent. Cape horses were first brought to southern Africa by the Dutch East India Company in 1652, though they didn't appear in Lesotho until the early 18th century, when they were captured from the Zulu and the Boers. However, it's widely believed that the Basotho pony was an established breed as early as 1870. Today it's estimated that there are over 100,000 Basotho ponies in Lesotho, the majority of which are used for transport through the rugged terrain.

NICHOLAS DEVORE // GETTY

⌃ COLOUR COORDINATION PAR EXCELLENCE

DI JONES // LONELY PLANET IMAGES

⌃ DRAKENSBERG DREAMING ON THE BACK OF A BASOTHO PONY

MYTHS & LEGENDS

Thaba-Bosiu, a steep mountain with a flat top that's rife with freshwater springs, is regarded by the Basotho as a sacred spot. After Moshoeshoe the Great and his followers built their mountain stronghold here in 1824, neither the British nor the Boers were successful in their siege attempts. According to Basotho legend, Thaba-Bosiu or the 'Mountain of Night' is a seemingly normal hill by day, but grows into a huge and unconquerable mountain as night falls.

IMPORT

↗ Food
↗ Building materials
↗ Medicine
↗ Petroleum
↗ Customs duties
↗ South African–paid wages

EXPORT

↖ Water
↖ Light machinery
↖ Farm vehicles
↖ Textiles
↖ Wool
↖ Migrant workers

TOP FESTIVAL

On 14 March, Moshoeshoe Day is celebrated, in commemoration of the founding father of Lesotho. The main festivities take place in Maseru and feature a colourful procession of Lesothans in traditional dress going from the royal palace to the Sotho Stadium.

ESSENTIAL EXPERIENCES

○ **Searching for ancient San paintings hidden in rock shelters near the scenic mountain village of Malealea**

○ **Visiting the grave of Lesotho's founding father, Moshoeshoe the Great, in the mountain stronghold of Thaba-Bosiu**

○ **Trekking through the rugged Drakensberg on the back of a sure-footed Basotho pony**

○ **Basking in the splendid isolation of Sehlabathebe National Park, Lesotho's first protected area**

○ **Shopping for tapestries and wool products at the craft industries centre of Teyateyaneng, the 'Place of Quick Sands'**

MAP REF // O14

BEST TIME TO VISIT **OCTOBER TO APRIL**

⌃ FIELDS OF COSMOS BLOOMING AT EASTER TIME, MALEALEA

DI JONES // LONELY PLANET IMAGES

WOMEN BUY THEIR EVERYDAY SUPPLIES FROM A LOCAL SHOP »

A WOMAN BEATS HER DRUM AMID THE SNOW »

HOW MANY CHILDREN CAN LEGALLY RIDE ON THIS? AN ABANDONED TRUCK MAKES THE PERFECT PLAYTHING FOR THE CHILDREN OF MALEALEA VILLAGE »

THEMES OF AFRICA

TEXT **MATT PHILLIPS**

ADRENALINE FIX ADVENTURE ACTIVITIES

⌃ RIDING WHITE WATER ON THE ZAMBEZI   ⌃ JUST PART OF THE SCHOOL IN GRAND BAIE, MAURITIUS   ⌃ TAKING A LEAP AT VICTORIA FALLS

THE FOOT THAT IS RESTLESS WILL TREAD ON A TURD.

Ethiopian proverb

The lion may be king of the jungle, but the safari doesn't have to rule the roost. Today, Africa offers up a world of adventure activities – surf down the world's biggest sand dunes, tread water with great white sharks or tiptoe past sleeping equatorial glaciers.

TREKKING

Trekking has long been at the top of Africa's adventure activities list – trekkers were bagging summits in East Africa as early as the late 1800s. Today, there are numerous opportunities for trekking, ranging from stunning coastal jaunts in South Africa to chilly mountain passes in Morocco. Besides the gorgeous journeys themselves, some treks offer unparalleled access to remote wildlife and unique cultural interactions unattainable to those who fail to unstick their behinds from their four-wheel drives.

Tanzania's Mt Kilimanjaro (5896 metres) is the highest summit in Africa and one of the continent's greatest sights; it lures hundreds of people up its slopes every year. When you see this snowcapped, gently sloping stratovolcano rising majestically up out of the baking African plains, you'll understand what all the fuss is about.

Although it's 697 metres shorter than Kilimanjaro, Mt Kenya (5199 metres) arguably offers better trekking. Once Africa's highest summit, it has been chiselled down by erosion into a melange of valleys, cliffs and summits. Of its three highest summits, only Point Lenana (4985 metres) can be reached on foot, but it offers views up to Batian (the highest summit at 5199 metres) and down to Lewis Glacier, a mere 16 kilometres from the equator. Mt Kenya's flora is as unique as it is beautiful – Unesco has declared the mountain a Biosphere Reserve.

Little visited but incredibly rewarding are Uganda's Rwenzori Mountains (or Mountains of the Moon). With 20 peaks exceeding 4500 metres, the Rwenzoris are Africa's highest mountain range. There are large alpine and rainforest zones which host an abundance of plant and animal life. Thick vegetation, rain and mud make trekking here more demanding than on Mt Kilimanjaro or Mt Kenya, though when the mists break and you glimpse the spectacular views of the main massifs and their glaciers, you'll forget the pain.

The Simien Mountains of Ethiopia resemble a verdant version of the Grand Canyon, with its high plateaus perched on the edge of Abyssinian abysses. Treks here offer glimpses of unique wildlife as well as intriguing interactions with remote highland people.

Morocco's mountains are riddled with trekking routes: you can stroll through the cedar forests of the Middle Atlas or climb the long, steep, rocky slopes in the High Atlas. Jebel Sarho, at the edge of the Sahara, offers a completely contrasting

trekking experience, with its landscape of mud bricks, arid plateaus and sculptural rock formations.

The Drakensberg mountains of South Africa and Lesotho also offer a plethora of great trekking trails. The Otter Trail, which runs along the coast on South Africa's Garden Route, is one of the continent's most beautiful and exclusive treks (only 12 people per day are granted access).

WHITE-WATER RAFTING

Thanks to the fact that some of the world's largest rivers course through the continent, Africa offers some of the most exciting (and frightening to some) white-water rafting on the planet. In fact, the Zambezi River's Batoka Rapids, which flow between Zambia and Zimbabwe, have been dubbed the wildest one-day white-water run in the world.

When the water level is low (October to December), the Zambezi is at its best. Rafts are launched within eyeshot of Victoria Falls, and the waters are still so frothy from their 100-metre fall that the site is simply known as 'The Boiling Pot'. You might think that starting next to one of the world's seven natural wonders would mean you've already experienced the best the trip offers, but you'd be wrong. The barrage of class-five rapids that follow will leave you gasping for breath and begging for more. Along the way you'll cruise beneath soaring basalt bluffs and past crocodiles sunning themselves on shore (toes in the boat!).

Challenging the Zambezi for supremacy is the source of the Nile in Jinja, Uganda. It boasts four seriously famous class-five rapids, along with more subdued sections for those not wanting to wash their insides as well as their outsides.

Less vigorous trips are also possible on countless other stretches of African water.

ROCK CLIMBING

Numerous desolate mountains that poke from Africa's plains and deserts have attained cult status in the climbing world. The dramatic north pillar of Kago Tondo within Mali's *La Main de Fatima* massif is justifiably famous. At 731 metres (and with a climb rating of 5.7 to 5.10b), it's one of the world's longest sandstone climbs. Equally striking is Namibia's Spitzkoppe, a 1728-metre tower of granite rising from the dusty Damaraland plains. Known as 'the Matterhorn of Namibia', it hosts a six-pitch 5.10a climb.

Climbers are also starting to creep into Kenya. Mt Poi (2050 metres), within Northern Kenya's remote Ndoto Mountains, offers four fabulous routes (5.12b to 5.13a) up its metamorphic gneisses. Fischer's Tower in Hell's Gate National Park has a few challenging climbs (5.7 to 5.11d) – eyes on the rock and off the zebras! Those wishing to summit Batian (5199 metres), Mt Kenya's highest peak, have several options including *Diamond Couloir* (5.8) and the *Diamond Buttress* (5.10a).

South Africa has the most developed climbing scene in Africa, with some 90 sites hanging throughout the country (even some ice climbs during winter!). Try your fingers and toes at Elsie's Peak near Cape Town (5.4 to 5.12d) – the view over the ocean is transcendent. Or head for Oudtshoorn and tackle the *Phallic Mechanic* (5.11c), *Tears for Fears* (5.12c) or *Seven* (5.14a).

The granite cliffs within Madagascar's Andringitra National Park are also home to some truly great climbs (5.7 to 5.13c), as are the walls of Morocco's arresting Todra Gorge.

DIVING & SNORKELLING

Whether you want to dive into a deep blue abyss or skirt shallow atolls, Africa has some of the planet's top diving and snorkelling locations. In the north are the famous Red Sea corals and aquatic life. Less known, but equally enticing, are the wrecks at the Gulf of Aqaba's entrance and in the Strait of Tiran, off Egypt.

Sudan's soft and hard corals are in perfect condition and host an array of unquantifiable aquatic life, including healthy populations of hammerhead shark. Explore Shaab Rumi, the reef lagoon chosen by Jacques Cousteau for his renowned Conshelf II project.

Eritrea's shallow coastal plateau, coupled with a limited fishing industry during the civil wars, has led to densities of aquatic life not seen anywhere else in the Red Sea. And just south in Djibouti, Ghoubbet al Kharab (a bay off the Gulf of Tadjoura) is one of the world's best places to swim with whale sharks.

East Africa's Indian Ocean waters are also laden with splendid dive spots. Kenya's Kisite, Watamu and Malindi national marine parks are all good options (especially for night dives), though visibility is severely limited between April and September. Tanzania's Zanzibar Archipelago hosts exceptionally diverse marine life – everything from hawksbill and green turtles to deep-sea species such as the Napoleon wrasse, barracuda and shark. There are also some tremendous wall dives off the island of Pemba.

Just south in Mozambique, the pristine coral atolls of the Quirimbas Archipelago have now been protected as a park and offer sublime dive opportunities. Less exclusive (and less pricey) dives can also be had at the more established Bazaruto Archipelago National Marine Park.

We'd also be remiss if we didn't mention that there are a plethora of dive options off the mainland's coast in the waters surrounding the island nations of Madagascar, Seychelles, Mauritius, Réunion, Comoros and Mayotte.

SKIING & BOARDING

No, we haven't lost the plot! Morocco's Oukaïmeden, in the High Atlas, and Mischliffen, in the Middle Atlas, are rough and ready resorts for some downhill action between December and February. Rewarding back-country skiing is also possible in the Middle Atlas, Toubkal Massif and on the Tichka Plateau. At Tiffendell, in the striking southern Drakensberg mountains in South Africa, snow-makers make downhill skiing and snowboarding possible during June, July and August.

If snow doesn't appeal, head for Namibia's Namib Desert and blaze down gargantuan dunes on a sandboard. It's serious fun, though it isn't nearly as easy to dig sand out of your nether regions as snow.

SURFING

South Africa is the king of Africa's surf scene, and Jeffrey's Bay wears the crown. Supertubes at J-Bay (as it's known) is reputed to have some of the world's speediest and most sublimely formed waves. Nearby Cape St Francis is almost as nice. Other sweet South African spots include Cape Agulhas, Durban, Port Alfred, Cape Town and the wild Wild Coast.

Namibia offers a few sweet rides in the chilly Atlantic, including one at Cape Cross that breaks continuously for several hundred metres. Cape Cross' lack of shark nets and thriving population of seals may make you think twice, though! Warmer waters are to be had in Mozambique with Tofinho, just around the corner from Tofo and near the charming town of Inhambane, boasting the country's best surf. Ponto d'Ouro, with a lovely long right point break, is a close second.

Morocco's surf pales in comparison, but the waters are still a whole lot warmer than Europe's! Anchor Point in Agadir, nearby Taghazout and several remote beaches near Tamri are good choices. If the wind is up, there's great windsurfing at Essaouira.

Less conventional, but entirely challenging, is surfing the Zambezi's standing waves within the Batoka Gorge at Victoria Falls.

ADRENALINE ACTIVITIES

There are sports that happen to elicit adrenaline, like surfing, boarding and white-water rafting, and then there are activities designed purely to stimulate its panicked production. Hopping into a small cage to face great white sharks in churning, chum-filled seas is certainly one such activity. It's possible east of Cape Town near Dyer Island. Also on South Africa's Garden Route is the world's highest commercial bungee jump. If that 216-metre bungee is too tame for you, head to Swakopmund in Namibia, hurl yourself from a plane and freefall over the meeting of the Atlantic Ocean and the dunes of the Namib Desert.

Although its 111-metre bungee has lost its lofty title as world's highest, Victoria Falls still produces more adrenaline than anywhere else on the continent. Along with the bungee jumping and white-water rafting, there is jet boating, abseiling, river boarding (hope you're thirsty!) and a thrilling gorge swing over the Zambezi that involves a 50-metre freefall and more g-forces than are worth thinking about!

TOP 10 ADVENTURE ACTIVITIES

- Enjoying the gods'-eye view while falling from the heavens – skydiving on Namibia's coast
- Going head to head with the Batoka Rapids while white-water rafting the Zambezi at Victoria Falls
- Completing the stunning Summit Circuit trek around the glacier-clad peaks of Mt Kenya
- Swimming in a sea of technicolour marine life and through World War II wrecks in Egypt's Red Sea
- Using your fingers, toes and a whole lot of skill to rock climb up the Kago Tondo pillar in Mali
- Staring Jaws in the face while cage diving off South Africa's Garden Route
- Avoiding demons while floating in the midst of whale sharks in Djibouti's cursed Ghoubbet al Kharab (Devil's Cauldron)
- Plummeting towards the bottom of the South Africa's Bloukrans River Gorge before the 200-metre bungee cord breaks your fall
- Seeing the sun rise from the 'Roof of Africa', a perfect end to a Kilimanjaro ascent
- Sandboarding down the face of a parabolic dune in the Namib Desert

THE PERFECT WAVE, BALITO BAY, SOUTH AFRICA

NO SURF? SANDBOARD DOWN NAMIBIA'S DUNES

THE BIG BLUE – A WHALE SHARK IN MOZAMBIQUE

TEXT NAOMI DOUMBIA

AFRICAN CULTURES & TRADITIONS

WEDDING DECORATIONS FOR THE BRIDE IN NUBIA ⌃

WHO IS THAT MASKED MAN? DOGON PEOPLE AT A BAMAKO FESTIVAL ⌃

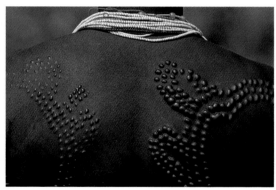

A SURMA TRIBE MEMBER SHOWS SCARS CAN BE BEAUTIFUL ⌃

**WE ARE ALL AFRICANS. FOR IT IS IN AFRICA THAT THE HUMAN RACE BEGAN...
IT WAS IN AFRICA THAT THE FIRST TOOL WAS INVENTED, THE FIRST FIRE LIT
BY A HUMAN HAND, THE FIRST CROP PLANTED, THE FIRST VILLAGE
ESTABLISHED, THE FIRST LANGUAGE SPOKEN.**

Thomas E Lawson

Africa, a continent alive with tradition and ancient ways, is not a story that can be narrated in one great epic. Rather, it's told in the lives of the African people, celebrated daily through astute proverbs, whimsical folktale, spirited music, ecstatic dance and passionate ritual. While African life is as vast and varied as the terrain itself – from the grassy savannas of the east to the arid deserts of the north or the lush rainforests of the west – it nevertheless remains connected by sacred customs. Shared African practices and beliefs are at the heart of what many affectionately call the Motherland.

In Africa's rural villages, the cycles of harvest, festival and ritualised family life continue their steady cadences – time and movement are soft and malleable, but they exist within an unyielding structure. Africa's traditions are etched in stone like cave art, and the grand artist who presides over them all is the mysterious supreme Spirit.

The world is full of gods in Africa, yet it would be difficult to find a religion anywhere on the continent that doesn't also honour one God. In African traditional religions, this God or Spirit is treated with the kind of deference and reverential space shown to village elders. Village elders aren't bothered with the latest sibling quarrel over the harvest hoe, and neither is God. Yet, while Spirit is grand enough to dwell in the vast, twinkling skies, it also resides in the ground we walk on, and every pebble, leaf, raindrop and star breathes Spirit. It's something that makes a lot of sense in a precarious world where paradox reigns supreme, and seemingly disparate parts create a harmonious whole.

The honouring of Spirit in Africa is ceaseless and pervasive, but is most observable through the offerings and prayers accorded the gods. The gods – more appropriately called the spirits or *jinè* – negotiate between our world and the spirit realm, and this sacred work is helped along with offerings of the most common food items found on any diner menu around the globe: chicken and beer. In African belief, spirits aren't too different from us: they like what we like. They especially enjoy meat (animal sacrifice), alcohol, clothing and, of course, money. Just like bringing a bottle of wine to a dinner party, an offering is considered good manners and a gesture of goodwill.

Other drinks you might provide a house guest, such as water or milk, are also acceptable gifts, along with the staples of any meal – sugar, rice, millet or flour, for example. Valuing the bread of life enough to give it away to the spirits is thought to be good practice: it's believed that if you give up something you need, you receive more of it. This 'show kindness to mother nature, and she will nurture you in return' philosophy might not go over well with corporate CEOs, but it's present throughout the continent under various names.

Ultimately, of course, the sacrifices are for Spirit, who doesn't need our offerings. The gifts serve to preserve a connection to the spirit world, to help the givers observe a reverence for life and nature and maintain a sense of the sacred in every word, gesture and action. Generally, individuals make offerings at the home of these spirits: in the ocean, at the base of a tree or in a mountain cave. You may not know the name of your mermaid in South Africa, but you can be sure that if you offer a libation in the ocean on any side of the continent, she will receive your offering. Be forewarned, however, about frivolously humouring the spirits. They don't take kindly to being thrown a bone here and there at your whim, like a stray dog. Once you make a pledge to them, essentially by offering a gift, you must continue to offer patronage or suffer the consequences – drought, fires, plagues, illness and other undesirable events. Communities don't take these upheavals lightly (especially since they tend to occur in biblical proportions in Africa!). The belief that 'everything happens for a reason', as the saying goes, is deeply held in much of the continent.

Observing the sanctity of life through an offering to the spirits is a daily ritual; but the passage of one of the four universal cycles of life always requires a special kind of ceremony. All four cycles generally begin and end with the beat of a drum: the drumbeat reproduces the rhythm of the life cycles, keeping the initiates connected to their path. All ritual festivities open with rhythmic music and communal dance.

The beginning of life, birth, brings the community together for the naming ceremony, to welcome the newborn with song, gifts and love. Children often inherit the names of ancestors, spirits or family members, and names are generally not without meaning, whether that's something as minor as the day of the week or as grand as the name of a revered prophet from the Islamic or Christian traditions.

Adult initiation begins the next cycle of life, an event that is not as pleasant, and perhaps deliberately unkind, as it aims to prepare children for the harsh realities of adulthood. Adulthood rituals often include circumcision and an extended rite of passage entailing fire handling and seclusion in the forest or in a nearby dwelling. The ritual seclusion is a symbolic break from the family and community: initiates leave the village as children, prepare during the seclusion for their roles as men and women, husbands and wives, leaders and elders, and return as adults. Children who do not undergo this ritual, particularly boys, cannot progress to adulthood, anywhere on the continent.

Marriage, perhaps the most exalted rite of passage in the life cycle, is often a marathon celebration, with festivities lasting up to several months. In Africa, marriage is seen as the sacred medium for channelling tradition: soon after the union, the couple aims to bring new life into the world to continue the bloodline, an act which is considered to be far more significant than any other meaningful mark a person can make in life. Children continue the family's lineage and strengthen the bond that connects the realms of spirit and life – seemingly dual worlds which are essentially one.

Women often fulfil a traditional female role in African culture, serving as the cooks, gardeners, herbalists, teachers, artists, shamans and providers. It's a role fundamental to the life of the community, and respectfully accorded its own domain: men stay out of the birthing room, kitchen, pottery barn and garden. While this segregation of roles and space is sometimes questioned by visitors to the continent, it's considered to help maintain not only a woman's sanity, but also the integrity and strength of the family.

Most sons in Africa never leave home, living with their parents, wife and children in one dwelling. New wives move into the family home to cook, clean and care for the children and grandparents. When the wife is eventually an elder herself, she (ideally) will enjoy the same nurturing and support from the younger women of the household, and in many cases will rest and benefit from the work of her children (karmic energy at its finest).

The final rite of passage, death, completes the circle of life, and the community both mourns and celebrates the crossing over of the spirit from this world into the next. The physical absence of the family member creates sadness, but the new status of the deceased in the realm of spirit is cause for great exuberation. The family benefits from having an ancestor to negotiate with the spirit world on their behalf, keep troublesome spirits at bay and serve as a kind of guardian angel for the home. Some ancestors appreciate their family so much, of course, that they return to it as newborns.

Generally, the overseers of these rites of passage are those with a type of mystical power – shamans. Shamans may be 'called' or may inherit their gifts, and depending on the region in Africa, may be a *griot* (or bard), blacksmith, hunter, artisan, priest or marabout, or some combination thereof. Essentially, the shaman both connects to and inhabits the world of spirits, and uses this ability to enhance and transform the life of the community.

The bards, who are primarily a fixture of West African life, serve to uplift, challenge, inspire, tease, educate and entertain the community with the verbal dexterity and cleverness of a New York rapper, the knowledge of a scholar and the antics of a circus clown. Their language and musical skills are masterful, like those of a symphony composer, and they can recite volumes of history – all from memory – often while performing music. Bards have the entertaining responsibility of poking fun at the traditions while at the same time safeguarding and honouring them.

Blacksmiths, or crafters of ritual objects and masks, embody and cultivate a mystical power through their work. Throughout Africa, iron, gold and various metals are considered numinous substances, and those who work with them are believed to have special knowledge of how to harness their energy for community living, festivities and ceremony. Often, blacksmiths are the creators of charms, weapons and tools; they also frequently perform the circumcisions in the community. Their powers are both awe-inspiring and frightening to the people they serve, and they're respected and feared accordingly.

Hunters, as they spend most of their lives in the bush, know the house manners of the wilderness. Negotiating with the tree spirits, dancing with the wolves and identifying herbal medicines, hunters use their knowledge of the bush for both healing and hunting for the community. To ensure safety and success in their pursuits, they adorn themselves with elaborate charms and consecrated clothing. Many hunters in West Africa, for example, wear garments made of mud cloth painted with powerful symbols as a kind of protective armour.

Africans consult shamans for their wisdom, revere them for their courage in dealing with the spirits, and often mistrust them for their immense power. As the sun is warmth and food for the earth, so the magic of the shamans is the light and energy source for the community, with which its members sustain and navigate their entire lives – Muslims, Christians and traditionalists alike.

Spirit permeates everything, and that energy can be used, or sometimes abused, retained and directed. Interestingly, the water-cooler talk of the shamans is remarkably similar in some ways to the theories of physicists about the nature of quantum particles: shamans hold that all matter is energy, but also that this energy is directly influenced by our beliefs. When a new religion visits hospitable Africa, like a welcomed guest, its practices and beliefs are comfortably assimilated into the existing customs. Indeed, the fascinating irony about oral traditions such as those in Africa is that they're inherently flexible and fluid. The Catholic rituals of baptism or the taking of communion, for example, can be easily accommodated in Africans' existing spirituality.

As a traveller to the mysterious continent, it might be tempting to visit a shaman for a reading. Be prepared: African seers aren't quite like the fortune-tellers or psychics with crystal balls you might find elsewhere. They don't advertise their services or hire unemployed teenagers to field their 1-900 calls. Shamans 'see' in countless ways and through various mediums. The genuine ones are tucked away off the beaten path, and may disappear into the forest for weeks or months at a time to gather their cauldron of ingredients or to listen to the whispers of the nature spirits. Also, the community as a whole has the opportunity, over a long period, to test the seers' ability to make accurate predictions for the wellbeing of society.

DANCING IN A MENSTRUAL CEREMONY IN ZAIRE

ALL THEIR WORLDLY GOODS: REFUGEES FLEEING BY CAMEL, SUDAN

BUTTONS AND BEADS: A NORTHERN MAASAI ORNAMENT

THE DONSOS CASTE, IN MALI, IS RENOWNED FOR ITS MEMBERS' HUNTING SKILL

Of course, you don't need to be a shaman in Africa to know how to read the signs. Birds squawking, dogs howling and lightning striking are all messages from the spirit world. Africans are often multilingual, but the continental language, more widely read and spoken than French or English, is spirit talk. All over Africa, individuals and communities consult the position of the stars, the behaviour of the village animals or the wind currents when planning just about any life event, whether trips, weddings, community gatherings or business ventures. From village to village, the signs signify different things, but throughout the land, the consensus remains: nature speaks.

Still, shamans have their own means of contacting the spirits: spirit channelling and cowry shell readings are the favoured methods (and have been for a millennium or two). Cowry shells were in fact originally used as currency. Their shape leaves little to the imagination and, most appropriately, they represent fertility and reverence for the feminine, and the strong matriarchal undercurrents of Africa. In fact, if there were only one symbol to represent all of Africa, it would be the ever-pervasive cowry. On goddess statues and fertility abodes, the cowry adorns a land where goddess traditions that predate other world religions by thousands of years continue to this day. Diviners toss the shells, like dice, on a mat and 'read' the configurations of their landing. Depending on the region, a diviner will employ up to 12, 20 or 40 shells.

Spirit channelling or communion occurs when a diviner, often a woman, invites a spirit to temporarily inhabit her to offer inspiration and guidance to the community. Shamans make special preparations for the inhabiting spirit by wearing protective clothing, charms and sometimes white, black or red body paint. Community members gather to welcome the spirit with songs, dances and drumming; there may also be an interpreter present to relay the spirit's message.

Ritual objects can also house spirits. Westerners may prefer to nestle up to their pet pooches: an African family may instead adopt a spirit abode for companionship and security. The abodes do often take the shape of one or more animals, and may live at the centre of an altar, as a statement about the centrality of the sacred in the home. The family provides the consecrated object or animal with regular offerings and sacrifice, and in return it provides guidance, security and prosperity. Successive generations may inherit the spirit abode, but the object becomes 'lifeless' once the offerings cease.

Visitors to the continent heading to the village market for bananas and rice might be startled to find displays of bat heads, hyena paws or snake fangs as well. Before you wince, consider that these seemingly disposable items are believed to be sacred, or at least be aspects of the sacred. They carry or embody a divine energy that can influence the self, others and the world at large. In Africa, charms are like clothing: without them, an individual is essentially naked and therefore vulnerable to the forces of nature. In village huts and city homes alike, amulets and talismans adorn children and adults about the neck, head and ankles, providing protection, blessing and power. They generally take the form of leather, cloth or metal pouches concealing their potent ingredients – not always animal parts, but also plants, sacred writings from the Quran or the Bible, or traditional songs or symbols.

Of course, African traditions don't just relay the story of Africa. African traditional religion remains strong throughout the continent, even for those who claim allegiance to other religions. But African spirituality has also migrated across the globe for centuries, from South America to the Caribbean and the southern states of North America – despite the lack of missionaries to spread their gospel, prophets to tout, martyrs or saints to claim, or even a written text for scholars to scrutinise. And beyond the obvious and not so obvious adherents of African traditional religion, Africa's music, art and culture reverberates like a primordial drumbeat across the vast land masses and deep seas, reaching out to all of humanity, connecting each of us back to our roots, calling us back to our ancestral homeland.

Naomi Doumbia PhD, is the author of *The Way of the Elders: West African Spirituality & Tradition*

TEXT JANE CORNWELL

AFRICAN MUSIC SACRED RHYTHMS

≫ ANOTHER STRING TO HIS BOW, CAMEROON ≫ HANDS UP: CELEBRATION OF THE SUNDAY CULT ≫ MAKESHIFT MUSIC AT A SAN RESETTLEMENT VILLAGE IN BOTSWANA

There are some African languages that have no word for music. Something so inherent, so elemental, doesn't actually need one. Here in this vast continent, rhythm, melody and harmony are an integral part of life – as natural as breathing and as vital to storytelling and communication as the spoken word. All of Africa's history is there in its music, as is its ethnic, cultural and linguistic diversity. Oh, and its natural world: the whistling thorn bushes of Tanzania, the loping gait of a camel across the Sahara, the crack of thunder over a thirsty veld. Across Africa, natural sounds are taken and incorporated into music, so that soundtracks to life become musical soundtracks as well. The often complex results might not always please the Western ear – but when it comes to traditional African music, Western standards don't apply.

The boundaries between life and art are blurred in Africa. Even speech has its musical uses: the link between language and music is so close in fact that instruments are sometimes tuned so that they are linguistically comprehensible. Not for nothing is the *tama*, the small, two-headed hourglass drum of the Wolof people of Senegal (known as the *kalengu* to the Hausa of Nigeria) called the talking drum! Music is often coupled with other art forms such as poetry or dance: the stomping feet of South Africa's Zulu warriors become the rhythm of the music, whose notes then turn into dance steps. Music can accompany work, religious, even political activities – 'Politics can be strengthened by music,' stated Nelson Mandela, 'but music has a potency that defies politics.' It can animate the life of the entire community.

In Africa everything moves to innumerable rhythms: the steady pounding of millet by Fulani women in the north of Senegal has its own metronymic beat. In the ancient Moroccan city of Fès, artisans pound metal, carve wood and stitch *baboush* slippers in familiar, long-practised cadences. Across the entire continent music marks everything from births, marriages and funerals to hunting, fishing and farming. African children quickly learn to imitate complex rhythms on minor and makeshift instruments, many of which they construct themselves from wood, hide or found objects. Their parents are known to improvise too: in Sierre Leone, empty Milo tins filled with stones were the core instrument for the genre called Milo-jazz. The South African musician Shiyani Ncobo grew up playing *maskanda* music on a guitar made from a tin can. In Cape Verde, women place a rolled-up cloth between their legs and beat it as part of their *batuco* music (the singer Lura does this live, with silver lamé).

African music lends itself to invention: Hausa children beat rhythms on the inflated bellies of live puffer fish. The Pygmies of Cameroon beat rhythms on river water. Everywhere, kids are shaking rattles, beating drums and playing instruments in adult groups. Children's musical games can aid the transition to adulthood: among the Dogon of Mali, a child sounding a bull-roarer is said to be 'calling the panther' – as a hunter might (the bull-roarer, a long piece of wood or metal tied to a string and swung in a circle, sounds like a panther's growl or a bull's roar). Instruments can also be functional: Malian superstar Salif Keita titled his 2002 album *Moffou* after the shrill one-hole flute he played to scare birds from his father's maize.

Traditional African music can be a source of magic and spirituality, healing and wisdom. 'I believe traditional music has a place in these modern times,' says Baaba Maal, a famous Senegalese singer, whose band Daande Lenol is made up of traditional players. 'To take something of the past and put it in the present teaches us something about ourselves.' Recent years have seen Maal and a few of his equally stellar contemporaries – Mali's Salif Keita, Guinea's Mory Kante – returning to their roots with acoustic albums. 'I wanted to sing about love,' says Salif Keita of 2005's critically acclaimed release, *Mbemba*, 'and use traditional instruments to make people dance.' Kante, a *griot* turned pop star – his 1988 house music–inspired song 'Yéké Yéké' remains Africa's biggest-selling single – is hailed for preserving and updating the musical traditions of his Malinke culture. His compatriots Ba Cissoko approach the kora (including the electric kora) with similar gusto.

Though the majority of Africans are musical, by no means all are actually musicians. In some societies musicians exist in semiprofessional groups, members of which earn their living both from playing and from working in totally different jobs. In other societies, music is the province of one social caste – the praise-singing *griot* of West Africa, say, who trace genealogies, recount epics and span generations in a manner similar to the medieval European minstrel. *Griot* (known as *jeli* in Mali) are acknowledged as oral historians – virtually all children know the epic of Sundiata Keita, the warrior who founded the Empire of Mali – and often as soothsayers, and they top the bill at weddings and naming ceremonies. Nevertheless, they occupy a lowly rank in hierarchical West African societies, and many big West African stars faced parental objections to their choice of career. Others such as Keita – a direct descendant of Sundiata and as such, not a *jeli* – made their reputations in exile. Over in equatorial Africa, by contrast, the player of the *mvet* harp-zither from Cameroon also relays great epics but – unlike his more obsequious counterparts further north – tends to say what he thinks, however crude it may be, and garners more respect as a result.

The existence of these *griot* is vital to societies that have no written records but hand down information from generation to generation. Fortunately, though ethnomusicologists continue to fret over the preservation of musical traditions and beliefs, Africa's remain in a largely healthy state – cohabiting, sometimes awkwardly, with a bold and impatient youth market. As with much of the globalised world, African cities do thump to the sounds of American hip-hop and rap; Eminem and 50 Cent are as popular here as they are Stateside. Yet the indigenous industry is also booming – Dakar in Senegal is home to over 2000 rap groups alone. Not for nothing did Daara J title their 2003 debut album *Boomerang*. 'Born in Africa, brought up in America, hip-hop has come full circle,' they say.

The only shared form of African musical expression, in fact, is popular music. There is no identifiable pan-African music in the traditional sense – though there are certain regional similarities. The movement of people into, out of and across the continent has enriched its musical make-up: North African music is heavily influenced by the Arabic-speaking world (its instruments are even held to be the original models for those of the West). Cairo's large *firqah* orchestras use centuries-old *maqam* scales (as heard in the classical poetry sung by the legendary Oum Kalthoum) and favour instruments such as the oud lute and goblet-shaped *derbouka* drum. Though danceable phenomena such as *raï*, *chaabi* and *al-jil* dominate North Africa, sub-Saharan traditions are not excluded: Morocco's *gnawa* brotherhoods, the descendants of sub-Saharan slaves, play pentatonic trance music using chants, hand drums, string instruments and giant metal *karakeb* castanets. Each year they invite Western jazz musicians to jam with them at the Gnawa and World Music Festival in Essaouira.

Islam has also made its mark on East and West Africa. The lush orchestration of the *taarab* ensembles of Zanzibar and Kenya have a distinctly Arabic tinge, as does the Swahili sound that proliferates between Uganda and Tanzania – though the rhythmic structure is not as complex as that of the Maghreb. West African music might be flecked with the muezzin's wail (listen to the glorious, swooping vocals of long-established stars such as Senegal's Youssou N'Dour or Malian songbird Kandia Kouyaté) but it's also highly rhythmic and drum-oriented, featuring call-and-response singing and vocal repetition. There's an emphasis on polyphony in Central Africa, where a number of Pygmy tribes sing their hearts out in relative isolation. South Africa probably has the greatest range of musical styles on the continent – not least its own flourishing jazz genre – but the rousing harmonies of the Zulu, Sotho, Pedi and Shangaan regions are the most identifiable.

Similar musical instruments are found throughout Africa: think drums, percussion, string, wind and self-sounding instruments. Precisely what form they take is dependent on geography: drums are more prevalent in forest areas than in savanna regions (oh, and if any instrument is representative of Africa, it's the drum). The *ingoma* drum choirs of Rwanda whack their gigantic instruments – made from rawhide and aeons-old umuvumu trees – with sticks the size of baseball bats. The dispersal of African slaves to the Caribbean and the Americas brought the likes of the *berimbau*, xylophone and *cuica* back to Africa; up in the former Portuguese colony of Cape Verde they sing *morna*, the local equivalent of the Portuguese *fado* (ciggie-puffing grandma Césaria Évora is *morna*'s undisputed queen). Angola boasts its own merengue, samba and accordion-fuelled music, called *rebita*. Gospel is hugely popular right across the continent, belted out everywhere from Lagos to Lilongwe.

The instruments of European colonialism – saxophones, trumpets, keyboards, guitars – have long been fused with traditional patterns. Popular music is best described as a product of African and external influences: jazz, soul and even classical music helped create the Afrobeat sound of the 'Black President', Nigeria's late Fela Kuti. The Malian bluesman Ali Farka Touré reaffirmed the role of the African *griot* by mixing wisdom with entertainment – and taking the blues back to its birthplace. (Touré was the continent's first artist to win two US Grammies, but his remarkable career was cut short by his death in February 2006.) Guitars helped invent Nigerian *juju*, Kenyan *benga* and Congolese rumba (which grew out of the Cuban rumba that made its way back across the Atlantic in the early 20th century). Horns – brass ones – jump-started Cameroonian *makossa* (check out master saxophonist Manu Dibango). Electric instruments gave rise to Senegalese *mbalax* and Ghanaian highlife. Ghanaian hiplife – hip-hop plus highlife – is now successfully exporting itself to its neighbours.

South Africa's giant recording industry rivals that of Europe and America (there are similarly large industries in Nigeria and Côte d'Ivoire) and embraces everything from *mbanqanga* (township jive) and Zulu *iscathimiya* call-and-response singing to the urban music phenomenon that is *kwaito*. And so the cross-fertilisation goes on: a new generation of township rap sits somewhere between *kwaito*, new-school and house music. Elsewhere, American hip-hop hybrids are sparking fascinating music revivals in Tanzania, Kenya, Angola and Guinea. Angola's favelas have given birth to *kuduro*, a breathless fusion of *semba*, rap and techno that has become popular in other Portuguese-speaking nations as well. Former Sudanese child soldier Emmanuel Jal has traded a Kalashnikov for a microphone; the Somalian rap sensation K'Naan (the first Somalian artist to feature on MTV) delivers fierce, percussion-fuelled protest songs. Both artists mark African music's growing social and political consciousness.

⌃ THE VICTORY ARMY CHURCH IN CONGO – STANDING-ROOM ONLY

⌃ HAIT HADDIDOU MUSICIANS GET THE PARTY STARTED, MOROCCO

⌃ A SOMBRE BEAT AT THE KING'S FUNERAL IN GHANA

NUBA TRIBESMEN CELEBRATE A PEACEMAKING FESTIVAL, SUDAN. ≪

As a political tool, music's lyrics and associations can wield immense power. Musicians are regularly expelled (or choose to exile themselves) from the likes of Algeria, Uganda and Zimbabwe for their political stance and beliefs. Paris in particular is full of exiled big-name African artists such as Angolan star Bonga, Ivorian reggae star Tiken Jah Fakoly and Algerian rock chanteuse Souad Massi. Conversely, African leaders often try and cash in on the popularity of their country's stars: Salif Keita, Baaba Maal, Oumou Sangare et al repeatedly decline requests to align themselves with the political parties of their countries. This doesn't mean that they balk at raising consciousness: everything from treating women with respect to the virtues of picking up litter and wearing a seat belt – oh, and a condom – has been broached by African songwriters. So has the problem of cassette piracy: a glance around any major African city reveals pirate operations on a massive scale.

The major record labels in Mali closed down in 2005 in protest at the fact that 95 per cent of the cassettes on the market are counterfeit. It allegedly takes just 24 hours from an album's official release for pirates to get their copies out on the streets, and despite government promises to crack down, the problem continues. (In Ethiopia in 2004 a well-organised strike by top musicians forced authorities into action, so that many musicians are now able to earn a living from their craft.)

Some genres, of course, are bent on helping listeners forget their environments altogether: Côte d'Ivoire's percussive, melodious and hugely popular Coupé Décalé sound was born during the politico-military crisis there. The likes of Sagacité, Papa Ministre and Mollah Omar sing of endless partying, easy money and unbridled happiness – and fill some of French Africa's biggest stadiums as a result.

It's simply impossible to overstate the influence of African music on other musical genres. Without African music there would be no Puerto Rican salsa, Brazilian samba or Trinidadian soca. No Cuban son, Jamaican reggae, American blues. No soul or gospel. No rock. The spread of African music has been compared to the giant baobab tree found in many West African regions. Its roots are African: traditional, historical, inherent. Its trunk is jazz and blues. Its branches are R&B, gospel, soul. Its leaves are Afro-cuban and calypsonian. Its fruits are rap, hip-hop, reggae, salsa, merengue and a host of genres too numerous to mention here.

To ensure that the musical traditions of Africa survive and grow, it is vital – to continue the analogy for a moment – that it be fed, watered and fertilised. Music in Africa is, after all, as natural as breathing.

The Motherland depends on it.

TOP 10 MUSICAL EXPERIENCES

- Learning kora, *djembe* drum and dance in the bright heat of The Gambia or Senegal: many companies offer 'real village experiences' in which participants live like locals, and sometimes, if there's an outing, entire villages will tag along

- Watching The Symmetric Orchestra – led by kora maestro Toumani Diabeté – play Le Hogon on Friday night in Bamako, Mali, then heading downtown to see the Super Rail Band at the Hôtel de la Gare, or Oumou Sangare at La Wassulu

- Hearing the *valiha* – the stringed bamboo zither – played in its island homeland of Madagascar, next to a forest alive with lemurs, chameleons, long-nosed snakes and giraffe-necked ladybirds

- Sitting on a sand dune under an endless, star-filled black sky at the Festival of the Desert in Mali, listening to Tuareg musicians bring it all back home to (well, 120 kilometres northwest of) Timbuktu

- Catching a five-hour concert by an internationally famous local hero – Salif Keita, Baaba Maal, Youssou N'Dour – and realising how different these are to the brief, shiny sets they deliver in the West

- Dancing to Afrobeat at the new Shrine club in Lagos, Nigeria, which – thanks to Afrobeat superstar Femi Kuti, son of the late great Fela Kuti – has risen from the ashes of the original venue

- Trancing out to the music of the *gnawa* brotherhoods in Essaouira – the gloriously windswept, medieval fortress town on Morocco's southern Atlantic coast – during the Gnawa and World Music Festival

- Watching dhow boats sail across a tropical horizon in Stone Town, while the Culture Musical Club, Zanzibar's leading *taarab* orchestra, play their lush combination of violins, oud, *qanun* and percussion

- Taking a pew for an emotional, hands-in-the-air, Sunday-morning gospel experience in a South African township church

- A night on the tiles in Kinshasa in the Democratic Republic of Congo, grooving to an urban traditional band playing ancestral rhythms on giant *likembe* thumb pianos plugged into amplifiers

TEXT DAVID ANDREW

AFRICAN WILDLIFE

» TEEN ANGST? AN ADOLESCENT MOUNTAIN GORILLA, RWANDA » CASUAL DRESS DAY FOR THE SECRETARY BIRD, KENYA » FASTER THAN A SPEEDING BULLET, KENYA

No other continent so instantly evokes a picture of large animals the way Africa does. And nowhere else on earth can you witness animals in such great numbers living in a totally wild state – millions of migrating wildebeest running the gauntlet of crocodiles at river crossings, stately giraffes and elephants grazing flat-topped acacias on vast, unpeopled plains, herds of buffaloes and antelopes large and small, and hundreds of bird species – all stalked by predators, including charismatic big cats like lions, leopards and cheetahs, and wild dogs, hyenas and mongooses, to name but a few.

Somehow the landscape looks right, as if we've been here before. And in a sense we have, for it's believed that this is the evolutionary crucible from which *Homo sapiens* – that's us – evolved. From apelike ancestors living in vast equatorial forests the first hominids ventured onto the savannas some six to 10 million years ago, and their co-descendants – the chimpanzees and gorillas – can still be seen today in the tropical rainforests of the Congo basin. Perhaps a collective memory draws people back to witness again the wildlife spectacle that greeted our ancestors and has remained more or less unchanged since then.

Africa the continent is too vast to absorb in one go, but a greatly simplified picture will help to understand how its wildlife – and ultimately its people – came to be where they are today. About 150 million years ago the supercontinent Gondwana broke apart to form several large continents, including Australasia, South America and Africa. (All of these modern landmasses contain biological relics, such as freshwater lungfishes and an ancient group of flightless birds called ratites,

which could not possibly have crossed oceanic barriers to colonise the new continents.) Once each group was cast adrift on its own isolated landmass, it followed a unique evolutionary trajectory. Africa, the largest fragment of Gondwana, drifted in ancient oceans long enough for its cargo of marooned animals (and plants) to evolve in isolation into thousands of unique species, such as elephants, rhinos and hyraxes. Monkeys and apes also originated in Africa, spreading to South America when the gap between the two continents was still relatively small. Then, around 10 million years ago, the northern part of the continent started to collide with what is now southern Europe and the Arabian Peninsula, and unleashed its animal cargo into Eurasia. Thus, elephants, rhinos, hippopotamuses and monkeys spread to the new lands – but the African indigenes were so well adapted to their continent that few of the large animals that evolved elsewhere were able to displace them from their niches. Only one deer species spread south from Eurasia to gain a toehold in Africa, and bears were never able to displace endemic predators such as lions and hyenas.

To further understand the African environment, picture it as a canvas on which a few strokes of colour have been made – dark green across the middle for the vast equatorial rainforests; a broad stripe of orange desert across the top of the continent and daubed onto the southwest corner; and a medium green for savannas to fill the spaces in between. These three broad regions expanded and contracted during alternating wet and dry climatic phases over many millennia, leaving pockets of rainforest and their wildlife stranded among savanna to evolve

AN IMPALA IS DWARFED BY A PASSING ELEPHANT, BOTSWANA ⩔

on their own and form still more new species. For example, some of the antelopes of southwestern Africa once roamed further north, but they were cut off from northern populations by expanding rainforests during one of the earth's wetter climatic phases. When drier conditions returned and the rainforest retreated again, these antelopes had been isolated so long that they were no longer able to interbreed with their northern relatives and new species resulted. Hundreds of such pockets occurred, some large, many small, divided by great rivers such as the Nile and Congo; pocked with titanic volcanoes such as Mt Kenya, Mt Kilimanjaro and Mt Cameroon; and further isolated by the great crack in the earth's crust – the Great Rift Valley – that stretches along a network of flooded valleys from the Red Sea through lakes such as Turkana and Tanganyika all the way to Lake Malawi.

Thus the stage was set for a continent whose evolutionary product is today unmatched anywhere in the world. Africa is home to more than 1100 mammal species, some 2400 bird species and hundreds of species of reptiles, amphibians and freshwater fish. Several bird families, such as the ostrich, secretary bird, turacos, shoebill, hamerkop and mousebird, are found nowhere else, and many other bird families have their greatest diversity in Africa. New species are still being discovered – a new species of monkey was described in Tanzania as recently as 2005 – and many more doubtless await discovery. Hundreds of mammals and birds are generalists that are found over much of the continent, but many others are restricted to just one or two countries or habitats, and some are so highly specialised they can exist solely in one area or on one food resource.

ISLANDS LITERAL & FIGURATIVE

Biologists sometimes use an island metaphor to explain Africa's extraordinary wildlife diversity. Oceanic islands are well known as centres of unique wildlife, and in Africa evolution has apparently worked overtime on 'islands' of terrestrial habitat stranded by geologic activity, climate change or even simply a river changing course. For example, large numbers of animals are endemic (found nowhere else) to the isolated Ethiopian uplands, the *fynbos* (a type of vegetation) of the southwest or the Congo rainforests, among others.

There are also true islands and archipelagos, such as Zanzibar, São Tomé, Comoros, Mascarenes and Seychelles, which are fascinating in their diversity and the endemic species both above and below the water's surface. Such archipelagos are particularly rich in endemic birds, whose ancestors flew from the mainland and over many generations adapted to their new island environments. Some islands, such as Zanzibar, even support distinct forms of medium-sized mammals, such as leopards, duikers and monkeys.

The largest and most spectacular of all Africa's islands, however, is Madagascar, a giant treasure-trove of endemic wildlife. Once part of the African mainland, Madagascar broke away and drifted south, and has been isolated in its present position for some 120 million years. Most famous of its inhabitants are the lemurs, monkey-like animals that are found nowhere else on earth. Lemurs have diversified into dozens of species ranging from tiny mouse-lemurs to the indri, a virtually tail-less lemur nearly a metre in length that looks like a cross between a koala and a giant panda. An indri's voice can boom nearly three kilometres across the forest to advertise its territory to other indris. Lemurs have adapted to nearly every niche in Madagascar's diverse forests, and include nocturnal species such as the bizarre aye-aye. The subject of local superstition, this weird-looking lemur listens with its batlike ears for grubs moving around under tree bark before extracting them with its greatly elongated middle fingers.

Madagascar's birds and reptiles have also taken some interesting evolutionary turns, and the island is famous for having the world's largest chameleons and unique birds such as mesites and ground-rollers. It was also once home to the largest bird species ever known, the extinct *Aepyornis* or elephant bird, which stood about three metres tall and laid eggs as big as a football. It roamed Madagascar's remote forests until only a few hundred years ago, and complete (but dried out) eggs are still occasionally found today.

A ROLLING TIDE OF GREEN
In Africa, as on Madagascar, forests provided an evolutionary hothouse and huge swaths of Africa's rainforests remain largely unexplored biologically. This is the least known and most inaccessible of Africa's natural habitats, and a visit to these primeval ecosystems, rich in birds and small mammals, is a privilege afforded comparatively few. As recently as 1901 a new species of large mammal, the okapi – a horse-sized member of the giraffe family – was discovered, along with the Congo peacock in 1936. (There were no known members of the pheasant family in Africa before this time – the peacock's existence shows Africa's ancient connection to other landmasses, where pheasants are still widespread.) Other denizens of the deep forest include pygmy hippos in West African rivers, distinctive forest-dwelling subspecies of elephants, buffaloes and bushpigs, and the bongo, a large and beautifully marked forest antelope. All of these generally retiring animals emerge from the forest into clearings called *bai*, naturally occurring grassy depressions that are often partly flooded and provide sweet grazing.

African primates are another group that maintains a stronghold in the huge rainforested basins that roll in green waves from the Atlantic coast to lap against the savannas of East Africa. Survival in this environment requires great agility, alertness and the ability to learn – all ingredients that propelled them on an evolutionary journey from 'primitive', solitary creatures such as today's galagos and bushbabies, to the monkeys and great apes, with their increasingly complex behaviours. From the deep green cathedrals of towering trees, monkeys eventually ventured into the surrounding savannas, and there developed complex social systems that enabled them to survive among the new suite of predators. Evolutionary relationships among African monkeys are complex and new species are probably still evolving.

For most travellers, of course, the number-one rainforest experience is the chance to get up-close-and-personal with gorillas – largest of the primates and distant relatives of humankind. But countries like Uganda and Tanzania also offer the chance to follow bands of wild chimpanzees through the rainforest and observe their wild, noisy antics. A greater contrast with gorilla-watching could not be imagined – while the gentle gorillas spend their time quietly chewing wild celery and belching, the hysterical chimps hoot, drum tree trunks and move at breakneck speed in bands through the forest. Another species of chimpanzee, the bonobo, has as yet barely made it onto the ecotravellers' circuit, even though it has been the focus of much scientific attention because it is so different to its sibling species. The bonobo is a gentle, vegetarian chimp that lives in a matriarchal society – its cousin across the Congo River is aggressive, meat-eating and kills its own kind.

THE WALK OUT OF THE FOREST
From miombo woodland to the familiar flat-topped acacias of East Africa – often with a vulture silhouetted in the crown – the savannas and their iconic wildlife are the 'real' Africa for most visitors. Right or wrong, this attitude is not surprising, since the great plains are where you will see most of the large mammals, nearly all of the predators and hundreds of bird species. This complex ecosystem is home to the greatest variety of large animals on earth, from knee-high antelopes such as dik-diks that wear pathways through the undergrowth, to the largest of all land animals: giraffes, elephants and rhinos. Grazers include zebras, buffaloes and a host of other antelopes large and small; and vegetarians are even found in the swamps, where the aquatic sitatunga antelope submerges to escape detection and has splayed hooves to enable it to walk on floating mats of vegetation. The largest of the aquatic grazing animals is the hippopotamus, which leaves its wallows by night to feed on grasses sometimes many kilometres from the water's edge. But the hoofstock is far outnumbered and even outweighed by the billions of blind termites that ceaselessly chew through plant matter. In turn, they provide a rich source of protein for unique animals such as the aardvark, pangolin and aardwolf, and a host of birds.

Despite its tranquillity and beauty, the savanna is a dynamic landscape shaped by fire, rainfall and even the wildlife itself. The pounding of millions of hooves over millennia has selected only the hardiest grasses for survival; the same grazers deposit vast amounts of manure that fertilise the soil after they move on. Fires set by lightning and the destruction of trees by elephants further encourage the grasslands, but eventually the elephants and vast herds move on and the shrubs and trees regrow, and so over the centuries the cycle is repeated across the continent.

Eating plants is hard work, however, and often requires special bodily functions: not surprisingly, predators simply eat the vegetarians instead. Lions are unique among cats because they form cohesive prides that hunt cooperatively and share the spoils. The secretive leopard is possibly the most adaptable of the large cats, occurring from rainforests to the edge of human settlements. The cheetah, famous for being the fastest of all land mammals, hunts alone by running down its prey. The dog family is also well represented on the continent, with three species of jackal and the African hunting dog, the most social of dogs, which hunts in packs and has an extraordinary success rate. Maligned and misunderstood, the spotted hyena is a superbly adapted animal and also hunts in packs, running down fleet-footed antelopes with a seemingly tireless, lolloping gait, and even challenging lions and leopards for their kills.

Trekking through the savanna wilderness on foot is one of the greatest wildlife experiences you can have anywhere on earth. Only this way will you really smell the earth and plants, see many small creatures that otherwise would elude you, follow footprints and get a feel for how our ancestors felt in face-to-face encounters with large animals. And when early hominids first ventured out of the tropical forests and began to walk upright on Africa's savannas, the world changed forever.

NATURAL & MANMADE DESERTS
As recently as Roman times there were giraffes, large antelopes and lions in North Africa, and zebras were often a sideshow at the Roman Circus. These animals have all since vanished from the northern rim of the continent, however, and centuries of deforestation and overgrazing have left a legacy of ever-expanding deserts in the Sahara and elsewhere. These areas have an interesting but less varied fauna than rainforests or savannas, although expanding human populations and overgrazing are exacerbating the process of desertification.

GREETINGS BETWEEN RHINOCEROSES, ZIMBABWE

A NILE CROCODILE LAZES IN THE SUN

GREAT LEAP FORWARD FOR THIS VERREAUX'S SIFAKA

A QUICK DRINK FOR LIONESSES IN CHOBE NATIONAL PARK, BOTSWANA

At the opposite end of the continent, the deserts of Namibia in the southwestern part of Africa are caused by cold-air convection, which sucks the moisture from the landscape and creates an arid landscape of rolling sand dunes with their own unique ecosystem. A suite of smaller animals – no less fascinating for their size – inhabits the Namib Desert and manages to survive these extraordinarily harsh conditions. Indeed, the whole southwestern corner of the continent supports many endemic species, including antelopes and predators not found elsewhere in Africa. The same cold waters that create these deserts support rich fish stocks, which in turn support a host of seabirds, sea lions and their predators – such as the great white shark of the southern oceans.

HUMAN IMPACT

Humans are perhaps the most amazing creatures to evolve in Africa, but they also pose the biggest threat – to both wildlife and themselves. Because human evolution occurred under the noses of other large animals, Africa's wild animals have learned to avoid people wherever possible, which is one explanation for why humans have not yet obliterated the wildlife of the great plains. It was a different story elsewhere: the spread of the upright ape across every continent spelt doom for hundreds of animal species. Many species familiar to tourists on safari were once also found outside the continent and are now cut off from their genetic relatives and beleaguered by humanity. Thus, for example, an isolated group of lions exists in India's Gir Forest; and a few cheetahs hang on in the deserts of Iran.

In Africa, the damage continues, despite the warnings of conservationists and the tireless work of volunteers. From a population of 40,000 in the 1970s, Kenya's rhino population has plummeted to a few dozen closely guarded individuals; they are now probably extinct north of the Congo Basin. Remarkably, however, animal extinctions have been comparatively few and a high degree of international interest can ensure that resources are quickly mobilised when a crisis arises. For example, the southern white rhino was brought back from the brink of extinction in South Africa through captive breeding and is now off the endangered list.

And that's not the only good news. Wildlife tourism is one of the biggest foreign exchange earners in many African countries, and is growing in undeveloped nations. It has long been realised that the involvement of local communities is essential to preserve and maintain national parks, police legislation and to study the wildlife itself. Tourist encounters with gorillas and chimpanzees are providing valuable foreign earnings for countries such as Rwanda, Uganda and Gabon, and teach local communities the value of preserving the forests and their wildlife. Increasingly sophisticated ecotourism developments are being initiated and run by local groups, helping to empower them financially and remove much of the mystery and superstition with which they have traditionally viewed wildlife.

TOP 10 WILDLIFE EXPERIENCES

○ Waking up to the raucous dawn chorus of indris – the world's largest lemur – sounding out their territories in the rainforest canopy at Madagascar's Réserve Spéciale d'Analamazaotra

○ Drifting silently on Botswana's Okovanga Delta in a dugout canoe past wallowing hippos, elephants bathing and birds erupting suddenly from towering reed beds

○ Watching birds in the equatorial rainforests of Mt Cameroon, home to many endemic species including the bizarre rockfowl, a bird unique to the African continent

○ Tasting the breeze as you stand downwind of 2000 kilograms of suspicious rhino, with nothing but grass between the two of you, while on a foot safari in Namibia's Damaraland

○ Floating in a hot-air balloon above East Africa's Serengeti-Mara ecosystem for a vulture's-eye view of wildebeest bleating and cavorting, hyenas in their dens and lions waiting in ambush

○ Being humbled by the sheer size and gentleness of a silverback mountain gorilla playing with his impish offspring on the slopes of Rwanda's Parc National des Volcans

○ Taking to the depths of the Red Sea in Egypt, Sudan, Eritrea or Djibouti and exploring reefs, wrecks and more aquatic life than you can shake a soggy finger at

○ Watching millions of flamingos feeding, preening, courting and honking among hippos and rhinos on the shores of Kenya's Lake Nakuru

THE AUTHORS

MATT PHILLIPS (COORDINATING AUTHOR)

Matt has shared campfires with hungry hyenas while on safari in Zimbabwe, crossed the Sahara in a couple of directions, dodged Mauritanian land mines in Mr Harry ('82 Land Rover), skydived over the Namib desert and wept for joy when an Ethiopian highlander successfully gave birth in his four-wheel drive. Matt's African experiences never seem to be ordinary or boring – that's why he's in charge of this colourful, definitive bible on the continent! And what an astounding team of fellow authors he's assembled. Matt has written about 26 African nations, including Lonely Planet's recent *Africa, Ethiopia & Eritrea, West Africa* and *Kenya* guidebooks.

DAVID ANDREW

David has been hooked on watching wildlife since his first visit to Africa at the age of 10. Since then he has also worked as a scientist in Antarctica, studied giant pandas in the wild in China, written or cowritten all five of Lonely Planet's *Watching Wildlife* guides, and edited *Wingspan* and *Wildlife Australia* magazines.

JAMES BAINBRIDGE

West Africa is James' patch. On the four visits he has paid to the region since he was 13, he has dug the dunes, dance floors and dysfunctional minibuses in a string of countries ranging from Morocco to Benin. His other Lonely Planet credits include *Africa* and *West Africa*.

TIM BEWER

After university, Tim worked as a legislative assistant before quitting capitol life in 1994 to backpack around West Africa. It was during this trip that the idea of becoming a freelance travel writer and photographer was hatched, and he has been at it ever since, returning to Africa several times for work and pleasure. He lives in Minneapolis.

JOE BINDLOSS

Joe was born in Cyprus, grew up in England, and has since lived and worked all over the place, though he currently calls London home. Joe's travels in Africa have taken him from Cairo to the Cape – he still rates seeing his first giraffe as one of his favourite travel experiences.

JEAN-BERNARD CARILLET

Say 'Africa' to Jean-Bernard and he will instantly have itchy feet. A Paris-based freelance journalist and photographer, he has been an Africa aficionado for more than 20 years and has visited 15 nations in West, East and Southern Africa, from Asmara and Zimbabwe to Djibouti and Somaliland. He has coauthored Lonely Planet's *Ethiopia & Eritrea* and *West Africa*.

PAUL CLAMMER

Paul first experienced Africa as a tender 19 year old in an overland safari truck, and has been returning regularly ever since. Rarely happier than when bumping along a dusty desert road, he has worked as a tour guide in the souqs of Marrakech, and has written a book about the delights of travelling in Sudan.

JANE CORNWELL

Jane is a Australian-born journalist, author and broadcaster. An anthropologist by training, she writes widely on the arts, travel and music for publications including the *Times,* the *Telegraph* and the *Australian.* She is a contributing editor on the world-music magazine *Songlines,* and has written about music for Lonely Planet's Africa publications.

ROB CROSSAN

Rob is a London-based travel writer who first discovered he had the knack of putting pen to paper whilst living in South Africa and performing as the nation's 14th-most-popular stand-up comedian. He has travelled extensively around Africa and these days contributes regular travel pieces to publications including the *Observer, CNN Traveller, Time Out* and the *Daily Telegraph.*

JAN DODD

Born in Africa, Jan picked up the travel bug early. Somewhere along the way she started writing guidebooks and providing content for magazines and websites. Africa still tugs, however, and recent forays have taken her to Morocco, Mauritius, Réunion and the Seychelles to update Lonely Planet guides.

NAOMI DOUMBIA

Author of the well-reviewed *The Way of the Elders: West African Spirituality & Tradition,* Naomi received her doctorate in comparative religions and spends most of her time writing in Africa and Asia. Through her work, Naomi aspires to bring to light the healing, transformative power of the world's mystical traditions.

MATT FIRESTONE

Matt is a trained biological anthropologist and epidemiologist, though his academic career was postponed due to a severe case of wanderlust. Although Matt hopes that this book will help ease the pain of others bitten by the travel bug, he fears that there is a growing epidemic on the horizon.

MARY FITZPATRICK

Originally from Washington, DC, Mary has spent over a decade living and working in sub-Saharan Africa, including Mozambique, Tanzania and Liberia. She has authored and coauthored numerous guidebooks covering these countries and other regions of the continent, and takes every chance she can get to travel south from her home base in Cairo.

MICHAEL GROSBERG

Michael found his way to Africa for the first time while in college. He later worked in South Africa and travelled all over the southern part of the continent. He is the author of the Ghana chapter for the Lonely Planet *West Africa* guidebook and has recently worked as a contributing author on the *Southern Africa* and *Tunisia* books.

ANTHONY HAM

Anthony's first trip for Lonely Planet was to West Africa in 2000, when he ate rat and fell irretrievably in love with the region. In the seven years since, he has returned often, alternating between West and North Africa, but always holding a passion for West African music and days of Saharan solitude. Anthony wrote Lonely Planet's *Libya* guide, as well as numerous chapters for *West Africa* and *Africa.*

ABIGAIL HOLE

Abigail was blown away by North and West Africa when researching Mali, Mauritania, Tunisia and Egypt for Lonely Planet's *Africa on a Shoestring.* Since then she's cowritten two editions of *Tunisia* and updated Lonely Planet's online guide to Mauritania. She has lived in London and Hong Kong, and now lives in Rome.

SIONA JENKINS

Siona arrived in Cairo for six months of Arabic-language study in 1989; she left 14 years later. A freelance journalist, documentary producer and writer, she has worked on a number of Lonely Planet publications, including its *Egyptian Arabic Phrasebook.* She is now based in London.

ROBERT LANDON

A year in Brazil introduced Robert Landon to the Portuguese-speaking world and served as gateway to West Africa's Cape Verde and Guinea-Bissau – two of the most extraordinary places he has visited in a life of travel. His work has appeared in the *Los Angeles Times* and *San Jose Mercury-News,* and on Travelocity.com.

KATHARINA KANE

When Katharina heard the haunting sound of a Fula flute during a London concert, her fate was sealed and she headed straight to West Africa. Katharina has worked on other Lonely Planet titles, writes for various world-music magazines, including *Roots* and *Songlines,* and produces world-music features for radio. She currently divides her time between Dakar, Cologne and London.

VESNA MARIC

Vesna Maric has worked on Lonely Planet guides to various countries, from Algeria and Tunisia to Albania, Macedonia, Hungary and former Yugoslavia. She has also worked on the *Cyprus, Andalucia* and *Bolivia* guides, and has written articles for *Elle* magazine and made radio features for BBC World Service.

HARRIET MARTIN

Born in Tanzania to Australian parents, Harriet lived in Southern Africa until she was 12. She then studied in Sydney, but the travel gene was never far from the surface. She backpacked and worked in South and Central America, the Middle East, India and West Africa, before returning 'home' to sub-Saharan Africa.

INDEX

NICK RAY
A Londoner of sorts, Nick comes from Watford, the sort of town that makes you want to travel. Nick has travelled through many countries in Africa over the years, but finds Uganda, Rwanda and Burundi to be small but perfectly formed. Nick currently lives in Phnom Penh, Cambodia, and has worked on more than 20 titles for Lonely Planet.

BRENDAN SAINSBURY
Brendan is an expat Brit based in Vancouver, Canada. He first discovered Africa back in the 1990s when he embarked upon a cross-continental hitchhiking odyssey that began in Cape Town and ended in Dar es Salaam, Tanzania. To date he has written for Lonely Planet about Cuba, Angola and the Congos.

NICOLA SIMMONDS
Nicola has worked in and backpacked around Indonesia, India, Europe, Japan, and Central and South America. She currently lives in Angola with her husband and two young children. During her time in the region she has managed to master water shortages, African bureaucracy and postwar chaos.

ANDREW STONE
Born in Zambia to a South African mother and with extended family in Southern Africa, Andrew has taken every opportunity to travel around this chunk of the continent, both under his own steam and as an author of Lonely Planet's *Southern Africa* guide. It's a tough call but his favourite country in Southern Africa is probably the otherwordly island nation Madagascar; his favourite place of all is St Marie, the old pirate island off the coast of Madagascar.

JUSTINE VAISUTIS
Justine's love affair with Africa began from the word go. Born in South Africa, she spent her adolescent years looking for jacaranda, dry summers and wildlife fixes. She has returned numerous times as an adult to explore the region and has worked on Lonely Planet's *Southern Africa* guide.

TONY WHEELER
Although it is more than 30 years since Tony wrote the very first Lonely Planet guidebook, he has never managed to find a cure for his travel addiction, which has recently taken him to the Central African Republic and a number of other off-the-beaten-track African destinations.

VANESSA WRUBLE
For most of her adult life, Vanessa has been a freelance writer, a humanitarian-aid worker, a TV correspondent and producer, an interactive artist, a renegade-street-event organizer, a Burning Man–festival enthusiast and, of course, a world traveller. She is currently at work on a book based on her blog from Sierra Leone (www.vanessawithoutborders.com).

THE AFRICA BOOK
SEPTEMBER 2007

PUBLISHER Roz Hopkins
COMMISSIONING EDITOR Ellie Cobb
PROJECT MANAGERS Adam McCrow, Ellie Cobb
IMAGE COORDINATOR Dana Topchian
IMAGE RESEARCH Pepi Bluck
DESIGN Mark Adams
LAYOUT DESIGNER Indra Kilfoyle, Mik Ruff
DESIGN MANAGER Brendan Dempsey
CARTOGRAPHER Wayne Murphy
COORDINATING EDITOR Vanessa Battersby
ASSISTING EDITOR Kate Whitfield
MANAGING EDITOR Annelies Mertens
PRE-PRESS PRODUCTION Ryan Evans
PRINT PRODUCTION MANAGER Graham Imeson

PUBLISHED BY
LONELY PLANET PUBLICATIONS PTY LTD
ABN 36 005 607 983
90 Maribyrnong St, Footscray,
Victoria, 3011, Australia
www.lonelyplanet.com

Printed through Colorcraft Ltd, Hong Kong
Printed in Malaysia

ISBN 978 1 741046 021

Text © Lonely Planet 2007
Photographs © Photographers as indicated 2007

All rights reserved. No part of this publication may be reproduced, stored in a retrieval system or transmitted in any form by any means, electronic, mechanical, photocopying, recording or otherwise except brief extracts for the purpose of review, without the written permission of the publisher.

Lonely Planet and the Lonely Planet logo are trademarks of Lonely Planet and are registered in the US Patent & Trademark Office and in other countries.

Although the authors and Lonely Planet have taken all reasonable care in preparing this book, we make no warranty about the accuracy or completeness of its content and, to the maximum extent permitted, disclaim all liability arising from its use.

PHOTOGRAPHS
Many of the images in this book are available for licensing from Lonely Planet Images.
www.lonelyplanetimages.com

LONELY PLANET OFFICES

AUSTRALIA
Locked Bag 1, Footscray, Victoria, 3011
Phone 03 8379 8000 Fax 03 8379 8111
Email talk2us@lonelyplanet.com.au

USA
150 Linden St, Oakland, CA 94607
Phone 510 893 8555 Toll free 800 275 8555
Fax 510 893 8572 Email info@lonelyplanet.com

UK
72-82 Rosebery Ave London EC1R 4RW
Phone 020 7841 9000 Fax 020 7841 9001
Email go@lonelyplanet.co.uk

PHOTO CREDITS
FRONT COVER Male lion, Selous Game Reserve, Tanzania; Staffan Widstrand // Nature Picture Library. **INSIDE FRONT COVER** (from left) The mausoleum of Moulay Ismail, Morocco; Jeremy Horner // Panos. Dancing Samburu men and women, Lorubae, Kenya; Mark Daffey // Lonely Planet Images. **BACK COVER** (from left) Young boys on Praslin Island, Seychelles; Mark Daffey // Lonely Planet Images. Town chief, Rusape, Zimbabwe; Steve J Benbow // Axiom. Koutoubia mosque, Marrakesh, Morocco; Doug McKinlay // Lonely Planet Images. Herd of giraffes, Etosha National Park, Namibia; AfriPics // Photographers Direct. **INSIDE BACK COVER** (from left) Young ostriches, South Africa; Imagebroker // Alamy. Sand dunes, Namib-Naukluft Park, Namibia; David Wall // Lonely Planet Images. **p2** (clockwise from left) Hairdressing in Burkina Faso; Trygve Bolstad // Panos. Chimpanzee, Sierra Leone; Nick Gordon // Photolibrary. Jewellery worn by Samburu girl, Kenya; Tom Cockrem // Lonely Planet Images. Quiver tree in Namib-Naukluft Park, Namibia; Andrew Parkinson // Lonely Planet Images. Sand dunes, Namib-Naukluft Park, Namibia; David Wall // Lonely Planet Images. **p3** A refugee from the Darfur region of Sudan walks near her family's tent home, Chad; Scott Nelson // Getty. **p5** A hunter rides his motorcycle home in full traditional dress just outside Bamako, Mali; Finbarr O'Reilly // Reuters. **p6** (from left) Herd of giraffes, Etosha National Park, Namibia; AfriPics // Photographers Direct. Djenné's Grande Mosquée, the largest mud-brick building in the world, Mali; Ariadne Van Zandbergen // Lonely Planet Images. Dancers perform the *tama* (drum) dance, Senegal; Olivier Martel // Corbis. **p7** Young women collect reeds during the Umhlanga (Reed Dance), Swaziland; Jochem Wijnands / Picture Contact // Photo Library. **p9** A man pours mint tea, Algeria; Giacomo Pirozzi // Panos. **p12** (from left) Carol Polich // Lonely Planet Images; Frank Herholdt // Getty; Sue Cunningham Photographic // Getty. **p13** (clockwise from left) Reinhard Dirscherl // Alamy; J Marshall, Tribaleye Images // Alamy; Adrian Sherratt // Alamy; Ariadne Van Zandbergen // Alamy. **pp20-1** Berber shepherd standing atop the Aït Benhaddou kasbah, Morocco; Dushan Cooray // Lonely Planet Images. **pp46-7** Man fishing in a small boat, Senegal; Hervé Gyssels // Photo Nonstop. **pp114-5** Chimpanzee, Gabon; Cyril Ruoso // Visual. **pp138-9** Locals walking along a path that winds down the escarpment; Patrick Horton // Lonely Planet Images. **pp202-3** Cheetah running on dune ridge, Namib Desert, Namibia; Winfried Wisniewski // Getty.